ne Ages of
ider Woman

THE UNIVERSITY OF
WINCHESTER

ALSO EDITED BY JOSEPH J. DAROWSKI

The Ages of Superman: Essays on the Man of Steel in Changing Times (McFarland, 2012)

The Ages of Wonder Woman

Essays on the Amazon Princess in Changing Times

Edited by JOSEPH J. DAROWSKI

McFarland & Company, Inc., Publishers
Jefferson, North Carolina, and London

LIBRARY OF CONGRESS CATALOGUING-IN-PUBLICATION DATA

The Ages of Wonder Woman : Essays on the Amazon Princess
in Changing Times / edited by Joseph J. Darowski.
    p.   cm.
Includes bibliographical references and index.

ISBN 978-0-7864-7122-5
softcover : acid free paper ∞

    1. Wonder Woman (Fictitious character)   2. Literature
and society—United States.   3. Comic books, strips,
etc.—United States.   4. Women in literature.
I. Darowski, Joseph J., editor of compilation.
PN6728.W6A74 2014
741.5'973—dc23   2013041458

BRITISH LIBRARY CATALOGUING DATA ARE AVAILABLE

Cover illustrations: Doug Wells (face) and Daniel Villeneuve
(inset arm) are © 2014 iStock/Thinkstock

Manufactured in the United States of America

McFarland & Company, Inc., Publishers
Box 611, Jefferson, North Carolina 28640
www.mcfarlandpub.com

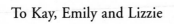
To Kay, Emily and Lizzie

Table of Contents

Introduction

Wonder Woman has had her comic book adventures published continuously for over seventy years, one of the longest runs in history. Wonder
Woman has a well-known appearance with her tiara and star-spangled
costume, but the character herself remains something of an enigma, seemingly for both audiences and creators. Despite more than seven decades of
published stories, a television series, regular appearances in animated shows
(though never an eponymous series like her DC Comics counterparts Superman, Batman, and Green Lantern), and a direct-to-DVD animated movie,
aspects of her character beyond her costume are difficult to pin down. Outside
of the comic book reading community Superman and Batman's alter-egos,
Spider-Man's creed, and even Iron Man's origin story are easily recognized,
no doubt aided by their multimedia adaptations. But Wonder Woman is recognizable but unfamiliar, an ambiguous icon, a symbol without definite meaning.

Some of Wonder Woman's lack of distinct identity arises from periods
in which the publisher has been at a loss for what to do with the character.
New creators come to the series with new directions and interpretations of
the character, often abandoning or ignoring previous storylines. Of course,
this is part of the nature of the American comic book industry. The same
process of write-establish-reboot-repeat has occurred for most long-running
superhero characters. However, in the case of Wonder Woman, the resulting nebulous identity has been more pronounced and problematic. This text
will help track the different ways Wonder Woman has been presented in her
comic book adventures, demonstrating the fluctuations the character has
endured.

This collection addresses, in chapters arranged chronologically, Wonder
Woman's evolution from her first appearance through DC Comics continuity
reboot in 2011. Often while tracking the thematic changes in the series there
are real-world issues that are clearly influencing the creators. World War II,
the Cold War, various stages of the feminist movement, and 9/11, for example,

can each be identified as having effects on the stories found in Wonder Woman stories.

The opening two essays use Wonder Woman comic books from the early 1940s as primary sources. In "William Marston's Feminist Agenda," Michelle R. Finn addresses the earliest Wonder Woman adventures in light of the feminist theories of the character's creator. Donna B. Knaff's essay, "A Most Thrilling Struggle: Wonder Woman as Wartime and Post-War Feminist," contextualizes the Wonder Woman stories from the World War II era with the evolving gender norms that were in flux at the time. The shifting wartime roles men and women were undertaking caused some to question traditional gender roles, a change that was not ignored by popular culture.

Moving forward, in "Containing Wonder Woman: Fredric Wertham's Battle Against the Mighty Amazon," Craig This writes about the changes Wonder Woman underwent following the attacks on the industry by Wertham. Following Wertham's assertions that reading comic books contributed to juvenile delinquency the comic book industry created the Comics Code Authority. The Comics Code Authority's strict guidelines dictated what could be shown in comic books, resulting in tonal transformations for most pre-existing characters in order to conform to the new standards.

Lori Maguire and Joan Ormrod both address the Cold War's influence on *Wonder Woman* comic books. Maguire's "Wonder Woman Comic Books and Military Technology After Sputnik" approaches the subject from the point of view of the space race and nuclear fears. Ormrod's "Cold War Fantasies: Testing the Limits of the Familial Body" focuses on issues of family identity and the culturally assigned gender roles from the period.

Recognizing the *Wonder Woman* comic books' transition away from romance oriented stories, Francinne Valcour's "Retiring Romance: The Superheroine's Transformation in the 1960s" covers the series' shift to stories more focused on super powers and adventure. Valcour positions this transformation in response to changes in reader expectations, industry patterns, and societal roles for women.

Undeniably one of the most famous Wonder Woman stories involves the Amazon Princess losing her powers but continuing to operate as a superhero with new martial arts skills. She loses her traditional costume and dons a new "mod" outfit, while her alter ego opens a fashion boutique rather than working in the military. This was an unsuccessful attempt by the creators to empower Wonder Woman as a female role model. Fittingly for one of Wonder Woman's most significant stories, there are multiple essays that focus on this tale. Jason LaTouche, Paul R. Kohl, and Peter W. Lee each address this period. In "What a Woman Wonders: This Is Feminism?" LaTouche examines the stereotypes that undermine DC Comics' attempt to empower Wonder Woman, including a reliance on outward beauty to provide personal worth, a need to please the men around her instead of standing up for herself, and Wonder Woman's emotionality, which is seen as one of her greatest weaknesses. Kohl's essay, "Wonder Woman's Lib: Feminism and the 'New' Amazing Amazon," addresses this period using feminist theorists such as Simone de Beauvoir, Trina Robbins, and Laura Mulvey. Lee's "Not Quite Mod: The New Diana Prince, 1968–1973" analyzes the gender roles in Diana Prince's relationship with her male partners (professional and romantic) and also analyzes reader reaction to this new version of Wonder Woman.

W.C. Bamberger's essay, "The Near-Awakening of Diana Prince," examines the final adventure for the depowered Wonder Woman. The novelist Samuel R. Delaney was hired by DC Comics to continue Wonder Woman's reimagining, and he simultaneously introduces sword and sorcery characters from an existing series of novels while trying to keep the feminist angle prominent in her stories. Without fully resolving his storylines, Delaney is replaced by Robert Kanigher as the writer of the series, and Kanigher immediately restores Wonder Woman's powers and costume.

Joseph J. Darowski's "'I No Longer Deserve to Belong': The Justice League, Wonder Woman and *The Twelve Labors*" uses a mid–1970s storyline in which Wonder Woman attempts to prove her worthiness to be a member of the Justice League to explore clumsy portrayals of the feminist movement, the male gaze, and voyeurism.

Ruth McClelland-Nugent's essay, "'Steve Trevor, Equal?' *Wonder Woman* in an Era of Second Wave Feminist Critique," delves into the letter columns printed in the back of comic books to gauge reader reaction to changes in *Wonder Woman*. These reactions reveal what were some of the most controversial themes in *Wonder Woman* including feminism, Wonder Woman's love life, and the potential resurrection of her long-time love interest Steve Trevor.

Matthew J. Smith touches on several of the different careers Diana Prince has had throughout the decades, but focuses primarily on her time working as an astronaut. "Working Girl: Diana Prince and the Crisis of Career Moves" uses a storyline from the late 1970s to address the portrayal of women outside of domestic roles.

D.R. Hammontree's "Backlash and Bracelets: The Patriarch's World, 1986–1992" explores *Wonder Woman* comic books from a period when there was some cultural rejection of, or at least resistance to, many of the social movements of the 1960s and 1970s. The feminist movement was redefined in this period, and as a feminist icon Wonder Woman was a pulled into this cultural renegotiation.

The 1990s saw many characters pass through a "grim 'n' gritty" phase, and in a manner of speaking Wonder Woman did the same. Nicole Freim's

"The Dark Amazon Saga: Diana Meets the Iron Age" considers a storyline in which Artemis replaces Diana Prince as Wonder Woman. The art, narrative, and themes of this story display many of the stereotypes of the era.

Jeffrey K. Johnson's essay, "Super-Wonder: The Man of Steel and the Amazonian Princess as the Ultimate 1990s Power Couple," explores the idea of a romantic relationship between Superman and Wonder Woman in terms of the gender roles the two characters assume. The two tales that are examined take place in alternative future timelines, one published in *Kingdom Come* and the other in *The Dark Knight Strikes Again*.

The next two essays in the collection use periods in which a singular writer's voice defined Wonder Woman's adventures. In "War, Foreign Policy and the Media: The Rucka Years," Fernando Gabriel Pagnoni Berns contextualizes Rucka's time as writer in post–9/11 America. Alison Mandaville's "Out of the Refrigerator: Gail Simone's Wonder Woman, 2008–2010" explores gender roles within the series in light of Simone's public comments on these same issues. Simone is one of the most prominent female writers in the comic book industry and the first regular ongoing female writer of *Wonder Woman*.

In the final essay, "Greek, Roman or American? Wonder Woman's Roots in DC's New 52," John Darowski and Virginia Rush explore the most recent reimagining of the Amazon Princess. The New 52 was a 2011 continuity reboot by DC Comics in which the entire narrative universe was reset and most characters had their previously established origins and personal histories reimagined. Wonder Woman's history, which has always included an eclectic blend of Greek and Roman mythology as well as American iconography and themes, was not excluded from DC's universe-wide revision. This essay explores this new iteration of Wonder Woman from a contemporary American point of view.

Throughout the collection the reader will find some variations on terms that are used interchangeably. Presently, there exists some debate about using the term "superheroine" or "female superhero" when describing a character such as Wonder Woman. Because no consensus has been reached within the academic community, much less within fandom and the culture at large, the editor left the choice of which term to employ to the discretion of each contributor.

Additionally, the adjective form of Amazon may seem to be a minor issue, but it should be addressed as it affects both the title of this collection and usage throughout the text. The term "Amazonian" appears to be the grammatically correct adjective form when referring to something associated with the Amazons. However, in the Wonder Woman comics it has been standard to refer to Wonder Woman as "The Amazon Princess" and not "The Amazonian Princess." Some contributors have elected to use the adjective Amazonian, while others have used the DC Universe-standard "Amazon." Again, the decision as to which term to use was left to individual contributors.

Finally, the creator of Wonder Woman was named William Moulton Marston, but he wrote Wonder Woman comic books under the pen name Charles Moulton. Depending on whether the authors cite Marston's work and statements outside of Wonder Woman comics, or cite a comic book that retained his use of the pen name, the names Moulton and Marston may be used when referring to the same individual.

Besides being an American popular culture icon, Wonder Woman is a fascinating subject for academic study. This collection provides insights into the evolution of the character, looking at individual periods of the character's published history and contextualizing it within the society of the time. This is but one method of analysis, among many, that could also deepen our understanding of Wonder Woman. *The Ages of Wonder Woman: Essays on the Amazon Princess in Changing Times* follows other academic considerations of Wonder Woman and, ideally, serves as yet another valuable tool in understanding a facet of American culture.

William Marston's Feminist Agenda

MICHELLE R. FINN

> *The social value of freeing woman from a harem-enclosed existence to a
> life of activity can be questioned only by those advocates of a "man's world"
> who wish to perpetuate its butchers and savage jungle law.*
> —*William Moulton Marston*

For second-wave feminists, who came to maturity in the 1960s, Wonder
Woman was a real icon, admired for her strength, courage, and can-do attitude
that stood as a welcome alternative to the more conventional model of femininity with which they grew up. "If we had all read more about Wonder
Woman and less about Dick and Jane," postulated Gloria Steinem in 1972,
"the new wave of the feminist revolution might have happened less painfully
and sooner" ("Introduction"). Although critics have argued that the superheroine's skimpy costume and the comic book's persistent bondage theme
undermine Wonder Woman's agency and relegate her to an object of male
fantasy, her creator's ideological agenda actually coincided with Steinem's
claim.

Believing that women's "natural" capacity for love, nurture, and self-
sacrifice would make them better leaders than men, William Moulton Marston
(1893–1947) created Wonder Woman to advance his vision of female empowerment. As he told the pioneer comic book historian Coulton Waugh in a
1945 letter, "Frankly, Wonder Woman is psychological propaganda for the
new type of woman who should, I believe, rule the world."[1] While the character's feminism is certainly open to interpretation, her creator's intentions
are clear. At a time when popular culture supposedly appropriated and defused
feminist ideas, Marston used Wonder Woman to promote women's political
power, economic independence, and social authority. Deliberate in his goal,

Marston hoped that Wonder Woman would inspire a real and permanent change in the social-sexual order.

Progressive Roots

Although Wonder Woman's first appearance was not until World War II, the philosophy that she embodied sprouted from the ideological seed of an earlier era. Studying psychology at Harvard in the mid–1910s, William Marston came of intellectual age at the height of America's Progressive movement and was heavily influenced by the spirit of reform that defined that historical period. A student of the eminent German scholar, Hugo Münsterberg, Marston espoused his mentor's belief that modern psychology, and the social sciences in general, should not only seek an academic understanding of human thought and behavior, but that they should be socially useful as well. Dedicating his career to helping people solve their personal and interpersonal problems, Marston shared his psychosocial theories on human progress with a wide audience through academic tracts, scholarly journals, self-help publications, advice manuals, mass-circulation magazines, a novel, and, ultimately, comic books.

Like many Progressive Americans, Marston believed that women were instrumental to bringing about a kinder, gentler civilization. Based on his study of people's responses to social stimuli, he concluded that women were fundamentally motivated by love, a constructive force that caused people to act out of concern for others. Men, Marston found on the other hand, were driven by appetite, a destructive impulse that fostered selfishness and greed. In the nineteenth century, such essentialist conclusions about the nature of men and women had supported the notion that each sex should function within its own distinct sphere of activity: men in the public world of industry and government, and women in the private world of home and family. Without disputing the biologically based polarity of sexual difference, Marston and other progressives challenged this traditional interpretation of sex essentialism. Concerned as he was with improving the human condition, Marston argued that "appetite emotion must first, last, and always be adapted to love" (*Emotions* 391). That is, he believed that women's love should reign over, not submit to, men's appetite.

Whereas the dominant perspective held that women's most valuable contributions to society were made through their roles as wives and mothers, Marston wanted female "love leaders" to supplant male "appetitive leaders" at the helm of governments and other social, economic, and political institutions. Bringing women out of their homes not only to vote, but to take over public life, he argued, was necessary for ensuring human progress and the well-being of civilization. As he explained in a 1942 article:

> If you conclude, as I do, that the only hope of permanent peace and happiness for humanity on this planet is an increased expression of love, and that women are the primary carriers of this great force, one of the problems we face is to provide women with more opportunity for using their love powers. The last six thousand years have demonstrated quite conclusively, I believe, that woman under the domination of man can increase but meagerly the world's total love supply. Our obvious goal, then, must be to devise social mechanisms whereby man is brought under the love domination of woman ["Women: Servants for Civilization" 44].

Because he felt that men's traditionally dominant position in American society had only fueled their proclivity for appetitive behavior, Marston did not consider men capable of becoming love leaders. Placing women's emancipation at the center of social evolution, Marston thus wished to overturn the traditional gender hierarchy and establish "a new code of conduct, based upon love supremacy" (*Emotions* 393). Wonder Woman was Marston's prototype for the female love leader.

Promoting Female Love Leadership

Using his pop-cultural heroine as a vehicle for his feminist agenda, Marston intended to spread his message of female love leadership to the widest and most impressionable audience possible. In addition to the fact that an overwhelming majority of America's youth, and a sizable percentage of adults, regularly read comic books in the 1940s, Marston invested his ideas in this medium because he believed that picture stories were an effective way of generating feelings and instilling values in a mass audience.[2] "[T]he picture-story fantasy cuts loose the hampering debris of art and artifice and touches the tender spots of universal human desires and aspirations," he explained. "Comics speak, without qualm or sophistication, to the innermost ears of the wishful self" ("Why" 36). Recognizing the particular influence comic books had over younger readers, Marston asked parents, "What life-desires do you wish to stimulate in your child?" ("Why" 40). A parent himself, Marston's answer to this question was clear:

> If children *will* read comics [...] isn't it advisable to give them some constructive comics to read? [...] The wish to be super-strong is a healthy wish, a vital, compelling, power-producing desire. The more the *Superman-Wonder Woman* picture stories build up this inner compulsion by stimulating the child's natural longing to battle and overcome obstacles, particularly

evil ones, the better chance your child has for self-advancement in the world. Certainly there can be no argument about the advisability of strengthening the fundamental human desire, too often buried beneath stultifying diver- tissements and disguises, to see good overcome evil ["Why" 40].

Seeing the power of comic books in their "visual stimulation of mass emotions" ("Why" 38), Marston hoped Wonder Woman would stimulate a widespread preference for women's love over men's appetitive self-interest, the most con- structive purpose he could imagine. Given this objective, it seems appropriate that Marston unveiled Wonder Woman in December 1941, the very month America entered World War II. As men once again led the nation into battle and bloodshed, Marston's plea for women's love leadership became all the more pertinent.

As a female role model, Wonder Woman was unlike any who had come before her in American popular culture. Most women who appeared in comic books in the early forties were secondary characters—sidekicks at best, but usually helpless victims in need of the male hero's rescuing. Wonder Woman, in contrast, took center stage. She did not require men to rescue her; she res- cued herself and whoever else needed her. A far cry from meek and helpless, Wonder Woman was stronger than men, with "a hundred times the agility and strength of our best male athletes and strongest wrestlers" (Marston and Peter, *All Star Comics* #8, 8). She could run, swim, fly a plane, rope moving objects with her lasso, and deflect bullets with her steel bracelets. Wonder Woman was also intelligent, brave, resourceful, and kind. In creating such a compelling figure, Marston hoped to inspire American women and girls toward a new, more powerful model of femininity. As he explained in *The American Scholar*:

> Not even girls want to be girls so long as our feminine archetype lacks force, strength, power. Not wanting to be girls they don't want to be ten- der, submissive, peaceloving as good women are. Women's strong qualities have become despised because of their weak ones. The obvious remedy is to create a feminine character with all the strength of a Superman plus all the allure of a good and beautiful woman ["Why" 42–3].

Combining "masculine" strength with "feminine" virtue, Wonder Woman was Marston's ideal love leader. She embodied his vision for a peaceful, matri- archal future.

The idea that women should rule men—or at the very least avoid being ruled by them—is a recurring theme in Marston's Wonder Woman stories, which he wrote under the pen name Charles Moulton from the comic's debut in 1941 until his untimely death from cancer in 1947. Before coming to America to "save the world from the hatreds and wars of men" (Marston and Peter, *Sensation Comics* #1, 18), Wonder Woman was Diana, princess of the mighty

Amazons. With her mother, Queen Hippolyte, Diana ruled Paradise Island, a secret land inhabited entirely by women. That Marston dubbed this man-free land "Paradise" is telling, as is his explanation for the peace and harmony that characterized the all-female civilization. As we learn in *Wonder Woman* #1 (Summer 1942), men are governed by Mars, the god of war, and wish to use violence to dominate others. "My men will rule with the sword!" Mars proclaims (147). Women, on the other hand, are guided by Aphrodite, the goddess of love and beauty, who counters Mars' aggression: "My women shall conquer men with love!" (147). While 1940s America was a far cry from the peaceful matriarchy that Marston envisioned, he was able to play out his fantasy of women's power in the Wonder Woman universe. The comic book's popularity enabled him to share that fantasy with a broad audience.[3]

Depicting his faith in women's leadership in a series of stories that took place over one thousand years in the future, Marston visualized a time when "men and women will be equal ... but woman's influence will control most governments because women are more ready to serve others unselfishly!" (Marston and Peter, *Wonder Woman* #7, 223). In this progressive future, women have banned lethal weapons, eliminated government corruption, and transformed prisons into rehabilitation centers. As Queen Hippolyte points out to her daughter in *Wonder Woman* #7 (Winter 1943), "men are much happier when their strong aggressive natures are controlled by a wise and loving woman!" (221). Whereas Mars expresses the socially conservative fear that women who followed the Amazon example would "escape man's domination completely! They will achieve a horrible independence! ... they'll grow stronger than men and put an end to war" (Marston and Peter, *Wonder Woman* #5, 37), this was just what Marston hoped would happen when he offered Wonder Woman as a role model to American girls.

As if he were worried that readers might miss his point, Marston was explicit and didactic in conveying his message of female empowerment. More than a mere role model, Wonder Woman literally told girls to be confident and believe in themselves, essential components in their ability to become strong and capable leaders. "You see girls, there's nothing to it," she explains while lifting a boulder in *Wonder Woman* #13 (Summer 1945). "All you have to do is **have confidence in your own strength!**"[4] "You can be as strong as any boy," she reassures little Olive North, and by extension her readers, in *Sensation Comics* #58 (Oct. 1946). Perhaps the most powerful message that Wonder Woman offered girls in the 1940s, however, was to "break your bonds!" So vital was this theme to Marston's feminist project to promote female love leadership that he featured it prominently, using the image of bondage — being tied up, chained, shackled, or otherwise restrained — in practically every one of his Wonder Woman stories.

Associated as it was, and still is, with sexual deviance, Wonder Woman's bondage theme has stood out to critics as fetishistic, if not sadistic. As Josette Frank from the Child Study Association of America explained to M.C. Gaines, the president of All-American Comics, in 1944, "Intentionally or otherwise, the strip is full of significant sex antagonisms and perversons [*sic*] ... Personally I would consider an out-and-out strip tease less unwholesome than this kind of symbolism."[5] Disturbed not only by scenes of Wonder Woman in chains, but also by images of her wrestling with wild animals or animalistic people while dressed in her skimpy super-costume, Frank was among the first — but would certainly not be the last — to argue that Wonder Woman was too sexually suggestive.

While acknowledging Wonder Woman's physicality, Marston rejected the claim that his character was unwholesome. Her costume, he explained, was athletic and functional. As for the bondage theme, he considered it necessary for teaching readers to distinguish between worthy and unworthy leaders: "As to chains and bonds — my whole strip is aimed at drawing the distinction in the minds of children and adults between love bonds and male bonds of cruelty and destruction" (Marston, "Letter to M.C. Gaines. Feb. 1, 1944"). Indeed, when considering the narrative context of Wonder Woman's bondage scenarios, we can see the various ways in which Marston used this controversial theme to advance his ideas about women's liberation and empowerment. In the Wonder Woman universe, bondage could be either good or bad, depending on who was doing the binding, who was being bound, and for what purpose.

When Wonder Woman was bound against her will by an evil adversary, as she frequently was, her ability to break free represented her determination to overcome various forms of oppression, most notably, male domination. Whether metaphorically — by busting the chains with which one of her male foes had bound her — or explicitly — through statements such as "Earth girls can stop men's power for evil when they refuse to be dominated by evil men!" (Marston and Peter, *Wonder Woman* #5, 79) — Wonder Woman encouraged her female readers to stand up for themselves and resist male control. Chains in Marston's Wonder Woman stories also represented the inner fears and insecurities that kept women from realizing their full potential. The jealousy and self-doubt that turn sweet Priscilla Rich into the evil and scheming Cheetah in *Wonder Woman* #6 (Fall 1943) are symbolized by her collection of chains. As Wonder Woman astutely points out, "Priscilla's hobby is collecting chains — mine is breaking them!" (111). Helping to boost Priscilla's ego and conquer the bitter and unhappy Cheetah within her, Wonder Woman's lesson was that girls must learn to love and accept themselves before they can share their love with others.

Without the will to get out from under that which oppressed them, girls' strength and confidence would never create the social changes Marston envisioned. Symbolized in the Wonder Woman stories as heavy ropes and chains, these oppressive forces were both external — like tyrannical men — as well as internal — like personal insecurities. Regardless of the form their oppression took, Wonder Woman encouraged girls to overcome it by being strong, believing in themselves, and meeting each challenge head-on. Ever the role model, Wonder Woman broke free from her fetters and showed other women how to do the same: "You see girls, it's easy to break bonds if you know you can!" (Marston and Peter, *Wonder Woman* #13). In this way, Marston enlisted the bondage theme to promote female liberation.

Bondage in Wonder Woman also served Marston's call for female love leadership and his belief that, as bad as it was to be controlled by malevolent forces, it was equally beneficial to submit to loving ones. Belonging to a nation of women who had earned the right to peace and eternal life by pledging their allegiance to Aphrodite, the quintessential love leader, Wonder Woman proved her own worth as a love leader by demonstrating in turn that she was properly bound to love and wisdom. Rewarded with a magic lasso that gave her the power to control others, Wonder Woman used this power to bind men and women to her love, with telling results. "With this great gift I can change human character," she marveled in *Sensation Comics* #6 (Jun. 1942). "I can make bad men good, and weak women strong!" (100). Such was the power of an effective love leader.

Subtitling his first Wonder Woman script "The Message of Love Binding," Marston stressed the importance of this concept to his editor, Sheldon Mayer: "In this theme I am using I fully believe that I am hitting a great movement now under way — the growth in power of women and I want you to let that theme alone — or drop the project." Believing as he did that love leaders would only exert their power over others in order to properly serve them, Marston used this "love binding" theme to promote the idea of submission to loving authority. He explained:

> Wonder Woman breaks the bonds of those who are slaves to evil masters. But she doesn't leave the freed ones free to assert their own egos in uncontrolled self-gratification. Wonder Woman binds the victims again in *love chains* — that is, she makes them submit to a *loving* superior ... Wonder Woman is trying to show children — who understand this far better than adults — that it's much more fun to be controlled by a loving person that [*sic*] to go ranting round submitting to no one[6] ["Letter to W.W.D. Sones"].

Marston demonstrated this idea most clearly in *Sensation Comics* #19 (Jul. 1943), when Wonder Woman's power is unleashed by a foe who unwittingly attempts to weaken her by removing her bracelets. "I'm not weak — I'm too strong," the mighty Amazon cries in dismay. "The bracelets bound my strength to good purposes — Now I'm completely uncontrolled! I'm free to destroy like a man!" (31). Threatening murder and demolishing property, it takes the power of Wonder Woman's own lasso to bring her back under control. "It's wonderful to feel my strength bound again," she proclaims. "Power without self-control tears a girl to pieces!" (Marston and Goodwin 34). Herein, claimed Marston, lay Wonder Woman's contribution to the "moral education of the young":

> The only hope for peace is to teach people who are full of pep and unbound force to *enjoy* being bound — *enjoy* submission to kind authority, wise authority, not merely tolerate such submission. Wars will only cease when humans *enjoy being bound;* (by loving superiors, of course)[7] ["Letter to M.C. Gaines Feb. 20, 1943"].

Advocating the right kind of submission to the right kind of leader, Marston used his bondage theme to help children, and adults, distinguish between constructive and destructive forms of power.

While Wonder Woman delivered a message of empowerment to her young female readers, the message she sent to boys was equally important in effecting a change in attitude towards women and their position in American society. Popular among children of both sexes in the 1940s, Wonder Woman taught boys that strong women like her were much more exciting and desirable than weak women like Diana Prince, the alter ego Wonder Woman adopted to protect her secret identity. As hunky Army Intelligence officer, Steve Trevor, bluntly points out: "Listen, Diana! You're a nice kid, and I like you. But if you think you can hold a candle to Wonder Woman you're crazy!" (Marston and Peter, *Sensation Comics* #1 30). Obviously as physically attractive (if not as excitingly dressed) as Wonder Woman, Diana's most evident deficiency was that she ostensibly lacked the superheroine's strength, courage, self-confidence, and agency. It was these qualities, more than her appearance, which earned Steve's, and other men's, admiration. This is not to say that Wonder Woman's physical beauty was unimportant. On the contrary, Marston considered Wonder Woman's attractiveness essential to her success as a love leader. "A woman character without allure," he explained, "would be like a Superman without muscle" ("Letter to M.C. Gaines. Sep. 15, 1943").[8] "Give [men] an alluring woman stronger than themselves to submit to and they'll be *proud* to become her willing slaves" ("Are Comics Fascist?"). As aesthetically appealing as she was impressive, Marston felt that Wonder Woman's character and appearance worked together to make her a worthy and effective love leader.

A Limit to Progress

"What woman lacks is the dominance or self-assertive power to put over and enforce her love desires," Marston explained to Coulton Waugh in 1945.

"I have given Wonder Woman this dominant force but have kept her loving, tender, maternal and feminine in every other way" (Waugh). Perhaps because Wonder Woman embodied some of the key characteristics mid-century Americans expected to find in an "ideal woman," they could more easily accept her as such. Yet certain aspects of Wonder Woman's conventionality suggest that Marston fell short of his feminist goals.

For starters, Wonder Woman failed to challenge the long-standing prejudice that the feminine ideal was white. Not only were Wonder Woman and her sister Amazons all fair-skinned, the Wonder Woman comic books reinforced racism by debasing minority characters. While the grotesque and evil "Jap" enemies that populated Wonder Woman's adventures were the most frequent illustration of this racism, the comic book was rife with other degrading characterizations, like the dim-witted African American porter and duplicitous Mexican "hussy" who make an appearance in *Wonder Woman* #1 (Summer 1942) (187). Hateful depictions of Asian, African American, and Mexican characters reinforced the racist association of "white" with "right."⁹ This inherent racism undercut Marston's message of women's freedom and empowerment and would have required minority readers to negotiate some serious obstacles in accepting, or rejecting, his comic book superheroine as a feminist role model.

On top of this racism, Marston's view that women deserved to be in power because they were intrinsically virtuous and would use their power to bring about peace and happiness further complicates Wonder Woman's feminist claims. Although Marston aimed to elevate women, arguments that base women's right to power on a set of assumptions about "the female character" ultimately reinforce the idea that women must adhere to the standards identified by the dominant culture as appropriately feminine. Those women who fail to meet society's expectations, whether by circumstance or by choice, risk being denied the rights that "acceptable" behavior would presumably earn them. For such individuals, Marston offered a rather unsympathetic solution: conform.

In *Wonder Woman* #7 (Winter 1943), Andra Moteeva's "insatiable ambition" to overthrow Primal Island's democratic government and become its supreme dictator evokes Steve Trevor's scorn: "You cruel, power-mad tyrant! You're not a real woman!" (233). To check Andra's unladylike self-interest and bring her to justice, the Council of Presidents sentences her to nurse's training, where she has to serve others until she "learn[s] to enjoy it!" A traditionally feminine occupation, nursing was supposedly in line with women's "natural" concern for others. Although it is arguably a positive attribute, to insist that altruism is something that all "real" women possess only reinforces the idea that a woman's needs are not as important as the needs of those around her. In celebrating women's selflessness, Marston undermined his mission to foster their "self-assertive power." The fact that he was yet another man seeking to impose his gender expectations on women further weakens his feminist appeal.

Careful to show that women's strength and assertiveness did not unsex them, Wonder Woman adhered to the dominant standards of acceptable femininity. Marston's Amazon princess was kind, nurturing, and self-sacrificing; she was also quite beautiful. Wonder Woman was tall and svelte and had a womanly, if athletic, body with "perfect 'modern Venus' measurements!" (Marston and Peter, *Wonder Woman* #6, 139). She had long eyelashes, painted lips, and long, thick shiny hair. She was also very fashionable and knew how to accessorize with earrings, bracelets, a tiara, and knee-high high-heeled boots. This keen fashion sense undoubtedly came from her interest in shopping, which was one of the first things she did upon arriving in America (Marston and Peter, *Sensation Comics* #1, 20). Occasionally yielding to a "girlish impulse," Wonder Woman could be caught dressing up and admiring her appearance from time to time.[10] She even mooned over Steve Trevor, who was known in their comic world as "the strong girl's weakness" (Marston and Peter, *Wonder Woman* #6, 118). Rather than emasculate Steve with her incredible strength, Wonder Woman often played the coquette, protesting for him to stop teasing her while thinking to herself "But I hope he won't!" (Marston and Peter, *Sensation Comics* #22, 166). Attractive, flirtatious, and occasionally frivolous, Wonder Woman delivered a healthy dose of traditionally expected femininity.

Regardless of whether or not Wonder Woman's femininity was the sugar coating that made her super strength, bold confidence, and self-sufficiency more palatable to her 1940s audience, her racism and adherence to sex essentialism detracted from Marston's call for women's liberation. As empowered as she was, Wonder Woman was not free to deviate too far from the standards of womanhood established by the dominant white, middle-class culture. Thus constrained, Marston's character reflected the limits of his feminist vision.

Change for the (Long-Term) Duration

In combining so-called "masculine" strength and capability with more stereotypically feminine qualities like altruism and beauty, Wonder Woman resembled another popular icon from the World War II era: Rosie the Riveter. Part of the propaganda that sought to mobilize American women specifically for the war effort, Rosie, like Wonder Woman, ventured beyond the domestic roles traditionally assigned to women. Her purpose was to inspire women to enter the workforce, replenishing the American labor supply while men were fighting overseas. Yet while Rosie and her real-life cohort were expected to resume their "normal" lives as housewives once the war was over and American men returned home, Wonder Woman had no intention of relinquishing her position. Unlike Rosie, who was only temporarily liberated from her home "for the duration" of the Second World War, Wonder Woman was Marston's model for a permanent change in women's roles and status.

Not only was Wonder Woman a more enduring character than Rosie, her contribution to the war effort was also more direct. Rosie's war job was to make planes, weapons, and ammunition that would help men win the war. She was the quintessential woman behind the man behind the gun. Wonder Woman, on the other hand, fought alongside men on the front lines of battle; she was the woman who led the man who held the gun. Defying convention that relegated woman to the role of man's submissive helpmate, Wonder Woman fought not for men, but for "liberty and freedom and all womankind!" (Marston and Peter, *All Star Comics* #8, 15). While the image of her leading the charge against the enemy seems to contradict Marston's argument that female love leaders would foster peace, Wonder Woman's ability to fight helped establish her credibility as a competent leader. At a time when most Americans rallied behind the war effort, Wonder Woman would have appeared weak, cowardly, and unpatriotic had she taken a pacifistic stand against it. Thus, Marston depicted his superheroine fighting Nazi and Japanese fascists, proving her commitment to democracy along with her courage and physical strength.[11]

Whereas Rosie suggested that women work in order to help men, Wonder Woman encouraged women to work because it enabled their independence from men. When misogynistic Dr. Psycho hypnotizes his wife, Marva, and forces her to help him in his plot to enslave American women in *Wonder Woman* #5 (Jun./Jul. 1943), Marva bitterly laments: "Submitting to a cruel husband's domination has ruined my life! But what can a weak girl do?" (51). Wonder Woman, of course, has the answer: "Get strong! Earn your own living—Join the WAACS or WAVES and fight for your country! Remember—the better you can fight, the less you'll have to!" Because Marston believed that women's economic independence was a necessary step towards their empowerment, he used Wonder Woman to encourage women and girls to pursue work outside of the home for the sake of their own autonomy and personal fulfillment. In doing so, his character directly challenged traditional gender roles in a way that Rosie did not.

In addition to her call for female independence, Wonder Woman's scorn for separate spheres further indicates that she was not one to comply with women's domestic containment in the post-war years. Although he subscribed to biological essentialism, Marston did not believe in a sexual division of labor. Advancing an argument that was later espoused by second-wave feminists, Marston insisted that husbands and wives should contribute equally to both the family income and the household chores.[12] He argued:

> The creation of children is not justifiable in a majority of unions between the sexes; but when the creation responses are justifiably undertaken, there is sound psychological ground for advising the woman to provide, beforehand, sufficient funds of her own to carry both herself and the child through the period of her physical incapacity for appetitive work. There is sound psychological ground, also, for requiring the male to share equally, at least, in the home work and the care of children [*Emotions* 395].

In insisting that married women and mothers continue to work "not at home with cook-stove and scrubbing brush, but outside, independently, in the world of men and affairs," Marston championed the feminist goal of combining family life with a career ("Women" 44).

Although Wonder Woman respected marriage and motherhood, she scoffed at the idea of women being confined to house and home. We can see this in *Sensation Comics* #9 (Sep. 1942). When Dan White mistakes Diana Prince for his wife and chains her to the stove to prevent her from going to work, she sarcastically quips: "How thrilling! I see you're chaining me to the cookstove. What a perfect caveman idea!" (134). Never having been a housewife and never hoping to be one, Wonder Woman was not about to retreat into domesticity after the war. On the contrary, she aspired to more prominent positions in public life, including, in one issue, the American Presidency. Her example would have been an appealing prospect to the number of real-life "Rosies" who discovered they actually wanted to keep working after the war's end.

Perhaps the most persuasive evidence that Wonder Woman was not just a temporary inspiration for a wartime change in women's roles, but a prescription for a long-term redefinition of American womanhood was the fact that her intended audience consisted primarily of children. Although children could participate in the campaign to buy war bonds and stamps, little girls were unable to support their country by taking war jobs, as adult women did. Rosie's "mobilization for the duration" message, therefore, did not apply to them; Wonder Woman's "girl power" message, on the other hand, did. As explained in an unpublished statement about Marston and the creation of the Wonder Woman comic book:

> "Wonder Woman" was conceived by Dr. Marston to set up a standard among children and young people of strong, free, courageous womanhood; to combat the idea that women are inferior to men, and to inspire girls to self-confidence and achievement in athletics, occupations and professions

monopolized by men.... Since millions of young people are reading "Wonder Woman" today, it is quite possible that their acceptance of this womanly ideal may alter our whole standards, in a few years, as to what is admirable in women. Children who admire the heroic type of woman will no longer have any use for the timid, physically weak, dependent and emotionally possessive woman of the old school, and will model themselves on the self-reliant, strong, comradely woman who can be honest and fearless because she is not dependent upon a man for her living ["Noted Psychologist"].

While it is unclear who wrote this statement, it captures Marston's intentions perfectly. Though he hoped to make his Wonder Woman line "as appealing to adults as it has proved to the juvenile readers of comics magazines" ("Letter to Coulton Waugh"), Marston ultimately offered his pop-cultural feminist icon to a young and still largely impressionable audience.

Marston sought to change Americans' understanding of ideal womanhood by instilling in children an appreciation for strong and independent women. Believing that a new type of role model would inspire girls to fulfill their leadership potential and that a new way of looking at girls would lead boys to participate in the reconstruction of traditional gender roles, Marston used Wonder Woman to teach American children that it was not only possible for girls to be strong and independent, but that this was, in fact, desirable. In contrast to Rosie the Riveter, a similar figure from the World War II period, Wonder Woman campaigned for a permanent change in the attitude toward and position of women in American society.

Despite its shortcomings, Marston's feminist vision proved relatively compelling for girls growing up in the 1940s. As testimony from readers suggests, Wonder Woman inspired real women to take control of their lives; speak up for themselves and others; seek fulfillment and economic autonomy in work outside of the home; develop their physical strength and athleticism; and meet challenges head on. Although it is difficult to know exactly what role Marston and his comic book creation played in fostering the feminist activism of the 1960s and 1970s, they were arguably successful in promoting a standard of femininity that was stronger, more independent, and more assertive than the traditional model. Whereas previous generations often valued female submissiveness and dependence, Americans today widely admire women who adhere to the Wonder Woman standard. It remains to be seen, however, whether this change in attitude can or will ultimately lead to the social-sexual revolution that Marston originally envisioned.

NOTES

1. While Waugh contacted Marston for details about Wonder Woman's creation, little of this ended up in his 1947 history of comics.

2. According to a survey conducted by the Market Research Company of America in 1944, the percentage of males who read comic books regularly was only slightly higher than the percentage of females, especially among children: 95% of boys and 91% of girls ages 6–11; 87% of boys and 81% of girls ages 12–17; 41% of men and 28% of women ages 18–30; and 16% of men and 12% of women age 31 and over. In addition to these regular readers, the survey estimated that an additional 13% of men and 10% of women over 18 were occasional readers. While these figures do not tell us actual numbers of male vs. female readers, it is clear that comic books were immensely popular among both boys and girls (and men and women!) at this time. ("Education" 89)

3. Debuting as a special feature in the last pages of *All Star Comics* #8 (Dec. 1941–Jan. 1942), Wonder Woman quickly rose to prominence, appearing as the cover story in the first monthly issue — and in most subsequent issues — of *Sensation Comics*, in Jan. 1942. By the following summer, she had rated her own quarterly publication, accomplishing in six months what it had taken her male predecessors, Superman and Batman, a year to do.

4. Emphasis in original.

5. Interestingly, Wonder Woman's bondage theme did not seem to concern Dr. Fredric Wertham, whose 1953 study, *Seduction of the Innocent*, sought to identify examples of social deviancy in comic books and sparked a federal investigation into a possible link between comic books and juvenile delinquency.

6. Emphasis in original.

7. Emphasis in original.

8. It is worth pointing out that Superman and other male superheroes were also physically appealing. Their tight costumes and prominent codpieces could reveal as much of their anatomy as Wonder Woman's outfit revealed of hers.

9. For the racist depictions of America's Japanese enemies during the Second World War, see Dower's *War Without Mercy* or Todd S. Munson's essay, "'Superman Says You Can Slap a Jap!' The Man of Steel and Race Hatred in World War II," in *The Ages of Superman: Essays on the Man of Steel in Changing Times*.

10. In *Sensation Comics #15*, Diana dons her Wonder Woman costume and remarks, "Isn't it silly how we girls love to dress up!" (Marston and Peter, "Sensation Comics #15" 146–7). In *Wonder Woman* #1 she receives her Wonder Woman outfit for the first time: "Diana, like any other girl with new clothes, cannot wait to try them on!" (Marston and Peter, "Wonder Woman #1" 156).

11. One should note, however, that Wonder Woman rarely killed her enemies; she was more likely to reform them, as Marston was quick to point out ("Why").

12. For second-wave feminist views on housework see Channing. See also Mainardi.

WORKS CITED

"Are Comics Fascist?" *Time*, Oct. 22, 1945. MS. Wonder Woman Letters, 1941–1945. Smithsonian Institution Libraries, Dibner Library of the History of Science and Technology, Washington, DC. (Hereafter SILDLHST)

Channing, Carol. "Housework." *Free To Be ... You And Me.* Arista Records, 1972.

Dower, John W. *War without Mercy: Race and Power in the Pacific War.* New York: Pantheon, 1986.

"Education: Comic-Coated History." *Newsweek,* Aug. 5, 1946: 89.

Frank, Josette. Letter to M.C. Gaines. Jan. 29, 1944. MS. Wonder Woman Letters, 1941–1945. SILDLHST.

Mainardi, Pat. "The Politics of Housework." *Women's America: Refocusing the Past.* Ed. Linda Kerber, Jane Sherron De Hart and Cornelia Hughes Dayton. 7th ed. New York: Oxford University Press, 2011. 701–03.

Marcello, Patricia Cronin. *Gloria Steinem: A Biography.* Westport, CT: Greenwood, 2004.

Marston, William Moulton. *Emotions of Normal People.* New York: Harcourt, Brace, 1928.

_____. Letter to Coulton Waugh. Mar. 5, 1945. MS. Wonder Woman letters, 1941–1945. SILDLHST.

_____. Letter to M.C. Gaines. Feb. 20, 1943. MS. Wonder Woman letters, 1941–1945. SILDLHST.

_____. Letter to M.C. Gaines. Sep. 15, 1943. MS. Wonder Woman letters, 1941–1945. SILDLHST.

_____. Letter to M.C. Gaines. Feb. 1, 1944. MS. Wonder Woman letters, 1941–1945. SILDLHST.

_____. Letter to Sheldon Mayer. Feb. 23, 1941. MS. Wonder Woman letters, 1941–1945. SILDLHST.

_____. Letter to W.W.D. Sones. Mar. 20, 1943. MS. Wonder Woman letters, 1941–1945. SILDLHST.

_____. "Women: Servants for Civilization." *Tomorrow,* Mar. 1942: 42–45.

_____. "Why 100,000,000 Americans Read Comics." *The American Scholar* 13.1 (1943): 35–44.

Marston, William Moulton (w), and Frank Godwin (a). "Sensation Comics #19 (Jul. 1943)." *Wonder Woman Archives* Vol. 3. New York: DC Comics, 2002. 21–34.

Marston, William Moulton (w), and Harry George Peter (a). "All Star Comics #8 (Dec. 1941–Jan. 1942)." *Wonder Woman Archives,* Volume 1. New York: DC Comics, 1998. 8–16.

_____. "Sensation Comics #1 (Jan. 1942)." *Wonder Woman Archives,* Volume 1. New York: DC Comics, 1998. 17–30.

_____. "Sensation Comics #6 (Jun. 1942)." *Wonder Woman Archives,* Volume 1. New York: DC Comics, 1998. 87–100.

_____. "Sensation Comics #9 (Sept. 1942)." *Wonder Woman Archives,* Volume 1. New York: DC Comics, 1998. 129–42.

_____. "Sensation Comics #15 (Mar. 1943)." *Wonder Woman Archives,* Volume 2. New York: DC Comics, 2000. 145–58.

_____. "Sensation Comics #22 (Oct. 1943)." *Wonder Woman Archives,* Volume 3. New York: DC Comics, 2002. 153–66.

_____. *Sensation Comics* #58 (Oct. 1946). New York: DC Comics.

_____. "Wonder Woman #1 (Summer 1942)." *Wonder Woman Archives,* Volume 1. New York: DC Comics, 1998. 143–97.

_____. "Wonder Woman #5 (Jun./Jul. 1943)." *Wonder Woman Archives,* Volume 3. New York: DC Comics, 2002. 35–79.

_____. "Wonder Woman #6 (Fall 1943)." *Wonder Woman Archives,* Volume 3. New York: DC Comics, 2002. 108–52.

_____. "Wonder Woman #7 (Winter 1943)." *Wonder Woman Archives,* Volume 3. New York: DC Comics, 2002. 195–239.

_____. "Wonder Woman #13 (Summer 1945)." *Wonder Woman.* New York: Holt, Rinehart and Winston, 1972.

"Noted Psychologist Revealed as Author of Best-Selling 'Wonder Woman,' Children's Comic." MS. Wonder Woman letters, 1941–1945. SILDLHST.

Steinem, Gloria. "Introduction." *Wonder Woman.* New York: Holt, Rinehart and Winston, 1972.

Waugh, Coulton. *The Comics.* New York: Macmillan, 1947.

Wertham, Fredric. *Seduction of the Innocent.* Laurel, NY: Main Road, 1953.

A Most Thrilling Struggle

*Wonder Woman as Wartime
and Post-War Feminist*

DONNA B. KNAFF

"In the green shimmering depths of the sea," begins a 1944 issue of Wonder Woman's comic book, "the girl from Paradise Island discovers a tunnel ... a phosphorescent passage that leads to hectic adventure ... the mighty Amazon maid plunges fearlessly into her most thrilling struggle for justice in this saga of girls under the sea" (Moulton, "The Saga"). The Amazon maid's phosphorescent passage could very well have symbolized Wonder Woman's entry into the popular culture of late 1941, plunging fearlessly into a struggle for justice for "girls" in crisis — set against a backdrop of the world in crisis. The Girl from Paradise Island first appearance and subsequent release of her eponymous comic book titled coincided with America's entry into World War II. Later, the Amazon Princess became a feminist icon because she represented the advances, often into formerly all-male domains, made by women during World War II.

Political cartoons and other graphic images had depicted the possible social catastrophes surrounding female advancement since before the creation of the United States (Franzen and Ethiel). Woman Suffrage, for instance, held a multitude of possible horrors: usually, cartoons depicted a woman in a tie, smoking a (Freudian) cigar and dominating a man, often her husband. In this logic, a woman with the masculine prerogative of the vote would naturally become masculinized, wearing pants and sitting in indelicate poses. If women became masculine the equal and opposite reaction was that men would then become feminine, adopting female duties and behaviors, like childcare and homemaking. The cartoons depicting and negotiating these fears addressed social paradigms about women's roles, about masculinity and femininity, and

22

they set an historical precedent in graphic art for later representations of women.

The girls who came of age in the World War II era had been raised by women who had been witness to the Suffrage movement (the Nineteenth Amendment, which granted women the vote, passed in 1920). The Second World War is widely accepted as a critical moment on the timeline of advances of women's rights and opportunities, but gender roles were contentious even during the war, partly because of the Great Depression. Women in the workplace hadn't lost nearly as many jobs as men did during the depression, and men had felt emasculated by women working when men were not (Canaday, 96). Men were still concerned about women invading their territory, and men and women both worried about the consequences of that invasion, wondering what would differentiate them if gendered tasks and traits were homogenized (Bailey, 114). The current theoretical notion — that women and men learn to "perform" their genders — was not an articulated concept.[1] It was, though, an extension of the longstanding fear: "male" work for women, especially in a civilian world where most young men were in the military or in defense work, often in a distant locale, might result in women's acquisition and retention of undesirable "masculine," "mannish," or "manly" qualities.

That anxiety became crucial when the American government heavily recruited women into formerly all-male spheres, like the military and production labor. Because in war, men enter the military in large numbers just as productive demands on society are at their highest, opportunities for women's liberation expand (Anderson, 3). Further, especially during World War II, it was to the government's advantage to increase visibility of those liberating opportunities. Working as a factory or farm laborer, though, or joining the military, required women to take on characteristics or attributes generally associated with men: their clothing (especially military uniforms), behavior, and/or languages, in addition to the formerly-male work itself. Ultimately, about 350,000 American women joined the women's branches of the military that had been created in 1942, and during the war, the number of women at work outside the home jumped from nearly 12 million in 1940 (over two million unemployed) to more than 18.6 million (less than half a million unemployed) in 1945. The proportion of all women who were employed increased from 27.6 percent to 37 percent, and by 1945 they formed 36.1 percent of the civilian labor force (Hartmann, 21). These numbers were intimidating, even to a nation with several million men in the (very masculine) military.

Wonder Woman also entered a male-dominated comic world during late 1941, coinciding nearly exactly with American entry into World War II. Beyond being merely an auspicious time for her to appear, her timing was critical. As comics historian Jeffrey K. Johnson notes, "By mid–1942, nearly all comic book heroes had changed into patriotic citizens that were willing ... to accept their new societal roles" (Johnson, 37). Her qualities — her balance of masculine traits with feminine ones, the way Steve Trevor and other male figures "managed" her masculinity; her maintenance of femininity no matter what — exemplified women's "new societal role" and married perfectly with what society expected American women to do. In fact, because of the historical context of her arrival, and because she appealed to adults as well as children, she combined femininity and masculinity in a way she only could have during the war.

The storyline of the "Saga of Girls Under the Sea" combines many of the elements of historic cartoons depicting women. There is fear of women's masculinity; fear men would become feminine in response, and management of that female masculinity — using the Amazon Princess to resolve or soothe those fears by comparing her to other women in the story. The plot goes like this: someone taps an undersea cable and sends a secret message to Army Intelligence, which Diana Prince, secretary to its commander, intercepts. She immediately understands the message as being for herself ("Tell Wonder Woman I need help!") and promptly jumps in her invisible airplane to trace the distress signal. Predictably, she runs into Steve Trevor flying *his* plane along the way (is there really just *one* route over the Atlantic Ocean?), and the two share information about the case. The "Ingenious Amazon" finds where the cable is tapped, locates a tunnel to the trouble spot (the lost city of Atlantis), and discovers that the queen of Atlantis, Octavia, is being jailed by her royal subjects. It seems power in the Atlantean region of Venturia has changed hands several times, from corrupt women to corrupt men and back again. Octavia's subjects have rebelled, thinking she is also dishonest, and Wonder Woman must save the queen from her own misled but miscreant citizens (Moulton, "The Saga")

The story works uniquely in a World War II context by comparing the Amazon Princess to Octavia and to her female subjects. While the Atlanteans show not only brute physical strength but trickery and poor sportsmanship — not ladylike behavior at all, Wonder Woman balances her masculine qualities with feminine ones. The Girl from Paradise Island, though, is "Stronger than Hercules," but she is "Beautiful as Aphrodite," as well. While she is "Swifter than Mercury," she is also "Wise as Athena" (Moulton, "Wonder Woman"). As an Amazon Princess, a warrior, she still exhibits femininity: she nursed Steve Trevor when he crashed on Paradise Island, after all, and later was a secretary, both normatively "feminine" occupations. Although during the war, she wears a uniform and conquers villains as a superhero, throughout the story, she wears not only her tight, short, revealing costume (blue spangled shorts, eagle-design halter top) but also red earrings, makeup, and lipstick. Her hair is coiffed, and she is never mussed (although she comes close once in the story, when she is electrified). Her legs are long and slim, her bust is pronounced, and her muscles, though toned, are not hulking.

When Wonder Woman first meets the Atlantean women in the story, one of them calls her "little weakling" and she calls the Atlantean "big girl," thus emphasizing the size differential between them, the Amazon is petite in comparison to the Atlantean, who is large and muscular. Throughout, the characters emphasize that difference, with the Atlanteans referring to Wonder Woman as "A dwarf," "Doll girl," and "This girl [who] is small but very strong" (Moulton, "The Saga" 12). The Venturian gender power structure is also reversed in the plotline: Venturian women are tall, with bulging musculature and square jaws (which in at least one image clamp large [again, Freudian] cigars), and are more aggressive than the Venturian men, who are referred to as "manlings" and are small, runty-looking, and bald (a sure sign of lack of masculinity, in World War II images).

In the past, both manlings and women have been dictators of Venturia, but now, the manlings have joined the anarchists because "Octavia makes all manlings slaves!" The Venturian women are shown to be devious, as when they invite Wonder Woman to a banquet, then attach electric wires to her Amazonian bracelets. They keep them on her until the manlings can connect fetters to the bracelets, which leads to the Amazon Princess's memorable declaration, "Men chained my bracelets together! By Aphrodite's decree, my Amazon strength is gone!" (Moulton, "The Saga").

This pronouncement demonstrates an important feature of Wonder Woman's acceptable masculinity as expressed in World War II-era graphic art: it is managed or regulated by men. The manlings who have chained her bracelets are slaves to women who ordered them to do so — the symptom of their overturned status in Venturian society — but nonetheless, it is their male prerogative to have this power over the Princess. Here in the upside-down world of Atlantis, where people lived under the ocean instead of on top or near it, and women ruled over men, it was probably not surprising to World War II readers that men abused their power over women — or that women abused their power over men, when they got the chance. Thus, the manlings abuse their power (under Aphrodite's decree) to chain up the Amazon Princess. The fact that the storyline implicitly disparages the manlings because they do so is a yet another example of how gender roles are negotiated in the story.

If the obvious moral of the story is about the use and misuse of power, the plotline of the saga is, in many ways, a cautionary tale of the ways *gender* is used and misused. Wonder Woman is strong, but her aggressive, tough qualities are balanced by her concern for others and for fairness. She is physically dominant, but in a way that comes from her inherent rightness and that de-emphasizes muscles and size as sources of that power. Juxtaposed against the burly and supremacy-intent female Venturians, the Amazon maid is tempered by her desire to correct wrongs and abuse and to give authority to those who deserve to rule, not to herself— the self-abnegating female ideal.

Male Atlanteans also, however, have had their gender role subverted. If idealized masculinity casts men as protective of women, with their "natural" domination over women demonstrated by a gentle (if paternalistic) discipline, the manlings have had to seize the throne by revolt, rather than having it as their birthright. Because their "normal" role has been perversely misconstrued, men's anger has taken the shape, in the Atlantean past, of making women pay for women's greater size and strength (they are "bigger than us men," as a male cigar-smoking former tyrant complained, making women kneel before his misbegotten throne).

The manlings' abuse of power is implicitly compared to Steve Trevor, who exhibits masculinity (and his influence over Wonder Woman) in a superior way: he uses it both to objectify her and to rescue and shield her. In the beginning of the story, when he and Wonder Woman "meet" over the Atlantic Ocean, he reacts to her leaping into his airplane from hers by saying, "Great Heavens, Beautiful, don't do that again! You nearly gave me heart failure!," both calling attention to her looks and fearing for her safety. After their talk, he queries her, "Leaving so soon? Please, Angel, tell me where you're going in case — er — I need you!" Wonder Woman responds, "Good old Steve — you mean in case I need you!" (Moulton, "The Saga" 3, 4). She understands his question to be one of male protectiveness — a patronizing attitude for him to have, given the fact that *she*, not he, is "Stronger than Hercules" and "Swifter than Mercury"— is a mere mortal man *still* stronger than a female superhero?? — but the plot shows implicit approval of his protectiveness here, too.

After Wonder Woman is chained, the wicked Venturians make her dance until she is fatigued, after which they hope to kill her. Because her Amazon strength is weakened by her man-applied chains, she eventually tires and the Atlanteans push her down — but she grabs a (rather phallic) sword and defends herself. This is almost a losing battle until "Ba-ang!— A shot rings out and severs the chain between Wonder Woman's bracelets!" (Moulton, "The Saga" 13). Steve Trevor has tracked down the clue the Amazon Princess gave him and has thoughtfully shot off her manacles. Both literally and symbolically, men have chained and freed women in the story.

"The Mighty Amazon, her strength restored," continues the story, then seizes the head rebel woman "in a grip of steel," growling, "You asked for plenty, Big Girl, and I'm not going to disappoint you!" Here again, the story points out the difference between Wonder Woman and her larger, more masculine adversaries. Steve Trevor and Etta Candy (who has, rather inexplicably, joined him in his search for Atlantis — perhaps she had a plane with the same route, too) help Wonder Woman beat up the remaining female rebels and manlings. Queen Octavia, still in chains, takes the oath of office as the democratically-elected president of Venturia, while the Girl from Paradise Island looks on, declaiming, "Bonds of love never make the wearer weaker — they give him greater strength!" (Moulton, "The Saga" 13).

I have discussed elsewhere some of the implications of Wonder Woman's propensity for bondage and chaining (Knaff 127–130). That propensity tracked through many of her comic book stories and has often been noted by fans and critics. The Amazon uses ropes and what she terms "binding games" on the Venturian women (Moulton, "The Saga"). While World War II readers of this tale, particularly children, might not have seen them as sexual, per se, they might also have interpreted those actions as at least naughty.

What binding and chaining represent in this story, however, are strength and responsibility. These are characteristics of citizenship that were very like those advocated by the U.S. government in its campaign to recruit women to the military and into civilian workplaces during the war. Working 48 hours a week or working in dangerous or uncomfortable circumstances was a bond that many women assumed in World War II, despite changes to their duties and gender-role behaviors that many of them might not have sought out, before the war. They did so, however, as expressions of patriotism, caring, or even as a way to defend men who were in the military and sometimes in grave danger. As *non sequitur* as Wonder Woman's declaration about "bonds of love" may have been, her words were also recognizable as part of a wartime vocabulary — not just of words but also of emotions. Wonder Woman's declamation spoke *to* and *for* the women of World War II, in her words and in her actions.

As World War II women instilled their values into their children, it was these strong qualities that also made the Amazon Princess a logical symbol to be adopted by the organized feminist movement. Wonder Woman appeared on the very first issue of *Ms.* magazine in July 1972, and the notion of the Amazon Princess as feminist icon brought her to life in different ways in the mid–1970s and beyond. The Girl from Paradise Island appeared as a television movie, a television series, a "posing doll," and all manner of Wonder Woman merchandise, from roller skates to Pez dispensers. She became a Mattel "Barbie," in 2000. A few years ago, D.C. Comics even licensed a "First Appearance" action figure wearing her original outfit, including her initial blue star-spangled skirt, red strapless top with eagle breast-plate, and high-heeled red boots ("First"). Because her audience identified with the fictional female superhero of World War II, Wonder Woman's status, qualities, and achievements became an important vehicle not only of wartime values but also of (long-term) postwar standards and aspirations.[2]

It was the Amazon Princess' origins in wartime, though — the critical moment of her arrival — that have helped to give her the staying power she has shown as a character. Because her appearance coincided with a moment in history when women were called upon to take on duties, responsibilities, and aspects of gender identity formerly in men's domain, her demonstration of "masculine" qualities was seen as appropriate for the times. Further, she was held to the same standards of female behavior as the World War II women she inspired and represented: her masculinity and power over men were managed, and she maintained her femininity no matter the circumstances. From her inception, beyond merely being entertainment for children, Wonder Woman represented a vision of *women's* qualities that were equal to or greater than men's, and exemplified a mix of *gender* qualities that adult women and men recognized as necessary to the Allied effort. Wonder Woman rode a wave of wartime feminism that permitted her to show that her greatest qualities were ones that helped win the war. Those same qualities enabled her use as an image of strength, self-reliance, and self-belief that were the basis of the Second Wave, pushing women further up the shore to equality. Much as the Amazon maid took on the Atlanteans, it was — and is — a thrilling struggle.

NOTES

1. "Performance of gender" is Judith Butler's concept from *Gender Trouble: Feminism and the Subversion of Identity* (New York: Routledge, 1990). It essentially says that we learn to perform our genders — that they are not as fixed as previously suspected, but that "masculine" and "feminine" are qualities that are behavioral, rather than essential.

2. For more on the concept of status and achievements becoming a vehicle of values, see Patricke Johns-Heine and Hans Gerth in *Creating Rosie the Riveter: Class, Gender, and Propaganda During World War II.*

WORKS CITED

Anderson, Karen. *Wartime Women: Sex Roles, Family Relations, and the Status of Women During World War II.* Westport, CT: Greenwood, 1981.

Bailey, Beth. "The Etiquette of Masculinity and Femininity." *From Front Porch to Back Seat: Courtship in Twentieth Century America.* Baltimore and London: Johns Hopkins University Press, 1988, 1989.

Canaday, Margot. *The Straight State: Sexuality and Citizenship in Twentieth-Century America.* Princeton, NJ: Princeton University Press, 2009.

"First Appearance" Wonder Woman Action Figure, D.C. Direct, D.C. Comics. Initial release Jun. 25, 2004.

Franzen, Monika, and Nancy Ethiel. *Make Way! 200 Years of American Women in Cartoons.* Chicago, IL: Chicago Review Press, 1988.

Hartmann, Susan M. *The Home Front and Beyond: American Women in the 1940s,* Boston: Twayne, 1982.

Johns-Heine, Patricke, and Hans Gerth, in Maureen Honey, *Creating Rosie the Riveter:*

Class, Gender and Propaganda During World War II. Amherst: University of Massachusetts Press, 1984.

Johnson, Jeffrey K. *SuperHistory: Comic Book Heroes and American Society.* Jefferson, NC: McFarland, 2012.

Kanigher, Robert (w), and Harry G. Peter (a). "The Man Who Shook the Earth." *Wonder Woman* Vol. 1 #57 (Jan. 1953). New York: DC Comics.

Knaff, Donna. *Beyond Rosie the Riveter: Women of World War II in American Popular Graphic Art.* Lawrence: University Press of Kansas, 2012.

Moulton, Charles (w), and H. G. Peter (artist). "The Saga of Girls Under the Sea." *Sensation Comics* #35 (Nov. 1944). New York: DC Comics.

Moulton, Charles (w), and H. G. Peter (artist). "Wonder Woman Arrives in Man's World." *Sensation Comics* #1 (Jan. 1942). New York: DC Comics.

Containing Wonder Woman

Fredric Wertham's Battle Against the Mighty Amazon

CRAIG THIS

William Moulton Marston created Wonder Woman because "not even girls want to be girls as long as our feminine archetype lacks force, strength, and power" (Marston 42). For Marston, "the obvious remedy is to create a feminine character with all the strength of Superman plus all of a good and beautiful woman" (Marston 42). This woman "would, should ... rule the world." Marston's Wonder Woman stories "exhorted women to become physically and mentally strong, promoted paid female employment, and critiqued ... over-masculinized aspects of American culture" (McClelland-Nugent 115).

Anti-comic book crusader and psychiatrist Fredric Wertham, however, saw Wonder Woman in a completely different light. "Wonder Woman," wrote Wertham, "is physically very powerful, tortures men, has her own female following, is the cruel, 'phallic' woman. While she is a frightening figure for boys, she is an undesirable ideal for girls, being the exact opposite of what girls are supposed to be" (34). This being "opposite of what girls are supposed to be" became the basis of Wertham's argument and attacks against Wonder Woman. Wertham's attempts to censor and limit the appeal of Wonder Woman and her feminism fall into the broader theme of containment, particularly the "domestic containment of women" in the 1950s (Wright; Gardner).

Containment

"Containment" was a term coined by George F. Kennan, an American diplomat to the USSR, in *Foreign Affairs* (1947), to describe a diplomatic policy whereby the United States would seek to prevent the Soviet Union from "using the power and position it won as a result of [World War II] to reshape the postwar international order" with respect to Germany and Japan" (Gaddis 4). The United States would achieve this containment through "adroit and vigilant application of counterforce at a series of constantly shifting geographical and political points" (Kennan 576).[1] While the containment policy did have its dissenters, notably Walter Lippman, the containment policy helped shape President Harry S. Truman's cold-war diplomacy (Gaddis).

Containment of Wonder Woman and her feminist views after World War II serves as an apt metaphor for what Wertham sought to do, not just with Wonder Woman but all comics. Wertham, an outspoken critic of comic books, could not put the comic book publishers out of business directly, but through a series of counterforces, both adroit and vigilant, he could contain the comic book industry and, as Kennan hoped with his policy, these counterforces would frustrate and force the comic book industry to either break-up or gradually mellow. Wertham's public attacks of comic books began almost as soon as the Cold War started. He presented his findings about the effects of comic books at a symposium entitled, "The Psychopathology of Comic Books" (Mar. 19, 1948) (Nyberg 32). A report of that symposium appeared on March 29, 1948, in *Time* magazine under the title, "Puddles of Blood" and in May 1948, he published an article, "Comics ... Very Funny" in the *Saturday Review of Literature* (Hadju 97–100). From that point on, Wertham promoted his anti-comic book crusade speaking whenever and to whomever would listen, such as the New York Joint Legislative Committee to Study the Publication of Comics and the U.S. Senate Subcommittee on Investigating Juvenile Delinquency as well as publishing articles in *Ladies Home Journal* and *Reader's Digest*. Eventually, he published his findings, thoughts, and opinions in *Seduction of the Innocent* (1954). This 400-page book outlined Wertham's criticisms of comic books, using data collected from various sources, including interviews of children and juvenile delinquents. Wertham's basic argument was that juvenile delinquency was on the rise in the United States and comic books were the cause (Wright).

Although *Seduction of the Innocent* was a much talked about book in 1954, it did have its detractors. Those detractors questioned Wertham's research and sources as well as his overall argument (Wright). And, while comic books had emerged just at the start of World War II, it seemed that World War II, as a social force, had contributed more to the juvenile delinquency rate than anything else. Children, whose fathers were off fighting the war or dead and whose mothers were trying to be single-parents and/or work outside the home, drifted off into juvenile delinquency due to the lack of attention (Diggins). The Great Depression and World War II had set in motion a cultural shift in American society that carried through the 1950s, despite its view as a placid decade (Wright).

The 1950s and Shifting Cultural Forces

Wonder Woman represented some of those shifting cultural forces in the United States through her appearance in comic books as a single, strong, independent, career-minded woman and the feminism she implied. The United States' involvement in World War II along with the preceding hard times of the Great Depression had "disrupted the rhythm and fabric of American society" (Diggins 22). In fact, Diggins argues that in the early 1940s "the American family experienced stresses and dislocations unknown since the American Civil War" (24). With men serving in the military, many women raised their children as single parents.

The stresses and strains of war also brought historic opportunities. With the demand for women to work, day care centers opened around the country. Women joined the work force welcoming the liberation from domestic drudgery. However, despite six million joining the workforce war effort, it was not the consciousness-raising event that feminists interpret it as. Women joined the war effort for a variety of reasons — patriotism, improve their economic standing, or boredom (Diggins).

Regardless, this shift in labor did not escape William Moulton Marston. In an interview with *Family Circle* (1944), Marston noted:

> Women now fly heavy planes successfully; they help build planes, do mechanics' work. In England they've taken over a large share of all manual labor in fields and factories; they've taken over police and home defense duties. In China a corps of 200,000 women under the supreme command of Madame Chiang Kai-shek perform the dangerous function of saving lives and repairing damage after Japanese air raids. This huge female strong- arm squad is officered efficiently by 3,000 women. Here in this country we've started a Women's Auxiliary Army and Navy Corps that will do everything men soldiers and sailors do except the actual fighting. Prior to the First World War nobody believed that women could perform these feats of physical strength. But they're performing them now and thinking nothing of it. In this far worse: war, women will develop still greater female power; by the end of the war that traditional description "the weaker sex" will be a joke-it will cease to have any meaning [Richard 15].

The characters of Diana Prince and Wonder Woman seemed to reflect this growing "female power" of women in the World War II workplace. Diana Prince, Wonder Woman's alter ego, worked as a colonel's secretary. Wonder Woman, on the other hand, represented the "strong-arm" women, who built planes and did mechanics' work: the Rosie the Riveter of the war effort. However, Wertham never attacked Diana Prince instead he attacked Wonder Woman as the greater threat to American society.

"Wonder Woman," wrote Wertham, "is a frightening image. For girls, she is a morbid ideal." Not only was Wertham bothered by her strength and independency, but also the scanty way she dressed. Wertham noted that children expressed that superheroes had "impure dress" or "no clothes on" and were "naked" or "not modest" (Wertham 177). Another boy, according to Wertham, in discussing a female character in a comic book said, "There is one that is sexy! Her legs are showing above the knees and her headlights are showing plenty!" (Wertham 178). Wertham reported that he asked a young boy who read comics what he wanted to be when he grew up and he reply was: "I want to be a sex maniac" (Wertham 173). If comic books turned children into "sex maniacs," as Wertham feared, then the publication of Alfred Kinsey's reports, *Sexual Behavior in the Human Male* (1948) and *Sexual Behavior in the Human Female* (1953), and *Playboy* magazine (1955) must have severely troubled him (Diggins 205–207). Not only did these publications promote women's sexuality, but also undermined the Victorian virtues of women — what women were supposed to be — pious, virtuous, domesticated, and submissive to fathers and husbands (Welter).

The submission of women to men in the Wonder Woman comics, in the form of actual bondage, was also attacked by Wertham: these "sadomasochistic fantasies may become a serious factor in the maladjustment of children" (Wertham 177). Marston, however, argued that the submission of Wonder Woman symbolized the bondage of women in American society (Pereira). Sadomasochism and bondage were huge themes and stem from Marston's belief that women were in bondage in society through the values and beliefs structures of society.

Domestic Containment Policy

The cultural bondage that Marston spoke about was found in the media of the day, such television, movies, and magazines. Television was still in its infancy, but television shows like *Father Knows Best* and *Ozzie and Harriet* portrayed a domesticated and contained woman, who stayed home and took care of the house and children (Diggins). Even the movies seemed to portray "contained" women. "While the social acceptability of women working increased in the 1950s," in the romantic comedies and popular love stories, when the girl got her man, she usually quit work (Coontz 61). In *All About Eve*, Bette Davis marries a man who loves her and she gives up her acting career while in the *Tender Trap*, Debbie Reynolds says, "A career is just fine, but it's no substitute for marriage" (Coontz 61).

The strength of the image of the domesticated and contained woman, however, could be found in popular women's magazines, such as *Cosmopolitan*, *Ladies' Home Journal*, and *Mademoiselle*, all of which sought to woo "their female constituency, promising the right and scientific ways to live" (Ehrenreich and English 4). Caroline Smith, in her examination of *Mademoiselle* (Sep. 1953), noted such containment articles as "Future for the Divided" (about the struggles of a woman who wants both a career and a family). The issue noted that women can have jobs outside of the family and combine those jobs with family duties, but women should think twice about their choice as taking a job "may conflict with one's husband." *Mademoiselle*, argued Smith, seemed to discourage women's navigation beyond the private sphere.

The "Future for the Divided" hinted at the issues facing the American family in the 1950s. While the 1950s have been viewed as a placid decade, it, in fact was a decade of struggle for the American family and women. In the wake of World II and with the emergence of the Cold War, the American family in the 1950s was a fragile institution as "attitudes toward proper roles changed dramatically ... and that change continued to affect women's lives into the 1950s" (Walker, 29). Further, social mobility became the focus for whites and civil rights focused on sanctioned inequality for both racial and sex groups. It was a period of profound tension and change.

Marston's Wonder Woman, created in 1941, seemed to speak to the confusion and tension that women felt during this period. Marston understood the "power of a single image ... [and] media manipulation" (Robinson 47). For Marston, that single image would be Wonder Woman and comic books would be the medium. However, in promoting feminism through the character of Wonder Woman, Marston argued "less about advocating gender equality and fighting sexism" and more about saying women were morally superior to men (Pereira 35). Women would rule the world with love, compassion, and justice. Marston foresaw a future in which women would be superior to men.

He projected that future with *Wonder Woman #7* (Winter 1943), which saw Wonder Woman being elected president in the year 3004. Through the marvel of the "life vitamin," which extended long life, Wonder Woman lived to the year 3000 and saw a woman elected president. However, the Man Party revolted against the new female president. Wonder Woman was able to crush the rebellion and protect the female president. Then, in the year 3004 Steve Trevor is nominated for president by the Man's Party while Diana Prince, sensing corruption by the Man's Party, decide to run against him. Professor Manly, a supporter of the Man Party, rigs the election in Steve's favor, but

Steve finds out about the tampering and confronts Professor Manly, who has Steve jailed. Wonder Woman comes to his rescue and proves the election results were tampered with. As a result Diana Prince is sworn in as president (Marston and Peter).

To Fredric Wertham, a female president was unacceptable. Not only were the gender roles reversed, but the outward hatred of males, as portrayed in Wonder Woman comics, clearly had homosexual undertones. To support his argument, Wertham referenced an editorial in *The Psychiatric Quarterly* (he does not provide a citation) stated that the "sadistic hatred of all males is plainly Lesbian" (Wertham 193). Thus, for Wertham, it was plain to see that "the lesbian counterpart of Batman may be found in Wonder Woman. The homosexual connotation of the Wonder Woman type of story is unmistakably psychological" (Wertham 192).

While the emergence of homophobia during the 1950s both in the attack on comic books and in the Red Scare served as another tool for right-wingers in their battle against lefts and liberals, it was also manipulated to contain women. The family was perceived as fundamental to American society in the United States struggle against the Soviet Union. Feminism, like homosexuality, was viewed as a threat to the heterosexual, patriarchal family. Thus, the Red Scare, while seemingly focused on communists, also attacked feminism out of fear of "women's increasing sexual and economic independence" (Storrs 119). Richard Hofstadter concurs that the 1950s Red Scare, among other things, expanded its reach to issues, like homosexuality and feminism, "to discharge resentment and frustrations, to punish, to satisfy enmities whose roots lay elsewhere than in the Communist issue itself" (41–42). Other historians agree with this assessment: Michael Heale argued that the 1950s Red Scare among other things defended a conservative sexual order while Kyle Cuordileone interpreted the Red Scare as anxiety about the threats to American masculinity because of, among many things, homosexuality. Others have shown that the Red Scare had as its basis white, Christian, heterosexual patriarchy families (MacLean; Nielsen). Many crusades seemingly fell under the umbrella of the Red Scare.

However, it is difficult to prove if Wertham's charges were driven by anti-communism rhetoric of the Red Scare. As Hadju writes:

> the controversy over comic books was neither a subset of the Red Scare nor a direct parallel to it ... McCarthyism, a movement out of the heartland to purge the country of modes of thinking associated with the Northeastern intelligentsia and the New Deal, was a form of anti-elitism as well as anti-communism. The sentiment against comic was near opposite, despite the urban New York origin of its target; it was a kinds of anti-anti-elitism, a campaign by protectors of rarefied ideals of literacy, sophistication and

virtue to rein in the practitioners of a wild, homegrown form of vernacular American expression [210].

Nevertheless, while a connection is there, the similarities between the two events cannot be dismissed: "witch hunts" and book burnings, congressional hearings, and the creation of loyalty oaths and the Comic Code Authority. The Comic Code Authority, adopted in 1954, "consisted of forty-one specific regulations that Comics Magazine Association of America (CMAA) President John Goldwater, labeled as problem areas" (Nyberg 112). Although not all forty-one regulations directly affected Wonder Woman, the Comic Code Authority did have two regulations that did:

• The treatment of love-romance stories shall emphasize the value of the home and the sanctity of marriage.
• Sex perversion or any inference to same is strictly forbidden (Nyberg 168).

Wonder Woman Contained

How much impact the Comic Code Authority had on the containment of Wonder Woman is difficult to say because before it was adopted in 1954, several events and forces within the comic book industry and the creative team of Wonder Woman impacted the future of Wonder Woman. These events along with Wertham's effort effectively contained Wonder Woman in the 1950s.

The most important of all the events was that in 1947, William Moulton Marston died of lung cancer. The editorship passed briefly to Sheldon Mayor before being handed to Robert Kanigher, who would hold the position of editor and writer of Wonder Woman for twenty years (Daniels 93). The loss of Marston and with it his original vision and dream for Wonder Woman was hard to replace and naturally would lead to changes in the portrayal of the character.

Other changes in the portrayal of the character resulted from the decline in the popularity of superheroes in the post-war United States. Even before Wertham's attacks, Wonder Woman, like so many other superhero comics, was declining in sales (Wright). The end of the war and the loss of recognizable villains, like Hitler, Mussolini, and Tojo, seemed to put comic book superheroes out of work. Many titles were ended. Kanigher, in his attempt to save the *Sensation Comics* title, turned the Wonder Woman storylines to romance, like the popular romance comics of the time, most notably Joe Simon and Jack Kirby's *Young Romance* (Wright 129). Kanigher seemed to play off that popularity with the controversial *Sensation Comics*, #94 (Oct. 1949), which had Steve Trevor carrying Wonder Woman; much like a groom would carry a bride across a threshold. Recasting the Steve Trevor-Wonder Woman relationship in the mold of the *Young Romance* comics, however, was not enough to save *Sensation Comics*, which disappeared, but Wonder Woman, as character and then as title continued.

Kanigher also dropped Etta Candy and the Holiday Girls from the Wonder Woman storylines. Etta Candy and the Holliday Girls had appeared in *Sensation* #2 (Feb. 1942). Etta was Wonder Woman's sidekick, but a bit bizarre. She was a student at Holliday College, where Wonder Woman asked Etta to round up "one hundred beautiful athletic girls" — the Holliday girls to fight — to fight Dr. Poison (Daniels 35). Etta was usually depicted carrying a box of bonbons and serving as president of the Beeta Lambda sorority. As president, she sat on a raised throne while watching new pledges kneel before her and get paddled by other sorority sisters. Etta even presided over a baby party, where college students dressed up as babies (Daniels 35).

Wertham, predictably, didn't like Etta or the Holliday girls. "Wonder Woman has her own female following," wrote Wertham, "the 'Holliday girls, i.e. the holiday girls, the gay party girls, the gay girls. Wonder Woman refers to them as 'my girls'" (Wertham 193). Whether homosexuals or not, by 1950, Kanigher eliminated them. In describing his decision, though, he seemed defensive. He argued that he didn't get rid of them. "It's a matter of the story," he continued. "It isn't as if I was an executioner. I wasn't" (Daniels 100). Whether he caved to Wertham's pressure or not is unclear. However, what is clear that Etta and the Holliday girls were no longer in the storyline and despite later attempts to be revived, they never returned.

Another change that focused on the shift from strong women to married women was the discontinuation of "Wonder Women of History" and its replacement with "Marriage a la Mode." "Wonder Women of History" had provided biographical sketches of famous women in history, such as Susan B. Anthony, Clara Barton, and Florence Nightingale. "Marriage a la Mode" highlighted marriage customs and ceremonies from around the world. Wonder Woman had become more and more fascinated with marriage in the storylines (Daniels 100). Yet, she continued to struggle with the confusion and desire to want a career and want to be married. Les Daniels argued that her confusion could be summed up in this comment by Wonder Woman from 1950: "According to Aphrodite's law, if I marry, I can no longer remain an Amazon. I'll become Diana Prince forever. Therefore, unless Steve falls in love with me as Diana Prince, we can never marry" (Daniels 101).

The dual character of the 1940s Wonder Woman/Diana Prince allowed Marston to focus on how women performed both typically male and female jobs in the wartime workforce. As stated previously, Wonder Woman resembled Rosie the Riveter while Diana Prince, colonel's secretary, encompassed the various roles that women held during the war. The 1940s Wonder Woman/Diana Prince, however, did not focus on the struggle between career and family and between career and marriage. The 1950s Wonder Woman/Diana Prince did portray the struggle of being a woman, trying to juggle career, family, and marriage, which Kanigher returned to over and over again.

In "Top Secret," *Wonder Woman* #99 (Jul. 1958), the struggle is right out there in the open. After Wonder Woman rescues Steve Trevor from yet another disaster, Steve says, "You must love me to risk your life for me like that, angel! When are you going to marry me? You know how I feel about you!" Wonder Woman responds, "I do, Steve, but I can't marry you — until my services are no longer needed to battle crime and injustice only then can I think about myself" (Kanigher). Despite being asked by the man she loves, Wonder Woman chooses career — battling crime and injustice — over marriage.

Later, in "Undersea Trap" *Wonder Woman* #101 (Oct. 1958), Wonder Woman watches as Steve Trevor saves himself from an impending plan crash. Wonder Woman comments that Steve Trevor doesn't really need Wonder Woman to help him. Steve replies, "But what if I did, Angel? What if I need your help — say three times a day?" (Kanigher). And, now the challenge is set: if Steve needs help three times, then Wonder Woman marries him. Now, Wonder Woman must juggle her love for Steve with her career. Performing her career choice — rescuing and saving people — with the man she loves threatens her career. And, after Wonder Woman has rescued Steve twice, a third rescue presents itself. It is then, and only then, that Steve Trevor realizes the dilemma he has created for Wonder Woman, noting, "But helping me this third time means she loses the wager with me" (Kanigher).

Kanigher wrote this constant struggle between career and marriage for Wonder Woman, but, unlike Bette Davis, Wonder Woman continued with her career. Yet, over and over again, Kanigher returned to this theme of struggle between career and marriage, which was really a struggle of Wonder Woman with herself— what she wants and what she desires and what she wants and what society desires.

Even when Kanigher focused on her career, he worked in elements that forced Wonder Woman to struggle with the tension of choosing between career and family. For example, in "The Million Dollar Penny," *Wonder Woman* #98 (May 1958), Wonder Woman must invest a penny and turn it into millions of dollars in 24 hours and then donate the proceeds to a charity for children. While she is not married, clearly the challenge brings with it matriarchal duties and desires — the protection of children.

This story line, along with the majority of the storylines, worked hard to show that Wonder Woman was a heterosexual, interested in men, marriage, and family. Another change in the comic, which reflects this storyline, was the creation of stories featuring Wonder Girl — Wonder Woman as a young girl. The development of this character followed the creation of two other girl characters — Marvel Girl and Supergirl — who served as side-kicks to their male counterparts, Captain Marvel and Superman, respectively. Just as Marvel Girl and Supergirl served to normalize Captain Marvel and Superman, deflecting concerns about their being single, so, too, did Wonder Girl normalized Wonder Woman, at least from the standpoint of the 1950s woman. Their popularity led to the "creation of Wonder Girl ... with her ponytail and a modest costume ... [that] coincided with the erasure of the Amazon background, which in itself indicates a soft-pedaling of feminist themes" (Robinson 79). Wonder Girl, being a teenage girl, enabled the writers to show that Wonder Woman had once been a girl with "one foot in the world of boyfriends and dating." In fact, Wonder Girl was the object of affection of Mer-Boy and Bird-Boy and these and other male rivalries for her affection carried forward into other Wonder Woman comics, such as "Wonder Woman Amazon Teenager" *Wonder Woman* #107 (Jul. 1959), "Battle of the Mer-Men, *Wonder Woman* #111 (Jan. 1960), *and* "Mer-Boy's Undersea Party," *Wonder Woman* #115 (Jul. 1960).

Although Wonder Woman was still single, independent, and focused on her career, these personal struggles and desires to become married gave the impression that she had become contained. In the words of one comic book scholar, Les Daniels, this period represented a "period of decline" for Wonder Woman that would exist until Wonder Woman's rebirth as a symbol of the feminist movement in the 1970s.

Conclusion

Wonder Woman emerged in the 1940s just as American entered World War II. As women entered the war production in various capacities, the image of Wonder Woman spoke to the promise of the future for women: strong, independent and career-minded. When the war ended, Fredric Wertham fought to contain that image of the strong, independent, career-minded woman for he felt it threatened the American family and American society. His attempts to contain Wonder Woman forced her, like so many women during the 1950s, to struggle with the tension between family and career. In the end, Wertham may have contained the symbol of the 1940s Wonder Woman — strength and independence — but the 1950s Wonder Woman —

having to choose between marriage and career — spoke to and inspired another generation.

NOTE

1. When first published in 1947, to protect George Kennan's anonymity, the article was attributed to the author "X."

WORKS CITED

Coontz, Stephanie. *A Strange Stirring: The Feminine Mystique and American Women at the Dawn of the 1960s.* New York: Basic, 2011.

Cuordileone, Kyle A. "'Politics in an Age of Anxiety': Cold War Political Culture and the Crisis in American Masculinity, 1949–1960." *Journal of American History* 87.2 (2002): 514–45.

Daniels, Les. *Wonder Woman: The Complete History.* San Francisco: Chronicle, 2000.

Diggins, John Patrick. *The Proud Decades: America in War and in Peace, 1941–1960.* New York: W.W. Norton, 1988.

Ehrenreich, Barbara, and Deidre English. *For Her Own Good: 150 Years of the Experts' Advice to Women.* Garden City, NY: Anchor, 1978.

Gaddis, John Lewis. *Strategies of Containment: A Critical Appraisal of Postwar American National Security Policy.* Oxford: Oxford University Press, 1982.

Gardner, Jeanne. "Girls Who Sinned in Secret and Paid in Public: Romance Comics, 1949–1954." In *Comic Books and the Cold War: Essays on the Graphic Treatment of Communism, the Code and Social Concerns,* edited by Chris York and Rafiel York, 92–102. Jefferson, NC: McFarland, 2012:

Hajdu, David. *The Ten Cent Plague: The Great Comic Book Scare and How it Changed America.* New York: Farrar, Straus and Giroux, 2008.

Heale, Michael J. *McCarthy's Americans: Red Scare Politics in State and Nation, 1935–1965.* Athens: University of Georgia Press, 1998.

Hofstadter, Richard. *Anti–Intellectualism in American Life.* New York: Knopf, 1963.

Kanigher, Robert (w), and Harry Peter (a). "SOS Wonder Woman." *Sensation Comics* Vol. 1 #94 (Oct. 1958). New York: DC Comics.

Kanigher, Robert (w), and Ross Andru (a)._____. "Battle of the Mer-Men." *Wonder Woman* Vol. 1 #111 (Jan. 1960). New York: DC Comics.

_____. "Mer-Boy's Undersea Party." *Wonder Woman* Vol. 1 #115 (Jul. 1960). New York: DC Comics.

_____. "The Million Dollar Penny." *Wonder Woman* Vol. 1 #98 (May 1958). New York: DC Comics.

_____. "Wonder Woman Amazon Teenager." *Wonder Woman* Vol. 1 #107 (Jul. 1959). New York: DC Comics.

Kennan, George F. ["X"] "The Sources of Soviet Conduct." *Foreign Affairs* 25 (Jul. 1947): 566–582.

McClelland-Nugent, Ruth. "The Amazon Mystique: Subverting Cold War Domesticity in *Wonder Woman* Comics, 1948–1965." In *Comic Books and the Cold War: Essays on the Graphic Treatment of Communism, the Code and Social Concerns,* edited by Chris York and Rafiel York, 115–128. Jefferson, NC: McFarland, 2012.

MacLean, Nancy. *Behind the Mask of Chivalry.* New York: Oxford University Press, 2001.

Marston, William Moulton. "Why 100,000,000 Americans Read Comics." *American Scholar* 13: (Winter 1943–44): 35–44.

Marston, William Moulton (w), and Harry Peter (a). "The Adventure of the Life Vitamin." *Wonder Woman* Vol. 1, #7 (Winter 1943). New York: DC Comics.

Nielsen, Kim. *The Un-American Womanhood: Antiradicalism, Antifeminism, and the First Red Scare.* Columbus: Ohio State University Press, 1988.

Nyberg, Amy Kiste. *Seal of Approval: The History of the Comics Code.* Jackson: University Press of Mississippi, 1998.

Pereira, K. L. "Female Bonding: The Strange History of Wonder Woman." *Bitch.* (Fall 2006): 35–39.

Richard, Olive. "Our Women are Our Future." *Family Circle* (Aug. 14, 1944): 14–17, 19.

Robinson, Lillian S. *Wonder Woman: Feminisms and Superheroes.* New York: Routledge, 2004.

Smith, Caroline J. "'The Feeding of Young Women': Sylvia Plath's *The Bell Jar, Mademoiselle* Magazine, and the Domestic Ideal." *College Literature* 37.4 (Fall 2010): 1–22.

Storrs, Landon Y. R. "Attacking the Washington 'Femmocracy': Antifeminism in the Cold War Campaign against 'Communists in Government.'" *Feminist Studies* 33.1 (Spring 2007): 118–152.

Walker, Nancy A. *Shaping Our Mothers' World: American Women's Magazines.* Jackson: University Press of Mississippi, 2000.

Welter, Barbara. "The Cult of True Womanhood: 1820–1860." *American Quarterly* 18.2 (1966): 151–174.

Wertham, Fredric. *Seduction of the Innocent.* Rinehart, 1954.

Wright, Bradford W. *Comic Book Nation: The Transformation of Youth Culture in America.* Baltimore: Johns Hopkins University Press, 2001.

Wonder Woman Comic Books and Military Technology After Sputnik

LORI MAGUIRE

On October 4, 1957, the Soviet Union launched Sputnik I, the world's first satellite, and this event provoked a panic in the United States. A period began in which the Soviets would score some stunning successes in the brand new space race: in November 1957, Sputnik II went up containing Laika, a live dog, and in May 1958 Sputnik III with a large array of scientific instruments. 1959 saw the launching of Luna I, the first spaceship to come near the moon and, even more importantly Luna III which sent back the first pictures of the far side of the moon. In 1960 there was the first Vostok unmanned spacecraft which would lead to an even more spectacular triumph in April 1961 when Yuri Gagarin became the first man in space. Worse still, many American efforts ended in disaster. Vanguard I, the first U.S. attempt to launch a satellite, failed in December 1957 as did the next undertaking in February of the following year. Explorer I restored some national honor in January 1958 but problems continued to plague the American space effort: a test rocket exploded at Cape Canaveral in February 1958; the launch of the first Thor rocket failed in August, as did that of the third in December.

Of course, things improved after this and the Soviets had a number of catastrophes as well. However, the disastrous Bay of Pigs invasion — which began just days after Gagarin's success — seemed to show that the nation's power was declining. Having firmly believed in their technological superiority, the Americans found themselves outstripped by the rival superpower. This led to a period of fear when the possibility of an invasion or surprise missile attack seemed terrifyingly real, and one of soul-searching with many criticisms of the educational system. There was much talk of a "missile gap." Reports and investigations all examined the state of American technology and scientific education and a new determination to conquer space and reach the moon developed. All of this undoubtedly played a role when, on May 25, 1961, the American president, John Kennedy, officially declared the goal of landing a man on the moon.

Coincidentally this roughly corresponds to the beginning of the Silver Age in comics and to a major makeover in the Wonder Woman series. Since 1948 Robert Kanigher had edited and written her adventures and his tenure has been criticized for making her much more in line with the domestic-oriented feminine ideal of the time (Knight 312; Daniels 93). Certainly Kanigher worked in a difficult period for comic books since the Senate Subcommittee Hearings on Juvenile Delinquency took place in 1954. Worse still, Fredric Wertham, in his highly influential book of the same year, *The Seduction of the Innocent,* had attacked Wonder Woman in particular (Brown 237). Kanigher had little choice but to tone down the stories and make them more in tune with conventional views. Kanigher himself insisted that he "worked instinctively" and, in fact, because of time constraints, probably went too quickly to plan ahead (Daniels 100). Furthermore, in 1958 Kanigher replaced Harry G. Peter, who had been drawing Wonder Woman from the start and recruited two young artists, Ross Andru and Mike Esposito, which meant that the comic book underwent a major visual change.

The Wonder Woman comics are a particularly interesting place to study the impact of Sputnik since — unlike superheroes such as Superman, whose alter ego was a journalist or Batman, reclusive millionaire Bruce Wayne — Diana Prince, Wonder Woman's secret identity, was in the American military and she worked for (and loved) Col. Steve Trevor, who held a high position in intelligence. Since Kanigher has stressed how quickly he wrote these episodes it is highly probable that current events related to the military had a disproportionate influence in his search for a story line. By the late 1950s, as we have seen, the most important subjects of debate were undeniably the "missile gap" and the Soviet achievements (as well as a number of U.S. failures). Indeed, during this period, Trevor frequently acted as a test pilot for new planes and rockets which very often malfunctioned — leaving him to be rescued by Wonder Woman. And since the "missile gap" bred fear, it is not surprising to see a large number of attempted attacks on the United States that, once again, only Wonder Woman could prevent. In the pages that follow we will consider the presentation of military technology, both American and hostile, and try to examine the chronological link between these stories and the actual events of the Soviet and American technological rivalries of the time, particularly with regard to the space race.

The Impact of Sputnik

Sputnik burst into the American consciousness with a spectacular impact, provoking more than a little panic. Its significance was widely understood and the achievement itself admired. But it also gave credence to Khrushchev's boasts about superior weapons and made the possibility of a Soviet attack seem more real. The Eisenhower administration initially tried to downplay Sputnik. For one thing, American officials were actually relieved that the Russians had chosen not to weaponize rocket technology and that they seemed more interested in waging a psychological war rather than a military one. The administration was also aware, through secret U-2 spy plane information, of the real state of Soviet military strength, which was substantially inferior to Khrushchev's boasts (Wang; Nojeim and Kilroy; Levine). But they could not reveal this information, which made it difficult for them to deal effectively with the outcry that followed. From left to right on the political spectrum, there were loud expressions of shock and worry. The labor leader Walter Reuther called it a "bloodless Pearl Harbor" (Levine 113). *Time* magazine quoted the Democratic hawk Sen. Henry Jackson as calling it "a devastating blow to the prestige of the United States as the leader in the scientific and technical world" ("Knowledge is Power"). Republican Senator Styles Bridges attacked American scientists for being too "beguiled by the peace and light emanating from the Kremlin" (Finney). In particular, the scientist Edward Teller insisted that the U.S. had suffered a massive defeat with Sputnik and needed to increase defense programs. These worries were immediately picked up in the press with *Life* going so far as to publish an article entitled "The Case for Being Panicky" (Price).[1]

Clearly Americans were worried and American pride had suffered a major blow from the Soviet achievement. The educational system came in for particular criticism (Dow; Clowse). *Time*, in an article called "Knowledge is Power" argued that America had fallen behind the USSR in some vital scientific areas (*Time*).[2] The launch of Sputnik also coincided with the Gaither Report "Deterrence and Survival in the Nuclear Age" which was prepared by the Security Resources Panel of the President's Science Advisory Committee. The report painted a gloomy picture of ever increasing Soviet power:

> The Gross National Product (GNP) of the USSR is now more than one-third that of the United States and is increasing half again as fast... This extraordinary concentration of the Soviet economy on military power and heavy industry ... makes available economic resources sufficient to finance both the rapid expansion of their impressive military capability and their politico-economic offensive by which, through diplomacy, propaganda and subversion, they seek to extend the Soviet orbit [Gaither].

Sputnik seemed to confirm the conclusions of the Gaither Report and gave weight to its insistence on the need to strengthen U.S. military capabilities (Snead). The report was top secret but excerpts soon leaked into the press (Roberts). Anxiety was compounded by the rush release shortly afterwards of the military subpanel report of the Rockefeller Fund's Special Studies Project directed by Henry Kissinger and including Edward Teller. It predictably called for a massive arms build-up against what they saw as Soviet military superiority. It also received a great deal of publicity including on the front page of *The New York Times* (Benjamin; Andrew). Naturally Congress also picked up on this and the wily Senate Majority leader and chair of the preparedness subcommittee of the Armed Services Committee, Lyndon Johnson, hoping to run for president in 1960, saw this as a good opportunity for publicity at the expense of the Republicans. He held hearings on satellite and missile programs from November 1957 to January 1958. Worse still, as we have seen, many of the initial American efforts failed. The early Vanguard failures were satirized in the press as "flopnik," "dudnik" or "kaputnik" (Divine, 1993, 71).

Not surprisingly, given all this publicity, Sputnik soon found its way into popular culture. Satellites turned up everywhere but, of course, especially in science fiction films, such as Roger Corman's *War of the Satellites*, or Paul Landres' *The Flame Barrier*. According to some estimates, as many as 43 such projects were announced on the day after Sputnik's lift-off (Doherty 152). Fear of nuclear war also resurfaced, notably in mainstream works, first in novels like *Two Hours to Doom* (Peter George, American title *Red Alert*) or *A Canticle for Leibowitz* (Walter Miller) and then in films such as *The World, The Flesh and the Devil* (1959) or *On the Beach* (1959).[3]

The Wonder Woman Comics

Certainly comic books, in general, showed the same trends in the period as other types of popular culture. In the Superman comics the relationship between kryptonite and nuclear radiation is clear (Maguire). Satellites also make an appearance there shortly after Sputnik. For example, Lex Luthor puts a satellite into orbit with the express goal of hurting Superman in a 1959 episode (Binder). Wonder Woman is, therefore, far from being an isolated example, but the theme appears particularly frequently because of the main characters' link with the U.S. military. Since role reversal is a major part of the comic, Steve Trevor is frequently rescued by Wonder Woman. It makes sense that he would be put in situations linked to what is happening in the news with regard to the military.

Wonder Woman was a World War II creation, first appearing in the January 1942 (and thus just before the U.S. entered the conflict) issue of *All Star Comics*. In this initial story, Trevor's plane crashes on Paradise Island although because of Nazi spies and not mechanical failure (Marston). Later, in the same issue, he is saved by Wonder Woman because he crashes his plane into the enemy. The following month he is captured while still wounded. As these examples show, at this period, spies were very frequently behind technological problems. This does show very real fears of America becoming a target for the Axis powers, in particular through betrayal from within, but it does not show worries about the quality of American military technology. However, in the late 1950s, while spies and invasion themes continue, a new preoccupation with malfunctioning equipment appears.

As early as January 1958 (which, given the delays in the comic book process meant it was probably written just after Sputnik), Wonder Woman passes earth's "first satellite station" as she enters outer space and satellites appear fairly regularly over the next few years (Kanigher, "Wonder Woman — The World's"). Furthermore, one can also see obvious reflections of feelings of national humiliation and worries about the U.S. falling behind in technology, especially with regard to the race for space. Over and over again Steve Trevor, military test pilot, experienced serious failures in new equipment. The actual testing of innovative technology became in itself dangerous and threatening. In the issue just mentioned, Trevor lost complete control of one such aircraft and found himself headed toward another test area—one for hydrogen bombs—just before an explosion. Significantly, there is no danger of that malfunctioning. Fortunately, Wonder Woman arrives in time to rescue him but, while sheltering him from the blast, she becomes radioactive. Having become a threat to earth, she goes into voluntary exile in space. But this has a positive result for she quickly discovers that evil aliens bent on conquering earth have taken over the satellite station. Naturally, she manages to defeat them and destroys the satellite in the process — upon which she discovers that she is no longer radioactive and can return to earth. Few stories illustrate so well the immediate impact of Sputnik: worries about falling behind in the technological race, anxieties about American technology malfunctioning, and the fear of satellites being turned into weapons that can endanger the very existence of the nation.

Similar stories appeared in succeeding months. In July 1958, Steve Trevor flies a "rocket plane — assigned to track a rocket through space" but very quickly the controls malfunction (Kanigher, "Stampede"). After announcing this, Trevor is cut off in midsentence. The narrator then informs us that "every observatory in the world is alerted to scan the skies for the missing pilot" but, of course, are unable to find him. Since he is in outer space Wonder Woman cannot just fly to his rescue so, rather oddly, she goes through a training session on Paradise Island. When she finally sets off after Trevor, her rocket ship also malfunctions. Eventually she discovers that this is all part of yet another alien invasion plot. Wonder Woman then manages to rescue Steve and save the earth. Here we have the theme of malfunctioning equipment combined with invasion fears. Interestingly enough, this time the problem does not stem from American mistakes but from alien activity — perhaps reflecting fears of sabotage and espionage from the outside.

In another episode the same month, a wing breaks off Trevor's plane as he is performing a stunt (Kanigher, "Top Secret"). The following issue saw little improvement. At a rocket testing, with Steve and Diana watching, something goes wrong and Wonder Woman must deflect the rocket to send it into orbit (Kanigher, "Wonder Woman's One Hundredth"). Then in October a giant rocket cone nearly lands on Steve and later, on the same day, while flying Gen. Darnell to a meeting, Trevor's plane catches fire (Kanigher, "Fun House"). It seems that American military technology was being plagued by disasters and most of these were not the result of outside sabotage but came from a problem with its actual conception and construction.

The Early 1960s

In the early 1960s the subject of American technological failure became less frequent although invasion fears continued. Undoubtedly much of the theme had been linked to rescuing Trevor and this occurs less and less often in these later years. There were more and more highly fantastic adventures centered around Paradise Island rather than in America. A number of episodes featured bizarre criminal villains too. In fact technological failure rarely appears as a subject in 1960 probably because of American successes. However, the so-called "missile gap" was a major part of the presidential campaign that year and the theme never completely vanished, although it sometimes appeared in a modified and less negative way. In 1961 it returns frequently perhaps because of the impact of American failure at the Bay of Pigs and the Soviet success with Gagarin. In January 1961, for example, Trevor is seen falling from a burning plane with a ripped parachute (Kanigher, "Three Wishes"). In April, Trevor is once again testing an experimental plane which is attacked by criminals (Kanigher, "The Island-Eater"). His parachute becomes entangled in the burning plane and he must be saved before it explodes. In May 1961, Wonder Woman and Steve head into space again in order to retrieve a new "ghost" satellite full of important data (Kanigher, "The Skyscraper"). This time Wonder Woman insists on taking the Amazon plane — perhaps because of the continual failure of American technology. This episode has more than

a little preachiness about the virtues of democracy for Eeeeyehhh, the brother
of the "rightful ruler of Saturn" plans on eliminating Wonder Woman so he
can seize control there. As such he exchanges the American capsule for his
own booby-trapped one. Eeeeyehhh exclaims with glee: "My brother and his
idiotic copy of peaceful democratic rule is doomed! And I shall rule with an
iron hand." Naturally, his plan fails and thanks to Wonder Woman's intervention, democracy is saved.

In October 1961, Trevor found himself in trouble again while testing yet
another new experimental plane (Kanigher, "Wonder Woman-Battle"). It caught
fire and now it was Steve's ejector seat that failed to work. The next month
Wonder Woman rescued an entire submarine crew after hearing their distress
signal (Kanigher, "The Unmasking). In April 1962 Steve lost control of his
ship once again while testing it (Kanigher, "Return"). In October 1964 a giant
rocket blasting off for Pluto malfunctioned (Kanigher, "The Last Day").

Admittedly, it was not always a problem with American technology that
caused the malfunction for, as we have already seen, aliens or criminals could
sometimes be responsible. In May 1963, for example, Queen Hippolyta saves
an injured American military plane only to discover that a Martian invasion
force had been responsible for the damage (Kanigher, "The Kite"). In at least
one case, Trevor himself was guilty. In November 1960, for example, fearful that
Wonder Woman was seeing someone else, he decides to follow her while testing a "new experimental ship's long range cruising capacity" (Kanigher, "Wonder Woman's Impossible"). Indeed, he finds her with a merman and is so
upset by this that he nearly crashes the plane against a whale. Steve then does
his best to save the plane, belatedly recognizing that "it's too valuable to our
country." He manages to do so but must make extensive repairs — and needs
Wonder Woman to bring him the necessary tools. In July 1963, Trevor deliberately pretends to have problems (notably with a parachute) in order to help
Wonder Woman recover her memory (Kanigher, "The Day Wonder Woman").
In other cases it is pure accident such as, in the February 1961 issue, Trevor's
airplane finds itself in the route of a falling meteor (Kanigher, "The Secret").

The Invasion Threat and the Nuclear Menace

Of course, with Sputnik and the succeeding Soviet successes making
people feel profoundly insecure it is not surprising to see, throughout popular
culture of the time, the strength of the invasion theme, most famously, perhaps, in science fiction cinema, but also in comic books. Once again, Wonder
Woman was no exception here. In the January 1958 issue already discussed,
aliens take over earth's first satellite station as a base for an invasion (Kanigher,

"Wonder Woman — The World's"). So, closely related to the theme of malfunctioning military technology is that of invasion. If America cannot properly defend itself and if hostile powers are ahead technologically, then the nation itself is seriously threatened. Numerous other examples can be cited. In May 1958, Wonder Woman saves the city from attack by an enemy submarine — and one which sends a "magnetically controlled" torpedo that follows her everywhere (Kanigher, "The Million"). In the July 1958 adventure mentioned earlier, aliens were ultimately behind the technical malfunction (Kanigher, "Stampede"). In October Wonder Woman is taken to the future — in the middle of an alien invasion of New York (Kanigher, "Fun House") — while, the following month, giants have missiles aimed at earth (Kanigher, "The Three"). In the February 1959 story, "Trial by Fire," another enemy submarine fires an atomic missile at the city while in another story the same month, "Key of Deception," Duke Deception leads the Martians in an attack on earth (Kanigher). And we saw in the previous section another Martian attack from 1963.

But the danger does not only come from without for, paradoxically, American nuclear power is viewed more as a threat to the United States than to potential exterior enemies. We have already seen how Trevor is nearly killed when his malfunctioning plane takes him over a testing place for the hydrogen bomb. Even more worrying is Multiple Man who is born from a nuclear test explosion. He is described as a "fantastic creature emerging from the blazing core of the nuclear explosion — a creature of unknown elements — assuming multiple shapes" (Kanigher, "The Impossible"). Multiple Man is one of the most fearsome enemies Wonder Woman has encountered. He is first seen in the rather bizarre episode of August 1961, rightly entitled "The Impossible Day" for Wonder Woman appears at the same time in three different versions of herself (Wonder Tot and Wonder Girl as well as her usual adult form) (Kanigher "Wonder Woman's One"). Unable to be reasoned with, Multiple Man speaks in a voice "like an icy wind blowing against one's face" in one incarnation and like "the breath from a furnace" in another. He is wholly evil and represents the various threats that atomic power poses to all humanity. Although defeated, he returns in April 1962 where he is described as "the nuclear villain," and again in May 1963. Multiple Man undoubtedly reflects the debate of the time around the impact of nuclear testing above ground. This would lead to the Nuclear Test Ban Treaty in 1963 after many years of negotiations.

Conclusion

The spectacular success of the Soviets with Sputnik called into question a very real complacency about the superiority of American education and technology and about the inevitability of their power in the world. This, in turn, increased feelings of vulnerability. These worries and fears found their reflection in the popular culture of the time and Wonder Woman comics is no exception — and, indeed, because of the main characters' work with military intelligence, a particularly interesting example of the phenomenon.

Progressively in the early 1960s, the failure of American technology recedes as a theme in Wonder Woman in the face of the obvious successes of the American space program. Fears with regard to nuclear power also recede after the Cuban missile crisis and the Test Ban Treaty. Anxieties about invasion remain although these too will make way for new worries and preoccupations as the decade progresses.

NOTES

1. It is interesting to note that Werner von Braun was on the cover of a special edition mainly devoted to Sputnik.
2. Significantly, Edward Teller was on the cover.
3. To be honest, fear of nuclear war had never really disappeared as a subject as the publication of the book *On the Beach* by Nevil Shute in 1957 shows.

WORKS CITED

Andrew, John. "Cracks in the Consensus: The Rockefeller Brothers Fund Special Studies Project and Eisenhower's America." *Presidential Studies Quarterly* (Summer 1998): 28:3.

Benjamin, Philip. "Arms Race Urged Lest Reds Seize Lead in Two Years." *New York Times,* Jan. 6, 1958.

Binder, Otto (w), and Al Plastino (a). "The Kryptonite Man." *Action Comics #249* (Feb. 1959). New York: DC Comics.

Brown, Jeffrey. *Dangerous Curves: Action Heroines, Gender, Fetishism and Popular Culture.* Jackson: University Press of Mississippi, 2011.

Clowse, Barbara Barksdale. *Brainpower for the Cold War: The Sputnik Crisis and the National Defense Education Act of 1958.* Westport, CT: Greenwood, 1981.

Daniels, Les. *Wonder Woman: The Complete History.* San Francisco: Chronicle, 2000.

Doherty, Thomas. *Teenagers and Teenpics: The Juvenalization of American Movies in the 1950s.* Boston: Unwin Hyman, 1988.

Dow, Peter. *Schoolhouse Politics: Lessons from the Sputnik Era.* Cambridge, MA: Harvard University Press, 1991.

Finney, John. "McElroy Assumes Role of Missiles to Spur Program." *New York Times,* Oct. 19, 1957, 3.

Gaither Report. "Deterrence and Survival in the Nuclear Age." Nov. 7, 1957. The complete text of the report is at http://www.gwu.edu/~nsarchiv/NSAEBB/NSAEBB139/nitze02.pdf (accessed Nov. 13, 2012).

Kanigher, Robert (w), and Ross Andru and Mike Esposito (a). "The Day Wonder Woman Revealed Her Secret Identity," *Wonder Woman # 139* (Jul. 1963). New York: DC Comics.

_____. "Fun House of Time." *Wonder Woman #101* (Oct. 1958). New York: DC Comics.

_____. "The Impossible Day." *Wonder Woman #124* (Aug. 1961). New York: DC Comics.

_____. "The Island-Eater." *Wonder Woman #121* (Apr. 1961) New York: DC Comics.

_____. "Key of Deception." *Wonder Woman #104* (Feb. 1959). New York: DC Comics.

_____. "The Kite of Doom." *Wonder Woman* #138 (May 1963). New York: DC Comics.

_____. "The Last Day of the Amazons." *Wonder Woman* #149 (Oct. 1964) New York: DC Comics.

_____. "The Million Dollar Penny." Part 3. *Wonder Woman* #98 (May 1958). New York: DC Comics.

_____. "Return of the Nuclear Villain —'Multiple Man.'" *Wonder Woman* #129 (Apr. 1962). New York: DC Comics.

_____. "The Secret of Volcano Mountain." *Wonder Woman* #120 (Feb. 1961). New York: DC Comics.

_____. "The Skyscraper Wonder Woman." *Wonder Woman* #122 (May 1961). New York: DC Comics.

_____. "Stampede of the Comets." *Wonder Woman* #99 (Jul. 1958). New York: DC Comics.

_____. "The Three Faces of Wonder Woman." *Wonder Woman* #102 (Nov. 1958). New York: DC Comics.

_____. "Three Wishes of Doom." *Wonder Woman* #119 (Jan. 1961). New York: DC Comics.

_____. "Top Secret." *Wonder Woman* #99 (Jul. 1958). New York: DC Comics.

_____. "Trial by Fire." *Wonder Woman* #104 (Feb. 1959). DC Comics.

_____. "Undersea Trap." *Wonder Woman* #101 (Oct. 1958). New York: DC Comics.

_____. "The Unmasking of Wonder Woman." *Wonder Woman* #126 (Nov. 1961). CD Comics.

_____. "Wonder Woman-Battle Prize." *Wonder Woman* #125 (Oct. 1961). New York: DC Comics.

_____. "Wonder Woman — The World's Most Dangerous Human." *Wonder Woman* #95 (Jan. 1958). New York: DC Comics.

_____. "Wonder Woman's Impossible Decision." *Wonder Woman* #118 (Nov. 1960). New York: DC Comics.

_____. "Wonder Woman's One Hundredth Anniversary." Wonder Woman #100 (Aug. 1958). New York: DC Comics.

Knight, Gladys. *Female Action Heroes: A Guide to Women in Comics, Video Games, Film and Television.* Santa Barbara, CA: Greenwood, 2010.

"Knowledge is Power." *Time* 70 (Nov. 18, 1957): 21.

Levine, Alan. *"Bad Old Days": The Myth of the 1950s.* New Brunswick, NJ: Transaction, 2008.

Maguire, Lori. "Supervillains and Cold War Tensions in the 1950s." In *The Ages of Superman: Essays on the Man of Steel in Changing Times*, edited by Joseph J. Darowski. Jefferson, NC: McFarland, 2012.

Marston, William Moulton (w), and Harry G. Peter (a). "Introducing Wonder Woman." *All Star Comics* #8, (Dec.-Jan. 1941–42). New York: DC Comics.

_____. *Sensation Comics* #2 (Feb. 1942). New York: DC Comics.

Nojeim, Michael, and David Kilroy. *Days of Decision: Turning Points in U.S. Foreign Policy.* Washington, D.C.: Potomac, 2011.

Price, George, "The Case for Being Panicky." *Life* 43:21 (Nov. 18, 1957): 125.

Roberts, Chalmer. "Secret Report Sees U.S. in Grave Peril." *Washington Post*, Dec. 20, 1957.

Snead, David. *The Gaither Committee, Eisenhower and the Cold War.* Columbus: Ohio State University Press, 1999.

Wang, Zuoyue. *In Sputnik's Shadow: The President's Science Advisory Committee and Cold War America.* New Brunswick, NJ: Rutgers University Press, 2008.

Cold War Fantasies

Testing the Limits of the Familial Body

JOAN ORMROD

From 1947 to 1967 *Wonder Woman* was written by Robert Kanigher — the longest writing stint of any writer in her seventy year history. Kanigher revamped the character in 1958 to fit a more cozy post–Wertham storyline where she lived a fantasy existence on Paradise Island. The images, drawn mainly by Ross Andru and Mike Esposito, softened Wonder Woman's image from a warrior woman to a teen romance heroine with a doe-eyes and full lips. Instead of warrior boots she wore Greek sandals tied up with straps around her legs. Kanigher also introduced more stories of life on Paradise Island and they must have been popular with readers because they featured in sixteen out of the twenty-three issues in this era. Also *Wonder Woman* appeared in the top thirty best-selling comics with a readership of over 200,000.[1] The demands by readers for more of these stories in letters pages demonstrate they must have resonated with some aspects of readers' lives in Cold War America. Despite her popularity, this era is one of the most overlooked in Wonder Woman scholarship, possibly because the stories were regarded as fairy tales told to a teenage female readership. Yet this era throws up some fascinating cultural paradoxes.

Wonder Woman posed a problem in 1950s and '60s because she challenged the perceived role of women as reliant on men in family life and the job market. As Diana Prince she was a career woman, her private life rarely shown. Arguably, Wonder Woman's domestic setting was Paradise Island where she learned dressmaking, played musical instruments and Amazon sports (although she admitted to being a poor cook). Here she also enjoyed adventures with her family battling mythic monsters. Wonder Woman's family consisted of her mother Hippolyta (Wonder Queen) and two siblings Wonder

Girl, Wonder Tot. Yet Wonder Girl and Wonder Tot were not siblings in a traditional sense. They were, in fact, younger versions of herself, produced through a magic camera introduced in *Wonder Woman* #124 (Aug. 1961). The magic camera, a product of Amazon technology, recorded limitless footage of Wonder Woman growing up. As explained in the comic book:

> HIPPOLYTA: These are shots of you as ... Wonder Tot ... walking down the steps of the palace! Now I'm going to run off shots of you as Wonder Girl in the same place, although in a different time, naturally! ... I've added pictures of you and me ... walking down those same steps! And spliced them all together so they run as one!
>
> WONDER WOMAN: Thunderbolts of Jove, mother! It ... looks as if the impossible is happening! As if the whole Wonder Woman family is together at the same time and the same place!" [Kanigher, "The Impossible" 3].

Through editing and splicing footage together at wonder speed and dubbing their voices in, Hippolyta and Wonder Woman were able to create adventures where she interacted with her younger selves. Thus, a fantastic story-within-a-story revealing the adventures of Wonder Tot and Wonder Girl was told within the pages of Wonder Woman's comic book.

That these adventures were fantasy enacted within a fantasy space, Paradise Island, seemingly ignored the realities of the Cold War, then at its height. It might seem that they also ignored a sea change in the superhero genre with Marvel Comics revision of the superhero.[2] However, this perception is mistaken on a number of points. Marvel comics revised superheroes so they reacted to real world events such as poverty, radiation poisoning, crime, and the perceived threat of communism. Yet in the early sixties, comic book sales show that the most popular superhero comics were still DC Comics' Superman and Batman. Marvel comics grew in popularity, starting to challenge DC Comics in 1965.[3] In the early sixties comedy, romance, uncanny tales and western comics were more popular than superhero comics. Paradise Island stories of genies, giants, mer-people and bird people were products of their time. However, while *Wonder Woman* stories were fantasies, they replicated the schizophrenic Cold War *zeitgeist* in their depiction of monstrous and grotesque bodies. It could be argued that monstrous and fragmented fantasy bodies populating *Wonder Woman* stories reflected disquiet amongst American people at threats to family stability and the growing possibility of nuclear conflagration.

Monsters in fairytale and legend perform dual narratives: they reflect cultural concerns but also patrol the borders of the known world to preserve power structures. (Stewart; Cohen; Warner). For instance, the Cyclops signifies the foreign in Classical Greece because they represent the opposite of

Greek democracy in their anarchic behavior, not to mention extreme individualism and cannibalism (Cohen). Just as monsters in Greek myths challenge the stability of cultural values, so the monsters in *Wonder Woman* pose a threat to home and family. In this era the family was the lynchpin of American culture, it maintained capitalism and the patriarchal status quo. Family members assumed essentialist gendered roles: the breadwinner father, the housewife mother, and developing children. However, peoples' affluent lifestyles in the booming economic climate of the late fifties were tempered by fears of nuclear holocaust. Like monsters and grotesque bodies in other fantasy genres of this era the monsters prowling Paradise Island function as reminders of Cold War realities.

To explore these ideas it is important to examine the cultural context of the stories' production. The grotesque body particularly that of the giant, will be discussed in fantasy and superhero narratives. Grotesque bodies cannot be contained and are frequently represented through doubling and fragmentation. Theoretical and cultural issues will be analyzed in a case study featuring Multiple Man, a shape-shifting giant born of nuclear explosion, who appeared in *Wonder Woman* comics from 1961 to 1963, three years when the comics achieved their best sales. Coincidentally, Multiple Man is also featured in the first story with the magic eye camera that is used to tell stories of Wonder Tot and Wonder Girl. These three years were also the height of American fears over nuclear catastrophe. Multiple Man terrorized Paradise Island and returned over several stories, seemingly indestructible, to test the Wonder Family to its limits.

Comics and Cold War Hysteria

In America, the late 1950s and early 1960s was a time of paradox politically, economically, culturally, and sexually. No sooner was Hitler defeated than America perceived a new threat to its own power and world stability in Russia. Anti-communist propaganda displaced the enemy "out there" to "the enemy amongst us." Cold War culture in America raised fears of nuclear catastrophe tempered by the fear that waging a full scale nuclear war constituted too great a threat to life on earth (Kuznick and Gilbert). It would be foolish to pursue an outright assault on the enemy nation for fear of retaliation on home soil. The conduct of war, therefore, changed after World War II and powerful nations transposed their conflicts to third nations such as Vietnam or Korea. Propaganda became a tool of this Cold War with a constant stream of rhetoric from both sides attempting to denounce their enemies' plans for world domination. In America this virtual ideological war translated into a fear and hatred of socialism and paranoia of the impending nuclear war. The McCarthy witch hunts and the mass media organized vitriolic attacks against communism and the enemies within, "Seeing the world through this dark, distorting lens and setting global and domestic policies to consider them fanciful as well as real threats was and is, then, the largest impact of the Cold War" (Kuznick and Gilbert 11).

The end of the fifties saw the greatest number of bomb shelters built in American backyards and "duck and dive" exercises carried out by American school children. This induced a contradiction in the ways children of this era were raised with fear and uncertainty on one hand and nurturing and permissive child rearing on the other (Tuttle). However, the apparent freedom of child rearing was countered by the constant rhetoric of danger in anticommunist propaganda. Atomic bomb rhetoric suggested there was nowhere to hide from nuclear fallout, "primal fears of extinction cut across all political and ideological lines" (Boyer xvii). However, much of the anti-communist rhetoric was based on deception by the Russian government. Khrushchev, the Russian leader, was the archetypal trickster, and he concealed the true extent of Russian weapons which amounted to only one-tenth of America stockpiles (Barson and Heller). The Cold War, therefore, was in many ways a virtual war with no hand to hand combat, its basis in fantasy.

A side effect of Cold War paranoia was a return to conservative values with the family as its focus. Fears of communism and the destructive potential of atomic power in the Cold War encouraged the channeling of sexual energies into family life and conformity (May). The most crucial elements in family life, the parents, were regarded as models for correct behavior but also deemed culpable for the problems faced by society and their offspring in later life. Women particularly had a difficult role as the moral focus of sexual discipline, "[female sexuality] had to promote both abstinence and promise gratification; it had to indicate its presence by absence" (Jancovich 117). However the introduction of the contraceptive pill in the early sixties, freeing women from the risks and shame of unwanted pregnancies, destabilized the double standard. Women's' roles as housewife and mother were particularly difficult, they were encouraged to stay home as housewives and support their husbands and children as the center of their existence, a role Betty Friedan was to lament:

> In the late fifties, a sociological phenomenon was suddenly remarked: a third of American women now worked, but most were no longer young and very few were pursuing careers... The suburban housewife ... was the dream image of the young American women and the envy, it was said, of women all over the world... She was healthy, beautiful, educated, concerned only about her husband, her children, her home [Friedan 432].

Dramas, sitcoms, and films represented motherhood as the only natural career choice for a woman. Conversely, fear of female power seemed all-pervasive, especially in the mother's poisonous effects on her male offspring. In *Generation of Vipers*, "momism" was condemned, likening the errant mother to monstrous women of myth, Medusa and Proserpine, the Queen of Hell (Wylie). Magazines such as *Ladies Home Journal* condemned idleness and frivolity in women as it poisoned the next generation (Meyerowitz).

Fathers, too, were constrained to be the ideal role model for their male offspring. However, masculinity was in crisis. *Playboy* for instance ran a campaign against the feminization of America, claiming that men were becoming soft and domesticated. Best-selling book, *The Decline of the American Male*, lamented the decline of American masculinity claiming the causes as the absent or workaholic father figure and over-dominant mother (Attwood, Leonard Jr. and Miskin). This position was reflected in *Better Homes and Gardens* (1958), which advised fathers to be on their guard against the over-dominant mother, "You have a horror of seeing your son a pantywaist, but he won't get red blood and self-reliance if you leave the whole job of making a he-man of him to his mother" (Kimmel 147).

The cultural constraints and ideologies of the Cold War had a great impact on comics production from the early 1950s. In a polemic against sex and violence in comics, *The Seduction of the Innocent*, psychologist, Dr. Fredric Wertham, proposed Wonder Woman and other powerful women characters were terrifying to young boys and a bad influence on female readership. Comics companies responded with the Comics Code Authority (CCA), a self-imposed set of regulations that limited salacious or violent content in comics and stories. At a stroke, comics' content was infantilized with stories founded upon family values and superheroes' crime-fighting activities shackled by the prohibition of excessive violence or sex. Superman and Batman suddenly developed families, girlfriends, best friends, pets and they had to negotiate the necessity for marriage with the needs of fighting crime. Like all bachelors in this period, male superheroes also had to demonstrate they were heterosexual by their desirability to women and a bachelor lifestyle. Their justification for bachelorhood was the fear of criminal retribution against their spouses. Wonder Woman, however, was a problem. As a woman she should have been eager to marry and fulfill her female role. The justification that she could not marry until all evil was eradicated seemed weak. Her family was out of reach of criminal's intent on retribution. Furthermore, her mother, an Amazon queen, was able to take care of herself. She could not marry and become a housewife as this would end her crime-fighting career. Kanigher's solution was to provide a family for her on Paradise Island. However, as noted above, it was a family of doubles: herself and her two younger selves.

Doubled and Monstrous Bodies

Wonder Woman in the Cold War features evil and benign doubled bodies in Wonder Woman's earlier selves (the Impossible Family), robots, mutating rays, magic and parallel worlds. Body splitting, doubling, and mutating are shown with little realistic explanation within the fantasy genre and are central to the mode as noted by Jackson (1998) who regards body fragmentation as a desecration of a homogenous identity (82). Identity fragmentation, especially of the protagonist, challenges the integrity of the narrative as this character is often the point of contact between the reader and the story. It highlights the problems of representation because it shows the impossible as possible. Jackson proposes that fantasy sates our desire for the imaginary order (Lacan), a stage of life before the subject becomes inducted into society when they feel free to express their darkest desires, act without restriction and experience plenitude, "Fantasies try to *reverse* or rupture the process of ego formation which took place during the mirror stage, i.e. they attempt to re-enter the imaginary" (90).

Fragmentation and doubling fall into two main categories in superhero comics. The *alter ego* splits the superhero identity whereas monsters and villains address issues that superheroes lack. Arguably superhero narratives were founded upon this rupture of identity and a desire to re-enter the imaginary, for what else is the superhero but an expression of wish fulfillment? Jerry Siegel, for instance, claims his idea for the Superman/Clark Kent dual identities originated from a teenage boy's desire to appeal to girls. As Reynolds notes, the secret identity is a crucial component of the superhero genre from the first Superman story (Reynolds 13–4). Connecting the necessity of the secret identity to warriors in myth, Reynolds suggests the secret identity is a way of limiting the hero, who must pay for his or her great powers. However, another reason for the *alter ego* is that it enabled the superhero/god to engage and empathize with the lives of ordinary people. In Moulton's original conception of Wonder Woman, Diana Prince as an efficient but dowdy military secretary presented a perfect foil for a powerful warrior woman. Where Wonder Woman was a glamorous maverick/vigilante figure, Diana Prince showed the possibilities for the ordinary woman's role in wartime.

Monsters also express the fragmented grotesque body in fantasy texts. They function as a culture's, and the hero's, "other." They also test the hero to demonstrate his heroism and superiority against obstacles[4] (Frye). The root of "monster" is from the Latin *monere* to advise or warn and *monstrum*, a warning. Their representation exposes cultural concerns. They test the power of the hero. They may also represent an aspect that the hero lacks. Monstrous bodies are aligned with the earth. In the act of becoming and this unfinished state, monstrous bodies refuse classification. The monster is the harbinger of a category crisis "they are disturbing hybrids whose externally incoherent bodies resist attempts to include them in any systematic structures" (Cohen 6). Thus, in their challenge to the classical body through fragmentation and disintegration and their existence between the fringes of the known and the unknown, monsters invite new ways of thinking about the world. They deny the certainty of "either/or," instead they suggest "and/or" (Derrida).

The giant's body presents a particularly interesting aspect of many of these issues. For instance, giants' bodies are often constructed through "infinity, exteriority, the public and the overly natural" (Stewart 70). As such they are usually earth monsters. Stewart notes how giants are connected with the landscape upon which they ascribe their existence through myths and legends. For instance, monuments such as Stonehenge or natural rock formations such as the Giant's Causeway are attributed to giants' battles or activities (Stewart 86). Giants also represent a specific type of fragmented body in its juxtaposition with the miniature because "the gigantic transforms the body into the miniature, especially pointing to the body's "toylike" and "insignificant" aspects" (Stewart 71).[5]

Fragmenting and Doubling in Paradise Island

The most popular monsters and grotesque bodies in the Paradise Island stories are in the double and the giant. These two types of fantasy bodies are identified in Wonder Woman's doubled identity and in the gigantic bodies of her antagonists. Of the former, Wonder Woman represented a doubled identity not, as noted above, with her secret identity, as was typical in the superhero genre. Rather, Wonder Woman's identity was split between herself and her two earlier incarnations as Wonder Girl and Wonder Tot. Wonder Woman could not enjoy a traditional family life predicated upon the heterosexual male breadwinner because no man was allowed to set foot on Paradise Island. Her father, like all Amazon men, was killed in wars.[6] This situation would be common in a post World War II America. To make up for her absent father, Hippolyta is presented as the exemplary mother, caring, wise and just — qualities that she also exhibits as a queen. Despite her regal responsibilities, Hippolyta is always represented as a "normal" mother with maternal concerns and fears. She is willing to sacrifice herself for her children who frequently claim she is the Wonder Woman.

Many foes are represented as monstrous and ugly for they represent a contrast to Wonder Woman. Where the monster is unfinished and grotesque,

Wonder Woman can literally claim to be perfect as a Greek statue, even though in this story arc she had an absent father, at birth Aphrodite, like a fairy godmother, gave her the gift of beauty.[7] Monsters were generally giants, who featured in 90 percent of the stories.[8] Stories featuring giants are organized around themes of the elements, fragmentation/duality, and gender. They exist on the fringes of Wonder Woman's world in other dimensions, in the oceans, in the air. Giants are nearly always male, childish and tend to be argumentative, aggressive, and stupid, replicating their representation in fairy tales (Prescott). They also frequently test Wonder Woman or her younger selves with earth or Paradise Island as the prize.

There were two types of testing tale: the hyperbolic exhibition and the antagonist's challenge.[9] The hyperbolic exhibition narrative demonstrated Wonder Woman's superior powers, intelligence and character in overcoming obstacles. These stories, expanded upon Wonder Woman's confirmation as a hero/ine "superior in *kind* [...] to the environment of other men, the hero is a divine being, and the story about [...her...] will be a myth" (Frye 33).[10] Often these stories featured Wonder Woman besting herself or a facsimile of herself. The antagonist's challenge features tests contrived by an opponent to defeat Wonder Woman and either take her place, rule the world or defeat the Amazons. For instance in "Wonder Girl in Giant Land," *Wonder Woman* #109 (Oct. 1959), Wonder Girl travels to another dimension when she hitches a ride on a rocket. In this dimension giants challenge her to compete with them for the fate of the earth. The giant and Wonder Girl present binary oppositions of the gigantic and miniature, the brutish and the intelligent. So when she competes against a giant, to leap across a chasm she hitches a ride on his back. Comparison of Wonder Woman's body with that of her giant foes is also represented in the comic through comparison of Diana's classically perfect body with the grotesque body of the giant, fragmented by the comic page panels. In her challenge to the giants, we see only their hands and feet which seem monstrous compared with Wonder Girl. However, it is Wonder Girl who is able to resolve the giants' disputes in a mature manner (Kanigher, "Wonder Girl").

In these trials Wonder Woman's victory is usually followed by her admonishment to the enemy to behave more peacefully. For instance, when Diana defeats Tooroo the space giant in "The Human Charm Bracelet!" from *Wonder Woman* #106 (May 1959), she tells his fellow giants, "Just because you are big, doesn't mean you can disregard the rights of those who are smaller than you! It is my command that you respect the rights of others and live in peace!" The space giants, cowed, respond, "You have taught us a lesson we shall never forget!" (Kanigher 16).

Multiple Man

Many of the issues discussed above can be identified in the Multiple Man story arc. Multiple Man, the Nuclear Man, was born of a nuclear explosion and could transform into anything he wished. Like many fantasy villains, Multiple Man was seemingly indestructible and survived being stranded in the past, frozen, hurled into outer space and melted. Multiple Man's story arc begins in the first magic-eye camera story, *Wonder Woman* #124 (Aug. 1961). The Wonder Family encounters a nuclear text explosion just off-shore of Paradise Island. They create a cyclone to disperse the fallout. However, they are unaware that a monster has been created in the heat of the nuclear explosion, "a creature fashioned out of unknown elements ... assuming multiple shapes" (Kanigher 5). Multiple Man's aim is to destroy whatever stands in its way. It assumes the shape of a missile heading towards Paradise Island. No matter how many times the Amazons destroy Multiple Man it returns in a different form, its mantra comes in the form of the chant typical of the oral storytelling strategies of the fairy tale, "Whatever I want — I take! Whatever stands in my way — perishes! Nothing can stop me —!" The only way Hippolyta can destroy the menace is to take it back in the past, to prehistory where she and her children defeat the creature (Kanigher, "The Impossible").

In the second Multiple Man story, "The Return of Multiple Man!" from *Wonder Woman* #129 (Apr. 1962), Hippolyta receives yet more requests for another impossible story and this time it begins with Multiple Man attacking a plane piloted by Steve Trevor. The Wonder family defeat it by creating a whirlwind which prompts Multiple Man to change into sand. The sand is gathered up but slips through their fingers before they can dispose of it. Multiple Man then transforms into an iceberg and then into a volcano. This time the Amazons create a vacuum through whirling around and funneling the creature into outer space (Kanigher "The Return").

The third Multiple Man story, "Attack of the Human Iceberg!" in *Wonder Woman* #135 (Jan. 1963),[11] begins when the Amazons are frozen by Multiple Man renamed, Nuclear Man the Nuclear Menace. Where the creature was silent or chanted in previous stories, in this tale he is more articulate, "It is you and your island ... which will be destroyed, Amazons ... so that I can make the world my plaything ... without hindrance from you" (3). In this story Wonder Woman invites a fictitious reader, Carol Sue, to join her on Paradise Island. The party, in honor of Carol Sue, is interrupted by an attack by Multiple Man. Multiple Man turns into a giant ball and crashes against the underside of Paradise Island producing an earthquake. He freezes the Amazons and grows to gigantic size. When the Wonder Family attack him they are frozen to his body. Wonder Woman escapes and melts Multiple Man with a volcano. However, the melting fragments of Multiple Man reform into a giant metal ball that crashes against the underside of Paradise Island creating another earthquake. The metal ball is catapulted into space by Wonder Tot, where Multiple Man reforms into a meteor shower, raining fire on Paradise Island. Wonder Girl catches the firestorm in a giant ice cone, dissipating Multiple Man's body. However, again he reforms, this time into a giant clam which traps the Wonder family. Wonder Woman uses her magic lasso to entwine and crack the clam. The story ends with Wonder Woman enjoying Carol Sue's party (Kanigher, "Attack").

A number of themes emerge from these stories that connect with fairy tale narrative, such as giants and oral storytelling techniques. Multiple Man narratives are similar in structure and storytelling to the fairy tale. For instance in all of the stories, Kanigher uses the narrative and oral storytelling structure of the rule of three: three daughters, each more powerful, clever, and strong than the last, three tests to be completed each more powerful and devilish than the last. Often the youngest, most vulnerable daughter proves the strongest. The Wonder Family competes against each other to outwit and destroy the nuclear menace, but they continuously rise to the tests he places on them. This story falls into the fairy tale "transformation chase" in a tale such as The Magician and his Apprentice or the "obstacle chase" such as "The Giant Without a Heart" or "The Two Magicians." In these types of stories the pursued character changes shape to evade capture and often this is countered by the pursuer, so a mouse may be countered by a cat, until one finally gives up (Thompson).[12] In the latter an evil giant or sorcerer can only be destroyed by discovering where he has hidden his heart or soul.

Multiple Man's body connotes fragmentation, the nebulous and the grotesque. As a shape-shifter, his body fluctuates between binary states, from the solid to the insubstantial, the hot to the cold, the giant to the miniature. He is born as an atom and, like the nuclear bomb, expands into a giant body. The dual nature of the giant as the binary opposite of the miniature is shown when comparing it with the Wonder Family, stuck to him like flies on flypaper. Like other giants in *Wonder Woman* of this era, he is impossible to contain within the comics panel as a unified entity. For instance, in "The Return of Multiple Man," his body is broken up by the panels down the left hand side of the page (Kanigher 4). This disrupts the reading of the page, arrows between the panels enjoin the reader to read down rather than from left to right across the page.

Like giants in folklore and the grotesque body discussed above, Multiple Man is constructed around discourses of the elements and earth. Multiple Man's giant body is reminiscent of the Classical Greek Titans, precursors and parents of the Greek Gods. The Titans are brutish and connected with the earth, nature and the infinity of the sky (Stewart). They represent the chaos that comes before the order and law installed by the Greek Pantheon, spearheaded by Zeus. As a shape-shifter, Multiple Man also defies classification. He is not just aligned with the earth — he is an elemental giant and can become part of the air, fire and ice. Multiple Man's body is transitory, ambiguous, and intangible. His voice is "something *felt* like an icy wind blowing against one's face" (Kanigher, "The Impossible" 7). In his second transformation, as a molten menace, Multiple Man's voice "is felt rather than heard ... a voice like the breath from a furnace" (Kanigher, "The Impossible" 11). In his flame form he is dampened by asbestos and the lead that is produced from this smelting is fashioned into a bracelet by Hippolyta. Hippolyta takes the bracelet into the past when it takes over her mind and there, Multiple Man transforms into a Tyrannosaurus Rex, its voice "like steam hissing from a locomotive" (Kanigher, "The Impossible" 21).

Multiple Man's fluid body form and shape, like all grotesque creatures, is unfinished and abject. Multiple Man, as a shape shifter disrupts boundaries — he transforms and his identity is nebulous, denying the notion of homogeneity. For example, in "The Return of Multiple Man," he is drawn as amorphous mass with no outline. His body is also fluid, changing from wind to sand, to water and ice. When the Wonder Family gathers up the sand forming his body, it trickles through their hands (Kanigher, "The Return"). In all these stories, Multiple Man, like the grotesque disrupts boundaries of body states, the possible and impossible life and death.

Conclusion

Wonder Woman's mythic roots link her character to the representation of monsters in fairy tale and myth. Shrinking and doubling connote an interior anxiety in the face of attack from exterior forces: giants and aliens. Monstrosity and unruly bodies in these stories are reflected in B movie science fiction films such as *The Attack of the Fifty Foot Woman* and *The Incredible Shrinking Man*. These representations also show similar cultural influences in comics from DC Comics Superman family, to Marvel Comics with their atomic age superheroes such as The Fantastic Four, The Hulk, and Spider-Man. However, in Wonder Woman, cultural anxieties over fragmented, splitting selves, are displaced from the alter ego, which is central to masculine heroes, into freakish and monstrous bodies that inhabit the frontiers of Wonder Woman's world.

Like all monsters, Multiple Man cannot die, a trace element remains, as Cohen notes "No monster tastes death but once" (5). The trace element is in the painting of a caveman showing the Wonder Family controlling the monster in "The Impossible Day!" (Kanigher). This image shows a trace of the monster but also blurs fact and fantasy for, the impossible day produced through the magic eye camera cannot possibly have happened. Yet the reality is recorded on wall paintings. Like all fantasy stories, as Jackson notes, one must accept the impossible and not seek logical explanations. The fantasy of the stories replicates the fantasy of the Cold War where nuclear weapons exist in the minds of people. Multiple Man tests the limits of the Wonder Family. They must be on constant alert should he reappear, though he was a creation of a story within a story. Just as Multiple Man attacks the Wonder Family within an impossible fantasy world, so American families existing in a fantasy Cold War must be on constant alert. In the real world children fruitlessly learn to survive a nuclear attack by the "duck and dive" method, families must build bomb shelters for a bomb that is never dropped, and nuclear weapons must be stockpiled for a battle that will never happen.

NOTES

1. Based on postal records of comics subscriptions, *Wonder Woman* from 1961 to 1963 was in the top 30 best selling U.S. comics with a readership of 213,000 to 230,000, the era when these stories appeared. Thereafter, when the tales were more concerned with her romantic relationship with Steve Trevor sales dropped out of the top 50 sales. By 1967 she did not appear at all in the top 100 (http://www.comichron.com/).

2. This could apply to DC heroes in general in this era. For instance, Superman stories revolved around his relationships with Lois Lane and Jimmy Olsen and the plots tended to concentrate upon trivia — protecting his secret identity or teaching his friends a lesson. Readers could also enjoy stories of Krypton, his home planet and homespun yarns of his life as a teenager in Smallville. However, unlike *Wonder Woman*, *Superman* and *Action Comics* were usually in the top three best-selling comics. *Wonder Woman* frequently did not appear in the top thirty best sellers.

3. According to postal sales, *Spider-Man* was the first Marvel superhero to enter the best-selling list top twenty in 1966 at number 16 (http://www.comichron.com/yearlycomicssales/1960s/1966.html).

4. Indeed, in 1974 Wonder Woman, like Hercules, completed twelve labors to prove herself worthy of rejoining the Justice League of America. This storyline is analyzed in the essay by Joseph J. Darowski in this volume.

5. This was been noted as early the thirteenth century when Jacques de Vitry wrote "just as we consider Pygmies to be dwarves, so they consider us giants... And in the land of the Giants, who are larger than we are, we would be considered dwarfs by them" (qtd. in Friedman 163–4).

6. The introduction of a father, possibly Theno, in *Wonder Woman* #132 as Hippolyta's long lost love, into the post–1958 storyline is significant. Where Marston had suggested Wonder Woman as the product of asexual reproduction, the father's authority is reinstated in what must have been within this socio-cultural context, a transgressive family.

7. Readers might also have been aware that in her previous incarnation, Wonder Woman was created as a clay statue and given life by Aphrodite.

8. Gigantic and shrinking bodies can be identified in other superhero comics of DC — for instance in Superman comics of this era, Superman sometimes has to deal with the manipulations of giants from the giant dimension and the effects of red kryptonite on his body and behavior. In the Superman family, Jimmy Olsen and Lois Lane comics dwelt upon freakish body mutations. Jimmy Olsen, for instance becomes an elasti-lad or a giant or an animal/human hybrid. Many

of these strange transformations were the result of Mort Weisinger's attempts to appeal to his youthful audiences. He often took the advice of children in focus groups when they suggested storylines. The mutating human body can also be attributed to fears of radioactive contamination.

9. These are my classifications as I have been unable to find any reference to types of testing of heroes by monsters and Gods.

10. Peter Coogan applies Frye's schema of the hero power of action within the narrative mode to the superhero genre concluding that "A super hero is a hero who is super or superior to other kinds of heroes ... just as a super model is superior to other types of models" (Coogan 49) However, given the diversity of heroic types and levels of power within the superhero genre, Frye's attempt to shoehorn all characters into one narrative mode is unworkable as a general model. In this case, I argue the narrative modes of fairytales and myth in Wonder Woman in this era would enable identification with the *mythos* comedy mode.

11. There are other Multiple Man stories such as "The Kite of Doom!" (*Wonder Woman* #138, May 1963), but they replicate most of the points raised in earlier issues. For reasons of simplicity therefore, I have not included any Multiple Man stories after "The Attack of the Human Iceberg!"

12. These two narrative classifications fall into Aarne and Thompson's classification. Aarne originally classified folktales by their structure, and her work was adapted by Stith Thompson.

WORKS CITED

Attwood, William, George B. Leonard Jr. and J. Robert Miskin. *The Decline of the American Male*. New York: Random House, 1958.

Bakhtin, Mikhail. *Rabelais and His World*. Bloomington and Indianapolis: Indiana University Press, 1984.

Barson, Michael, and Steven Heller. *Red Scared! The Commie Menace in Propaganda and Popular Culture*. San Francisco: Chronicle, 2001.

Baudrillard, Jean. *Simulations*. New York: Semiotext(e), 1983.

Boyer, Paul. *By the Bomb's Early Light: American Thought and Culture at the Dawn of the Atomic Age*. New York: Pantheon, 1985.

Cohen, Jeffrey Jerome. "Monster Culture (Seven Theses)." In *Monster Theory*, edited by Jeffrey Jerome Cohen, 3–25. Minneapolis: University of Minnesota Press, 1998.

Coogan, Peter. *Superhero: The Secret Origin of a Genre*. Austin: MonkeyBrain, 2006.

Derrida, Jacques. "No Apocalypse, Not Now (Full Speed Ahead, Seven Missiles, Seven Missives)." *Diacritics* 4.II (1984): 20–31.

_____. *Of Grammatology*. Baltimore, London: Johns Hopkins University Press, 1997.

Englehardt, Tom. *The End of Victory Culture: Cold War America and the Disillusioning of a Generation*. New York: Basic, 1995.

Friedan, Betty. *The Feminine Mystique*. London: Gollancz, 1963.

Friedman, John Block. *The Monstrous Races in Medieval Art and Thought*. Cambridge: Harvard University Press, 1980.

Frye, Northrop. *Anatomy of Criticism: Four Essays*. Princeton, NJ: Princeton University Press, 1957.

Jackson, Rosemary. *Fantasy the Literature of Subversion*. London and New York: Routledge, 1998.

Jancovich, Mark. *Rational Fears: American Horror in the 1950s*. Manchester: Manchester University Press, 1996.

Kanigher, Robert (w), Ross Andru (a) and Mike Esposito (a). "Attack of the Human Iceberg!" *Wonder Woman* #135 (Jan. 1963). New York: DC Comics.

_____. "The Human Charm Bracelet!" *Wonder Woman* #106 (May 1959). New York: DC Comics.

_____. "The Impossible Day!" *Wonder Woman* #124 (Aug. 1961). New York: DC Comics.

_____."The Kite of Doom!" *Wonder Woman* #138 (May 1963). New York: DC Comics.

_____."The Return of Multiple Man!" *Wonder Woman* #129 (Apr. 1962). New York: DC Comics.

_____. "Wonder Girl in Giant Land!" *Wonder Woman* #109 (Oct. 1959). New York: DC Comics.

Kimmel, Michael. *Manhood in America: A Cultural History.* New York, Oxford: Oxford University Press, 2006.

Kristeva, Julia. *Powers of Horror: An Essay in Abjection.* New York, Guildford: Columbia University Press, 1982.

Kuznick, Peter J., and James Gilbert. "U.S. Culture and the Cold War." In *Rethinking Cold War Culture,* edited by Peter J. Kuznick and James Gilbert, 1–13. Washington and London: Smithsonian Institution, 2001.

Lacan, Jacques. *Ecrits: A Selection.* London: Tavistock, 1980.

MacDonald, J. Fred. *One Nation Under Television: The Rise and Decline of Network TV.* New York: Pantheon, 1990.

May, Elaine Tyler. *Homeward Bound: American Families in the Cold War Era.* New York: Basic, 1998.

Meyerowitz, Joanne. "Beyond the Feminine Mystique: A Reassessment of Postwar Mass Culture 1946–1958." *Journal of American History* 79.4 (1993): 1455–82.

Nadel, Alan. "Cold War Television and the Technology of Brainwashing." In *American Cold War Culture* by Douglas Field, 146–163. Edinburgh: Edinburgh University Press, 2005.

Prescott, Anne Lake. "The Odd Couple: Gargantua and Tom Thumb." In *Monster Theory,* edited by Jeffrey Jerome Cohen, 75–91. Minneapolis: University of Minnesota Press, 1998.

Reynolds, Richard. *Superheroes: A Modern Mythology.* London: Batsford, 1992.

Seed, David. *American Science Fiction and the Cold War: Literature and Film.* Edinburgh: Edinburgh University Press, 1999.

Stewart, Susan. *On Longing: Narratives of the Miniature, the Gigantic, the Souvenir, the Collection.* Durham, NC, and London: Duke University Press, 1993.

Thompson, Stith. *The Folktale.* New York: Holt, Rinehart and Winston, 1946.

Tuttle, William M. "America's Children in an Era of War, Hot and Cold: The Holocaust, the Bomb, and Child Rearing in the 1940s." In *Rethinking Cold War Culture,* edited by Peter J. Kuznick and James Gilbert, 14–35. Washington and London: Smithsonian Institution, 2001.

Warner, Marina. *Fantastic Metamorphoses, Other Worlds.* New York, Oxford: Oxford University Press, 2002.

Wertham, Fredric. *The Seduction of the Innocent.* London: Museum, 1955.

Wylie, Philip. *Generation of Vipers.* New York: Rinehart, 1955.

Retiring Romance

The Superheroine's
Transformation in the 1960s

FRANCINNE VALCOUR

In November of 1965 the plot of DC Comics *Wonder Woman* changed swiftly and dramatically. From the late 1950s the comic book had focused on love, romance and family as its major themes. Indeed, in the early 1960s the comic book no longer solely featured Wonder Woman, but expanded to include the adventures of Wonder Girl, Wonder Tot and Wonder Queen. Each member of this Wonder Family appeared in the *Wonder Woman* comic book in adventures that typically highlighted their relationship with romantic suitors. Then, abruptly in 1965, the editor of the comic book eliminated the Wonder family and their love interests. New stories featured Wonder Woman exclusively, placing less emphasis on romance and highlighting the superheroine's Amazon skills and adventures similar to the traditional escapades and villains of the original 1940s Golden Age *Wonder Woman* comic books.

Wonder Woman's transformation, though seemingly abrupt, proves logical when placed within the larger context of American society and the comic book's production. By the mid–1960s significant factors brought the 1950s perception of women's ideal as wife and mother into question. By eliminating the Wonder Family and placing emphasis on the superheroine's mission and Amazon skills, the comic book reflects the changing role of women in American society. The shift in *Wonder Woman* also came at a time when important changes occurred in the comic book industry, as editors and creators found success in reviving Golden Age heroes and experimenting with new styles to capture readers' changing interests. As editor of *Wonder Woman*, Robert Kanigher proved aware of and motivated by fans' desires. When fans openly

66

criticized the Wonder Family in the pages of *Wonder Woman*'s letter column, Kanigher responded by transforming the comic book.

Responding to the societal and cultural milieu of the United States and the comic book industry, Kanigher enacted dramatic changes that transformed *Wonder Woman*'s emphasis on domesticity and romance into stories highlighting the title character's Amazon skills and adventures. *Wonder Woman*'s editors have historically struggled to identify and create what readers desire from a female superhero. Chronicling the ways in which Wonder Woman transformed in this period thus offers insight into the readers' and the editor's changing ideal of a female superhero and women in general in the 1960s.

Romantic Adventures

Between the late 1950s and 1965 *Wonder Woman* issues devote significant emphasis describing the origins and adventures of the Wonder Family, which included tales of an adolescent Wonder Woman, called Wonder Girl, and an even younger version of the same character called Wonder Tot.[1] With these new stories the comic book moved away from the predominant theme of defending democracy that permeated the early 1950s issues to an emphasis on the superheroine's interest in romance and domestic life. From its inception in 1941, *Wonder Woman* always encompassed a dynamic of romance. In fact, Wonder Woman's forbidden affection for Steve Trevor drove the superheroine to come to America and procure the secret identity of Diana Prince. In the late 1950s and early 1960s, however, Wonder Woman's affection for Trevor is a more significant plot element and the superheroine also acquires additional suitors who compete for her affection. Indeed, the domestic overtones of the Wonder Family are exaggerated and Wonder Woman's (and Wonder Girl's) subsequent dilemma of romance eventually supplants the traditional villain versus superhero plot line.[2]

The comic book's emphasis on romance is clearly illustrated through Wonder Girl's adventures. Soon after Wonder Girl appears in the pages of *Wonder Woman* she meets Ronno, a Mer-Boy (half man, half fish). At first glance, Ronno is smitten with Wonder Girl as he exclaims, "You are the prettiest fish I have ever seen!" (Kanigher, Andru and Esposito, "Amazon Teen-ager!" 2). Later, Wonder Girl again meets Mer-Boy while completing Amazon training. Observing her feats of danger, Mer-Boy vows to "keep an eye" on Wonder Girl, and even attempts to aid her when he feels she is in danger (Kanigher, Andru and Esposito, "Amazon Teen-ager!" 4). He assures Wonder Girl that he will always be nearby if she should need him. After this first meeting, virtually all Wonder Girl stories focus on Mer-Boy and their developing romance.

Mer-Boy and Wonder Girl's romance is soon complicated when Wonder Girl meets Bird-Boy (half bird, half boy) who also reveals his affection. The complication begins immediately, when Bird-Boy, on first meeting Wonder Girl, asks her to a dance. Wonder Girl consents to his offer, but soon remembers her previous commitment to a date with Mer-Boy. As she tries to explain her dilemma to Mer-Boy, Bird-Boy appears. Wonder Girl is torn, literally, between Bird-Boy and Mer-Boy as each pulls her towards them (Kanigher, Andru and Esposito, "Mer-boy vs. Bird-boy!" 4). When they again ask Wonder Girl to choose between them, she pleads. "Mer-Boy! Bird-Boy! You're both so wonderful — How can you expect me to choose between you? G-Give me a little time — to make up my mind! Please?" The narration caption above reads, "Has ever a teenager's heart faced with such a choice?" (Kanigher, Andru, and Esposito, "Mer-boy vs. Bird-boy!" 10). Future adventures of Wonder Girl offer similar plot lines, pressuring Wonder Girl to choose between suitors vying for her affection.

Wonder Girl's seemingly vacillating attitude toward Mer-Boy and Bird-Boy and romance in general presents a complex picture, yet the overall message of Wonder Girl's relationships in the early 1960s proves that all women, including superheroines, eventually fall in love and suffer the burden of choosing a man. Indeed, Wonder Girl gains this knowledge directly from Wonder Woman. After several issues of Mer-Boy and Bird-Boy competing for Wonder Girl's affection, the three are captured by the evil fisherbird who mounts them for display on his castle wall. After Wonder Woman rescues all three, Mer-Boy and Bird-Boy once again demand Wonder Girl choose between them. Unable to answer, Wonder Girl asks Wonder Woman to help her choose. "Sorry," Wonder Woman responds, "that's something every girl has to decide for herself! I have enough trouble myself!" (Kanigher, Andru, and Esposito, "The Phantom FisherBird Part IV!" 24).

Wonder Girl not only learns from Wonder Woman, but parallels her romantic life in significant ways. While Wonder Girl contemplates her relationship with the bickering and competing Bird-Boy and Mer-Boy, Wonder Woman gets caught in her own romantic tug of war. Much like the younger version of herself, Wonder Woman's adventures in the early 1960s hinge on her connection to male suitors.

The competition for Wonder Woman's affection begins when Steve Trevor meets Manno, the Merman. In November 1960, after Wonder Woman turns down Trevor's proposal for marriage (a recurring event in the 1950s), Trevor becomes suspicious that protecting democracy is not the only reason for her refusal. He immediately suspects another man rivaling for her affection. To investigate his fears, Trevor follows Wonder Woman to Paradise Island, her Amazonian home. His jealousy grows when he spies Wonder Woman receiving flowers from another man, a Merman. "It's a Merman!" Steve gasps. "A handsome devil! Look at the way she's smiling at him — and he gives her a bouquet! They know each other all right! He must be my rival!"(Kanigher, Andru, and Esposito, "Wonder Woman's Impossible Decision!" 6).

Much like Wonder Girl's relationship with Mer-Boy in the early 1960s, insecurity quickly turns to jealousy and rivalry. Without questioning Wonder Woman's relations with the Merman, Trevor overreacts. "I'll bet that flippered half-fish, half-man is telling Wonder Woman how beautiful she is! And how wonderful he is! And what a great pair they'd make!" (Kanigher, Andru, and Esposito, "Wonder Woman's Impossible Decision! Part II" 7). Though she explains that Manno is her friend from childhood, like "the boy next door," Trevor feels no relief. After she leaves him, he laments, "Looks like I'll never have a chance of meeting Manno, the merman! And proving to Wonder Woman that I'm as good a man... How can I win over a rival if we can never meet? It's not fair!" (Kanigher, Andru, and Esposito, "Wonder Woman's Impossible Decision! Part II" 10). Trevor is immediately jealous and willing to compete for Wonder Woman, even though Trevor has yet to meet Manno, knows nothing of his intentions and learned from Wonder Woman that the two are merely friends.

Later, when Trevor finally meets Manno, they immediately and simultaneously seek Wonder Woman's affection. To resolve the debate, they ask Wonder Woman to choose. Much like her younger counterpart Wonder Girl, Wonder Woman is unable to decide. As the caption reads: "Wonder Woman smiles an enigmatic smile, which can only be found on a Mona Lisa." To her suitors and the reading audience she declares: "I'll exercise my women's prerogative by leaving it up to you to decide!" (Kanigher, Andru, and Esposito, "Wonder Woman's Impossible Decision! Part IV" 25).

In this first encounter between Manno, Trevor and Wonder Woman, the Amazon establishes Wonder Woman's relationship with men and opinion of romance and domesticity in the early 1960s. From the moment Manno and Steve Trevor learn of each other they continuously fight for Wonder Woman's affection, as she looks on. No longer torn by Trevor's constant push for marriage, she is comfortable and seemingly pleased over their competition for her affection. While early issues focused on her internal struggle between career and marriage, she is now a more self-confident and powerful player in the love triangle. Furthermore, Wonder Woman's "enigmatic smile" and coy retort parallel Wonder Girl's own security in indecision.

Period of Transition

By 1964, Kanigher's constant focus on Wonder Woman's and Wonder Girl's romantic quandary transforms. Increasingly, the superheroine appears hesitant to embrace marriage and domesticity as offering true happiness. Although marriage and romance seem inevitable in the late fifties and early sixties and the Amazon seems delighted by male attention and competition, by 1964 the comic book and the superheroine increasingly offer evidence that marriage may not offer true fulfillment.

Wonder Woman's building skepticism toward marriage and domesticity is clearly illustrated in one comic book issue where Steve Trevor, in a dream, marries Wonder Woman. On the day of their wedding, Wonder Woman is barraged for hours by publicity, while fans call her name and request her autograph. Visibly annoyed, Trevor comments: "Wonder Woman — Wonder Woman — Don't they know you're Mrs. Steve Trevor now?" (Kanigher, Andru, and Esposito, "Wonder Woman's Surprise Honeymoon!" 6). Before the couple can reach their honeymoon and Wonder Woman can change from her wedding dress, the superheroine is called to face danger. After defeating the villain she is once again bombarded by publicity, while Trevor watches visibly exasperated. Later, Trevor becomes further annoyed as Wonder Woman offers her dress and their car to a couple in trouble. (Kanigher, Andru, and Esposito, "Wonder Woman's Surprise Honeymoon!" 7–9).

At last Wonder Woman and Trevor find themselves alone on their honeymoon. Trevor is finally calmed. "Soon Wonder Woman will serve me my first Amazon meal! I'll bet it will taste like nothing on Earth!" (Kanigher, Andru, and Esposito, "Wonder Woman's Surprise Honeymoon part II!" 10). Happy that his new wife is off to cook, Trevor sits back in a rocking chair with his feet up. Yet Trevor's ideal meal served by his new bride falls short. "This toast's burnt! The meat's raw! The jello's hot! This coffee's cold!" (Kanigher, Andru, and Esposito, "Wonder Woman's Surprise Honeymoon part II!" 10). Crying, Wonder Woman sobs to Trevor, "Y-Y-You n-n-never asked me whether I c-c-could cook!" (Kanigher, Andru, and Esposito, "Wonder Woman's Surprise Honeymoon part II!" 11). Trevor consoles his bride by stating that he will do the cooking and that perhaps the couple should go for a swim to forget the incident. Yet even on the beach Wonder Woman's behavior falls short of Trevor's conception of an ideal wife. While sunbathing the Amazon notices an enemy submarine firing a missile at the United States. Wonder Woman abandons her husband to save the country, without thinking of her husband's desires in a wife. After averting peril Wonder Woman returns to Trevor, who because of sun glare, could not see the missile, the peril, or the Amazon's feat, but sits aggravated by his missing "restless bride." He expresses his anger as she approaches. "You were right! It's not only unfair — but downright mental cruelty to be married to you!" Just then Trevor wakes from his dream of being married to Wonder Woman. Later, he confesses to the superheroine, "I dreamed I was married to you ... and it was a horrible experience!" (Kanigher, Andru, and Esposito, "Wonder Woman's Surprise Honeymoon part II!" 14).

Trevor's "horrible experience" in being married to Wonder Woman, if but only in a dream, offers insight into both Wonder Woman and the comic book's editor's expectations in marriage and domestic life by the mid-sixties. Though she appears to know the traditional ideal and duties of a wife, she resists conforming. Even while married, the superheroine continues her duties of fighting crime and helping citizens, although she is aware that her actions displease her husband. When her cooking upsets Trevor, she does appear visibly upset. She even agrees to Trevor's offer to cook for them from that moment on, rather than declaring that she will learn how to cook herself. Though she understands what Trevor expects, she is unwilling to transform to what Trevor and *Wonder Woman's* editor reveals as the ideal wife. Hence, Trevor's dream of marriage is a "horrible experience" because he becomes aware of the gap between Wonder Woman's aspirations and his own ideal. Her action demonstrates resistance when offered a direct opportunity to commit to romance and domestic life.

By 1965 the comic book's resistance to romance and domesticity grows substantially. Indeed, in an issue entitled "The End — or the Beginning," *Wonder Woman* experiences a dramatic and seemingly abrupt change. The story begins with crowds of people holding signs in front of a large office building. Their protests concern the comic book and the editor's treatment of the superheroine. Meanwhile, inside the office building Wonder Girl, Wonder Tot, Mer-Boy, Bird-Boy, Manno, Birdman and others stand before the *Wonder Woman* editor Robert Kanigher. After expressing his affection for the characters, Kanigher "retires" them and symbolically places photos of each character in a drawer and closes it. Outraged, Wonder Woman exclaims "Merciful Minerva! Y-you've done it! You've really done it! You've killed them all! You've only left my mother — and Steve! What are you going to do with us?" "You'll soon see," responds Kanigher (Kanigher, Andru, and Esposito, "The End — Or the Beginning!" 7). The next frame shows the three remaining characters and Kanigher standing on the balcony of the office building overlooking the earlier disgruntled fans. "Okay fans," Kanigher declares, "You've won! Starting with the December Wonder Woman no. 159 — we're going to make comics history! We're going to recreate the golden age! (Kanigher, Andru, and Esposito "The End — Or the Beginning!" 8).

To those regular readers of the comic book, Kanigher's decision to "retire" several regular *Wonder Woman* characters may have seemed abrupt or even shocking. Yet, a close analysis of the comic book and the changes happening in the comic book industry as well as American culture in the years before this dramatic day sheds light on Kanigher's behavior.

Why the Change?

The latter half of the 1950s and early 1960s produced myriad changes for super hero comic books initiated by falling profits. The first major effort to remedy lagging sales came from DC and involved reviving popular Golden Age heroes, hoping to tap into a dual market of both older fans that read the original comics as a kid in the 1940s and the present day younger comic book fans (*Fifty Who Made DC Great*, 31). DC originally revived The Flash, a popular Golden Age hero. Their strategy included modernizing the hero, incorporating more realism and the growing interest in science, while retaining the original premise of the character. The revived character debuted in Showcase comics, and then gained its own title in 1959 initiating what comic scholars and fans refer to as the "Silver Age" of comics. In the following years DC would apply the revival strategy to other characters, including The Green Lantern and The Justice League of America (Wright, 183). Marvel Comics also found success with *The Fantastic Four*, which featured new, complex characters that acted distinctly different from the traditional superhero (Jacobs and Jones, 52–54).

Reviving Golden Age heroes proved profitable and encouraged other editors to also incorporate the Golden Age style into their comics. Though the success of revived comic books influenced Kanigher's elimination of the Wonder Family and incorporation of the Golden Age style in *Wonder Woman*, another aspect of the comic book industry clearly influenced Kanigher's decision: the growing importance and changing desires of fans as exhibited through fan mail and fanzines.

Fan mail was not new to the comic industry, yet it wasn't until the late 1950s that reader's input started appearing in the pages of comic books. Initially, the majority of letters printed in DC's comics, including *Wonder Woman*, came from young readers. Typically these letters commented on how much the reader enjoyed the story and heroes, or asked unrealistic questions that revealed their youth. For example, early fan mail produced in Wonder Woman asked if the reader could acquire the same superpowers that the hero possessed or asked to visit Paradise Island and Wonder Woman herself.

By the early 1960s, DC witnessed a growing number of older readers sending letters to the editor. Indeed, these older fans manifest a desire to influence the direction of comic books and the characteristics of the superhero/ine. Concomitantly, comic book editors saw a direct benefit from listening and reacting to fan comments. These older, more mature readers could offer insight into what readers wanted, and thus what might sell best (Schwartz, 3).

Comic book producers, including Kanigher, could also monitor fan interests and potential sales through newly established fanzines, like *Alter Ego*. Fanzines allowed readers to express their thoughts and comments on comics, but also connect with other readers. In his first mailing, founding member Jerry Bails sent *Alter Ego* out free to a growing mailing list largely assembled from the DC letter columns. *Alter Ego* included articles on comic books written by Bails, Roy Thomas and other comic book fans. To satiate those fans looking for copies of comics missing from their own collection Bails also began the first advertising fanzine, *The Comicollector* in September 1961 (Schelly, "Jerry Bails" Ten Building Blocks of Fandom 5). Soon after these two publications other writers and artists began producing additional fanzines. Thus comic fanzines illustrate a grassroots movement on behalf of comic fans and the comic book industry to cultivate a strong comic book fan community. By the mid–1960s a visible and active fan community existed that interacted with, and influenced comic book creators.

In 1961 *Alter Ego* published the first Alley Awards, reflecting readers' opinion of comic books published the previous year. Award categories included "Best Regularly Published Comic Book" (won by *The Justice League of America*). The "Worst Comic" award went to *Wonder Woman*. As Roy Thomas reflected: Wonder Woman had no competition, amassing almost 20 percent of the total votes — a considerable feat, since all of these were write ins! The selection is probably much deserved; the stories are abominably weak and trite, what with Wonder Girl and Wonder Tot (Thomas, 46).[3]

An analysis of the letters sent into *Wonder Woman,* and Kanigher's response to these letters, reflects fan sentiment represented in the Alley Awards and their increasing influence on the comic book's production. Starting in October 1965, letters appearing in *Wonder Woman* progressively include criticism towards the comic book. For example, one letter sent to *Wonder Woman* from Robert Allen during this time period asks Kanigher to revamp *Wonder Woman* to a Golden Age style. Allen offers a detailed analysis of why the current Wonder family oriented *Wonder Woman* proves unsuccessful and encourages Kanigher to create a more independent and strong superheroine. Moreover, Allen asks to, "Make the stories more mature and make Steve Trevor WWs only man and make her love him but still not marry him; keep up suspense" (Kanigher, Andru, and Esposito, "I — The Bomb").[4]

When placing the *Wonder Woman* story line within the context of fan comments sent to the editor, it is not surprising that Kanigher chose to abruptly and dramatically change the comic book. Clearly readers showed dissatisfaction with the Wonder family and its emphasis on romance, marriage and domesticity. Indeed, as Allen states, fans desired a superheroine like that in the 1940s Golden Age issues, one who interacted more with villains than suitors and showcased her strength and super skills, not her romantic intentions. Their choice in a stronger, more independent superheroine and Kanigher's agreement with this choice proves especially significant considering women's changing experience in American culture in the 1960s.

The United States in the 1960s is often described as a decade of upheaval, a time when grassroots movements led by a predominantly young, educated generation created a revolution through social movements concerning all manner of rights. Yet the majority of what may be considered the upheaval of the 1960s took place in the second half of the decade and continued into the 1970s. This is especially true of the women's movement, which arguably won some of its major victories during this time. As a result, public perception of women's changing roles and needs would not reflect the ideals of the women's movement until later in the sixties. Indeed, in considerable ways, the perception of American women generated in the suburban focused 1950s lingered into the early 1960s.

By 1965 significant events helped challenge the 1950s perception. In 1963 Betty Friedan published *The Feminine Mystique*, which identified women's discontent as housewives. Friedan described what she called "the problem that has no name," in which women responsible for the daily toils of motherhood asked themselves, "Is this all?" (Friedan, 11). *The Feminine Mystique* became a best seller and excerpts appeared in several women's magazines. For many women, Friedan voiced concerns they had kept silent for years.

While Friedan brought considerable public attention to women's opinion on the domestic ideal, other factors also shed light on women's changing desires and needs. In 1961 President Kennedy initiated the Presidential Commission on the Status of Women. The Commission's goal consisted of designing strategies to contest sex discrimination in government and private employment. The Commission published its final report, entitled *The Presidential Report on American Woman*, in 1963, the same year that Friedan published *The Feminine Mystique* (Linden-Ward and Green, 8).

The following year women's experience in paid labor gained further attention with the inclusion of sex in the Civil Rights Act of 1964. Though the decision to include sex as a category in the legislation produced controversy and debate, the act eventually passed, prohibiting discrimination in employment on the basis of race, color, religion, national origin and sex. The inclusion of sex proved significant. In the coming year, the Equal Employment Opportunity Commission formed to implement the act's provisions and investigate complaints of discrimination (Rosen, 72). Unfortunately, the EEOC proved lax in halting gender inequity prompting some politically motivated women, including Betty Friedan, to create a non-governmental organization that focused on combating discrimination. In 1966 the National Organization for Woman (NOW) formed to work towards equality between the sexes (Rosen, 75).

By the time Betty Friedan and her colleagues formed NOW in 1966, issues of women's experience in the public and private realm had received considerable attention. The publication of *The Feminine Mystique*, as well as passage of federal legislation, including the Equal Pay Act and Title VII of the 1964 Civil Rights Act, and individual activism, raised the public's consciousness regarding women's issues and questioned the earlier perceptions of women shaped in the 1950s. It is not surprising that within this climate of changing perceptions of women's roles Robert Kanigher's characterization of *Wonder Woman* also transformed. Perhaps in transforming Wonder Woman, Kanigher hoped to create a superheroine that more accurately reflected the changing status of women in the United States.

By the end of 1965 *Wonder Woman* does project a significantly different superheroine, whose adventures highlight her career as a superheroine rather than her romantic interests. In the late 1950s and early sixties Wonder Woman and Wonder Girl appear preoccupied by romance, while self-conscious and jealous of their suitor's affection for other women. By 1962, the superheroine's self-consciousness dissipates as both Wonder Girl and Wonder Woman appear to enjoy suitors competing for their affection. Yet, within a year the comic book begins offering evidence of the superheroine's resistance to marriage and family and her inability to fit the ideals of wife and mother. Then Kanigher eliminates the Wonder family and the comic book's heavy emphasis on romance and domesticity and creates a comic book similar to the Golden Age Wonder Woman. These stories emphasize the classic Wonder Woman themes, including distinct villains with diabolical plans and an emphasis on Wonder Woman's Amazon skills and paraphernalia. In these stories Wonder Woman meets Dr. Psycho and the Cheetah (both popular villains in the 1940s) and predominantly uses her bracelets and lasso to defeat enemy foes. And Wonder Woman's romantic struggle (now only including Steve Trevor) falls to the background as Wonder Woman's mission as a superheroine takes center stage.

In tracing the comic book within the larger context of its production from the late fifties to 1965, Kanigher's decision to transform the comic book appears influenced by three major factors. First, the early 1960s saw significant innovation within the superhero genre. The success of Marvel's new heroes and DC's revived Golden Age heroes offered Kanigher a tangible example of what readers would buy. In a sales driven industry, Kanigher had to see the inclusion of Golden Age elements as a possible chance to boost sales.

Secondly, *Wonder Woman's* metamorphosis proves clearly influenced by Kanigher's increasing recognition of fan culture and fan interest. Throughout the first half of the 1960s Kanigher exhibits a growing investment in his readership, first by including letters in the comic book and then by encouraging criticism from older readers and executing the changes they desired. As fans became more influential in the comic book industry, through letters and fanzines, Kanigher responded to their desire for a stronger, more independent superheroine.

Finally, *Wonder Woman's* transition reflects changes happening for women in American society at the same time. By 1965 significant elements brought women's experience into the public arena and challenged the dominant perception of women's role as wife and mother made popular in the 1950s. Thus the comic book's transformation to stressing Wonder Woman's role as superheroine and not just a woman focused on marriage and domesticity reflects the transformation concerning women's perceived role occurring in the larger American society in the 1960s.

NOTES

1. Between 1959 and 1965 Kanigher devoted a significant portion of *Wonder Woman* issues to describing the origins and adventures of the Wonder Family. This story line begins in an Apr. 1959 issue, which reveals the "secret origins" of Wonder Girl, including her acquisition of superpowers as a child. This issue also describes how Wonder Girl built a ship, which the Amazons used to sail away from the land of war to Paradise Island. After the initial issue, stories of Wonder Girl appear frequently, highlighting her Amazon training and relationships with male suitors. Soon after Wonder Girl's arrival, other characters appear in the Wonder Woman series. In May 1961 Wonder Tot debuts, representing Wonder Woman as a toddler with superpowers. These "imaginary stories" offer tales of the superheroine at a younger age. Eventually, these three versions of Wonder Woman, Wonder Tot, Wonder Girl and Wonder Woman came together with Queen Hippolyta to create the Wonder Family. At first glance, readers may wonder how three different versions of Wonder Woman (at different ages) could appear in *Wonder Woman* at the same time to create the Wonder Family. Indeed, even Robert Kanigher appeared vague on its happening. Yet, Kanigher's explanation fit in with his emphasis on imaginary tales and fantasy. At first Kanigher allows multiple versions of Wonder Woman to appear simultaneously by having one character view others through a time and space machine. Soon Kanigher provides a more fantastic rational, as his artist Mike Esposito explains. Diana procures a camera "and as Wonder Woman grew up from Wonder Tot to a Wonder Girl to her present day, she set it on automatic and photographed them all in the same scene." Kanigher compared the process of bringing multiple versions of Wonder Woman together to splicing film (Daniels, Wonder Woman, 113).

2. DC experienced many changes in the 1950s as publishers contended with the attack on comic books for their perceived promotion of crime, sexual explicitness and juvenile delinquency. This assault reached its peak in the mid-fifties with the publication of Dr. Fredric Wertham's attack on comic books in *The Seduction of Innocent*, the 1954 Senate Subcommittee investigation on juvenile delinquency and the subsequent comics code. For some comic books, including *Wonder Woman*, the effort to evade criticism while promoting sales meant adapting more romance oriented story lines much like the increasing popular teen and romance comics. While the comics crusade affected *Wonder Woman*, analysis of the impact falls outside the scope of this article.

3. It is significant to note that Robert Kanigher never publicly responded to *Wonder Woman* receiving the "worst comic award."

4. It is important to note that when analyzing the impact and influence of *Wonder Woman* letters that letter content is not an accurate reflection of fan base. DC, and specifically, Kanigher, chose which letters appeared and therefore it is difficult to determine if the selection accurately represents the numerous letters the comic book received. Indeed, the letters could have been manufactured, although it seems that letters published came from legitimate fans. Yet, the

ambiguous process seems significant. DC and Kanigher held the power of deciding which letters appeared and whether they contained praise or criticism. Thus the letters displayed in *Wonder Woman* potentially offer two notable factors: fans' reception of the comic book and what DC wanted readers to believe fans felt about *Wonder Woman*.

WORKS CITED

Benton, Mike. *Superhero Comics of the Silver Age.* Dallas: Taylor, 1991.

Bridwell, E. Nelson. *Superman: From the Thirties to the Seventies.* New York: Crown, 1971.

Chafe, William Henry. *The American Woman: Her Changing Social, Political and Economic Roles, 1920–1970.* New York: Oxford University Press, 1972.

Daniels, Les. *Comix: A History of Comic Books in America.* New York: Outerbridge and Dienstfrey, 1971.

_____. *Superman, the Complete History: The Life and Times of the Man of Steel.* San Francisco: Chronicle, 1998.

_____. *Wonder Woman, the Complete History: The Life and Times of the Amazon Princess.* San Francisco: Chronicle, 2000.

D'Emilio, John, and Estelle B. Freedman. *Intimate Matters: A History of Sexuality in America.* New York: Harper and Row, 1988.

Fifty Who Made DC Great. New York: DC Comics, 1985.

Fleisher, Michael L. *The Encyclopedia of Comic Book Heroes: Wonder Woman.* New York: Macmillan, 1976.

Friedan, Betty. *The Feminine Mystique.* New York: W.W. Norton & Company, Inc., 1963.

Gilbert, James. *A Cycle of Outrage: America's Reaction to the Juvenile Delinquent in the 1950's.* New York: Oxford UP, 1986.

Infantino, Carmine, and J. David Spurlock. *The Amazing World of Carmine Infantino: An Autobiography.* Lebanon, NJ: Vanguard, 2001.

Jacobs, Will, and Gerard Jones. *The Comic Book Superheroes: From the Silver Age to the Present.* New York: Crown, 1985.

Jones, Gerard. *Men of Tomorrow: Geeks, Gangsters and the Birth of the Comic Book.* New York: Basic, 2004.

Kaledin, Eugenia. *Mothers and More: American Women in the 1950's.* New York: Free, 1989.

Kanigher, Robert (w), Ross Andru (p) and Mike Esposito (i). "Amazon Teen-Ager!" *Wonder Woman* #107/1 (Jul. 1959). New York: DC Comics.

_____. "The End — Or the Beginning!" *Wonder Woman* #158 (Nov. 1965). New York: DC Comics.

_____. "I — The Bomb." *Wonder Woman* #157 (Oct. 1965). New York: DC Comics.

_____. "Mer-Boy vs. Bird-boy!" *Wonder Woman* #144/3 (Feb. 1964). New York: DC Comics.

_____. "The Phantom FisherBird." *Wonder Woman* #150/4 (Nov. 1964). New York: DC Comics.

_____. "Wonder Woman's Impossible Decision!" *Wonder Woman* #118/1 (Nov. 1960). New York: DC Comics.

_____. "Wonder Woman's Surprise Honeymoon!" *Wonder Woman* #127/3 (Jan. 1962). New York: DC Comics.

Kessler-Harris, Alice. *Out To Work: A History of Wage-Earning Women in the United States.* New York: Oxford University Press, 1982.

Lee, Stan. *The Origins of Marvel Comics.* New York: Simon and Schuster, 1974.

Linden-Ward, Blanche, and Carol Hurd Green. *American Women in the 1960s: Changing the Future.* New York: Twayne, 1993.

Matthews, Glenna. *"Just a Housewife": The Rise and Fall of Domesticity in America.* New York: Oxford University Press, 1987.

May, Elaine Tyler. *Homeward Bound: American Families in the Cold War Era.* New York: HarperCollins, 1988.

Meyerowitz, Joanne. *Not June Cleaver: Women and Gender in Postwar America, 1945–1960.* Philadelphia: Temple University Press, 1994.

Murray, Will. "Of Robots, Amazons and Dinosaurs ... Andru and Esposito." *Comic Book Marketplace* 78 (May 2000): 20–5, 66–7.

_____. "The Wonder Woman Who Was Lost." *Comic Book Marketplace* 78 (May 2000): 44–54.

Nyberg, Amy Kiste. *Seal of Approval: The History of the Comics Code.* Jackson: University Press of Mississippi, 1998.

Pustz, Matthew. *Comic Book Culture: Fanboys and True Believers.* Jackson: University Press of Mississippi, 1999.

Rosen, Ruth. *The World Split Open: How the Modern Women's Movement Changed America.* New York: Viking, 2000.

Rupp, Leila J., and Verta Taylor. *Survival and the Doldrums: The American Women's Rights Movement, 1945 to the 1960s.* New York: Oxford University Press, 1987.

Schelly, Bill. *Fandom's Finest Comics: A Treasury of the Best Original Strips from the Classic Comics Fanzines, 1958–1975.* Seattle: Hamster, 1997.

_____. *The Golden Age of Comic Fandom.* Seattle: Hamster, 1995.

_____. "Jerry Bails' Ten Building Block of Fandom." *Alter Ego* 25 (Jun. 2003): 5–9.

_____. *Sense of Wonder.* Raleigh: TwoMorrows, 2001.

Schwartz, Julius, and Brian M. Thomsen. *Man of Two Worlds: My Life in Science Fiction and Comics.* New York: HarperCollins, 2000.

Snyder, Robin. "The Golden Gladiator: Robert Kanigher." *The Comics Journal* 84 (Oct. 1983): 51–85.

_____. "The Golden Gladiator: Robert Kanigher Part II." *The Comics Journal* 85 (Nov. 1983): 71–100.

_____. "Who Created the Silver Age Flash?" *Alter Ego* 10 (Sep. 2001): 37–41.

"Superfans and Batmaniacs." *Newsweek,* Feb. 15, 1965, 89.

Thomas, Roy, and Bill Schelly, eds. *Alter Ego: The Best of the Legendary Comics Fanzine.* Seattle: Hamster, 1977.

Weist, Jerry. "A Short History of Comic Fandom and Comic Book Collecting in America." In *The Overstreet Comic Book Price Guide,* 26th ed., compiled by Robert Overstreet, A104–5. New York: Avon, 1996.

Wright, Bradford W. *Comic Book Nation: The Transformation of Youth Culture in America.* Baltimore: Johns Hopkins University Press, 2001.

What a Woman Wonders

This Is Feminism?

Jason LaTouche

In the early 1970s Wonder Woman was adopted as a symbol of the women's movement. To many feminists who had grown up reading her comic books, Wonder Woman stood as a strongly positive role model for female empowerment. This appropriation of Wonder Woman as a feminist icon was cemented when she was featured on the cover of the first stand-alone issue of *Ms.* magazine in July 1972. Striding over the Earth like a colossus, protectively carrying a piece of a town, including an ambulance, safely in her magic lasso, this Wonder Woman was worriedly keeping a Vietnam-style rural war zone from encroaching on an idealized American-style small town emblazoned with a gigantic "Peace and Justice in '72" billboard. In this one image, Wonder Woman is presented as a feminist agent of social change: a supporter of social welfare, an opponent of war and violence, and a symbol of female power, strength, and wisdom.

This feminist appropriation was made even more explicit later that year in the book *Wonder Woman* (Steinem). Spearheaded by *Ms.* magazine co-founder Gloria Steinem and produced in conjunction with National Periodical Publications (DC Comics), *Wonder Woman* contained extensive editorial commentary, a lengthy introductory essay, and an even lengthier anthropological interpretive essay all attempting to situate Wonder Woman as an icon of female empowerment. In her introductory essay, Steinem writes:

> Wonder Woman symbolizes many of the values of the women's culture that feminists are now trying to introduce into the mainstream: strength and self-reliance for women, sisterhood and mutual support among women, peacefulness and esteem for human life, a diminishment both of "masculine" aggression and of the belief that violence is the only way of solving conflicts [2].

To illustrate these values, *Wonder Woman* reprinted thirteen stories from the *Wonder Woman* comic book series.

However, the Wonder Woman stories and imagery being used in *Ms.* magazine, *Wonder Woman*, and other feminist literature was not the contemporary Wonder Woman that existed in the comic books at the time. Instead, the feminist movement appropriated the Wonder Woman of the early to mid–1940s as their symbol of feminist virtue.

This was a particularly revealing decision as the character of Wonder Woman had undergone a remarkable transformation in the years immediately prior to her adoption as an icon by the women's movement. Beginning in 1968, editors Jack Miller and Carmine Infantino and writer Dennis O'Neil had revamped the Wonder Woman character in an attempt to revive its flagging sales (Daniels 123).

This revamp was intentionally designed to modernize the character and make her more approachable. As part of this transformation, Wonder Woman's Amazonian sisters and their Paradise Island homeland leave Earth for a parallel dimension. By refusing to go with them and choosing to stay on Earth, Wonder Woman is compelled to surrender her powers. This entails her becoming an everyday human with everyday needs. So Wonder Woman rents an apartment and starts her own business to pay for her living expenses. Still a hero, she starts to train in martial arts and carries on her good works by becoming a freelance crime fighter cum secret agent.

All of these changes were made with the idea of creating a more empowered character. O'Neil characterized his work on this transformation "as taking a woman and making her independent, and not dependent on superpowers. I saw it as making her thoroughly human and then an achiever on top of that, which, according to my mind, was very much in keeping with the feminist agenda" (Daniels 126).

The failure of this "feminist" transformation of Wonder Woman to resonate within the actual feminist community points to the problems contained within the character during this period. The late 1960s and early 1970s new Wonder Woman was a character caught between worlds. A character that was ostensibly feminist, a business owner, a secret agent, a woman making her own choices and way in life, but in reality a character that at its core embraced many of the sexist values and roles the women's movement was fighting against.

By the time of the transformation of the Wonder Woman character in 1968, a revived women's movement was flourishing within the United States. Throughout the 1960s, women's groups successfully mobilized for legal changes designed to eliminate sexual discrimination. In 1963, Congress passed the Equal Pay Act. The following year, due in large part to pressure exerted by the National Woman's Party, sex was included among the protected classes under Title VII of the Civil Rights Act of 1964 which banned discrimination in employment and in access to facilities such as stores and restaurants (Rosenberg 187).

Such successes were both fostered by and helped to foster the growth of women's rights organizations. In addition to innumerable local consciousness-raising groups, new regional and national groups such as the National Organization for Women were being formed. Indeed, by the time of the transformation of the Wonder Woman character in 1968 these groups were engaging in highly public examples of social activism such as that year's highly visible protest of the Atlantic City Miss America beauty pageant (Rosenberg 192). In fact, by 1968, due in large part to these political activities of women's movement feminists, ideas of gender roles within the United States were beginning to toward more feminist beliefs, particularly among younger, college-educated individuals (Ferree and Hess 79).

So the creators of Wonder Woman were not out of sync with the times in envisioning a more modern, feminist Wonder Woman. In fact, given the increasingly college-aged readership of comic books in the late 1960s their readership was increasingly primed to be open to such a depiction.

The failure of the character to resonate with this group speaks to the problems with the way in which Wonder Woman's creators went about depicting a feminist superhero. While feminism was a broad movement with many diverse interests and goals there were some key ideas that bridged the majority of the community. The women's movement was fundamentally challenging the idea of traditional gender roles and the constraints these roles placed on women both at home and in the public sphere. As part of this critique, the women's movement was challenging the ways in which systems of belief and action that were seen as feminine were devalued in favor of those that were perceived as masculine, such as emotion versus action (Johnson 124). In conjunction with this idea, feminists were seeking to upend the traditional gender roles of men as the leaders and actors in society and women as their followers and cheerleaders. In sum, women's movement activists were calling for equality of opportunity and respect for the capacities of all people, men and women, to lead, to follow, and to participate on all levels of society (Ferree and Hess 27).

Such an agenda required changes in the cultural systems that supported sexist practices. To this end, feminists were calling for changes in sexist language that diminished the role of women in society and for an end to the public status of women as visual objects to be consumed by men (Ferree and Hess 161, Rosenberg 192). They were calling for women to be viewed for all their capacities, intellectual, physical, moral, rather than for the limiting roles of sex object and subordinate that had been the primary role of women since World War II.

The cover of the very first issue introducing the new Wonder Woman, *Wonder Woman* #178 (Sep.-Oct. 1968), established that the "feminist" agenda of her editors and writers might not be fully aligned with that of the feminist activists of the women's movement. On a cover with a psychedelic green background, bold groovy lettering announces, "Forget the Old ... The New Wonder Woman Is Here!" The new Wonder Woman stands in the center of the cover holding a dripping paint can with a brush. Behind her is a poster showing a mock up of an old style Wonder Woman comic book such as would have been used for the issue in the past. This cover has been crossed out with the blue paint the new Wonder Woman is holding. The old style cover shows two images of the old Wonder Woman, one in her traditional superhero costume of calf-length red boots, eagle emblazoned bodice and blue starred shorts and the other dressed in the military intelligence uniform of her secret identity, Diana Prince. So the "old" Wonder Woman had been left behind, crossed out, her superhero role and military intelligence role discarded. In their place, the cover of the new Wonder Woman seemed to offer a new role, Wonder Woman as a passive personification of beauty.

Indeed, this new Wonder Woman stands inactive on the cover, even the act of crossing out her old images having already been completed. She stares straight out at the reader, hand on tilted hip, fully made up with thick eye shadow, lipstick, fingernail polish, and elaborately coiffed hair. Rather than being dressed in a uniform that promises she will fulfill an important role in society, she instead stands dressed in trendy mod fashions, tight black leggings and micro mini dress.

This is an image of a Wonder Woman that asks to be valued for her beauty and not her intellectual, physical and moral abilities. As the issues of the new Wonder Woman series unfolded over the next few years this idea of the central importance of Wonder Woman as an objectified woman valued primarily for her beauty, a woman who is seen primarily through the lens of her physical appearance and how this appearance appeals to men, became the central way in which the character was addressed.

In the very first issue with the new Wonder Woman, *Wonder Woman* #178 (Sep.-Oct. 1968), Wonder Woman goes undercover at a nightclub to try to track down a woman she thinks can help her free her boyfriend who has been wrongly imprisoned. In order to go undercover, Wonder Woman, in her Diana Prince secret identity, gets a makeover, emerging from trips to a salon and several boutiques declaring, "Wow! I'm gorgeous! I should have done this ages ago!" (O'Neil "Wonder Woman's Rival" 10). Indeed, once she arrives at the nightclub her self-evaluation is validated as men proceed to throw themselves at her.

This idea of her beauty driving men mad with desire is repeated again and again throughout the story, and indeed the series, and the new Wonder Woman loves it. "Ha! The new me sure turns 'em on!" she crows as a man she just met declares, "For a [gorgeous] chick like you, I'd take a trip to the moon!" (12).

By the end of the issue, she has managed to free her boyfriend Steve Trevor from prison only to find that whereas before he was uninterested in Diana Prince, her newly glammed up Diana Prince persona has now sparked Steve's interest. As Wonder Woman, in her superhero guise, cuddles with Steve on a couch, he tells her that Diana Prince is "so much more than I what I thought she was — in fact, I think I'll ask her out one of these days and really get to know her" (23).

Wonder Woman reacts to this news by becoming jealous of herself, thinking, "I'll lose him forever if I don't do *something* to keep him interested in *me!*" (23). In this manner she buys into the idea that her worth is tied to her physical appearance and her ability to attract a man's attention.

This idea of Wonder Woman's objectification by men and her willing complicity in this objectification becomes a recurrent theme throughout the run of the new Wonder Woman series. As she relinquishes her superpowers and takes on the Diana Prince role on a permanent basis she starts to be referred to almost exclusively in terms of her physical beauty. She is repeatedly called such things as a "beautiful young woman" and a "good looking dame" (O'Neil, "Wonder Woman's Last"), a "sharp looking chick" (O'Neil, "A Death"), and "a comely wench" (Sekowsky "The Last").

In fact, the more she attracts this male attention, the more highly invested Wonder Woman becomes in her physical appearance. The objectification of the new Wonder Woman was clearly evident in the sexualizing of her clothes. Wonder Woman, a woman who is a superhero, a woman who worked for years in military intelligence, now adopts as her "combat uniform" such outfits as the thigh-high, high-heeled black boots and a lace up blouse she wears in *Wonder Woman* #181 (Mar.-Apr. 1969) and the tight white micro mini dress she wears in *Wonder Woman* #187 (Mar.-Apr. 1970). She even justifies these highly sexualized outfits as good for crime fighting declaring, "one good thing about minis is they give you plenty of room for knee action!" as she attacks an assailant in *Wonder Woman* #187 (Mar.-Apr. 1970) (7).

Even her crime fighting accessories are put into service as markers of female beauty. Rather than having a utility belt filled with functional pouches and containers like Batman, the new Wonder Woman seeks out an old contact from her military intelligence past to provide her with gimmicked jewelry: bracelets, necklace, and earrings that are secretly bombs, acid containers, and other useful devices premiere in *Wonder Woman* #181 (Mar.-Apr. 1969). Hence, even her weapons become feminized.

Other women in the Wonder Woman strip are treated in the same manner. Wonder Woman's main antagonist in these early stories is Dr. Cyber, the female leader of a group of female villains. In their first appearance, Dr. Cyber's gun toting female crooks are referred to as her "beauteous band of henchmen" and one is distracted by the man she is holding hostage at gunpoint by such comments as, "I wouldn't dream of escapin' from a doll like you, baby!" (O'Neil, "The Wrath"). A similar idea of the power of male interest is contained in another story in which the witch Morgana enchants a group of men to fight viciously with each other for the affection of a homely woman. As the men brutalize each other around her, the woman beams and giddily says, "They're fighting over *me*—and Morgana did it—she's so *wonderful!*" (Sekowsky, "Morgana" 14).

The editors further hammer home the point that physical beauty and the desire of men is the key attribute of the new Wonder Woman in a response to a letter to the editor criticizing the changes in the character and calling for a return to the old Wonder Woman. In reply to the letter writer's comments the editors respond, "You can't mean that! You mean you really want that dowdy, grim, short, fat, square, frumpy Wonder Woman back?" (Sekowsky, "The Last" 10).

For Wonder Woman and indeed all the women in her book their value lies in being visually appealing to men and not in their social roles and positions. Wonder Woman is only of interest to men because she is pretty and not because she is a powerful, noble superhero.

This marginalization of the character with its concomitant diminishment of her superhero role continues in the language that is used to address her. Echoing the feminist critique of sexist language, the new Wonder Woman, and indeed all the women who appear in the book, are almost always referred to as "girls," "chicks," and "dames." Feminist critics challenged this infantilizing and marginalizing language because they argued it helped to diminish the role of women by symbolically placing them in less serious and subordinate roles.

In fact, this was precisely the case for the new Wonder Woman. Wonder Woman had for years fought all manner of super-powered villains, evil geniuses, and enraged gods and goddesses. She had trained with the Amazons in all manner of physical abilities and combat techniques. Yet when she becomes the new Wonder Woman she loses all her training and skills and becomes fearful, timid, insecure and dependent on the men around her to save her and guide her.

In fact, even before she was stripped of her superpowers the new Wonder Woman was already deferring to the men around her. The very first issue of the new Wonder Woman, *Wonder Woman* #178 (Sep.-Oct. 1969), finds Wonder Woman in her superhero garb at a party with her boyfriend Steve Trevor. At the party a lecherous drunken man insults Wonder Woman and then wraps his arm around her and propositions her. Wonder Woman does nothing to stop him and passively watches as her boyfriend Steve Trevor punches the man to the ground. Even though she's the superhero, Steve Trevor is the one that acts to "save" her (O'Neil, "Wonder Woman's Rival").

Once she loses her superpowers in *Wonder Woman* #179 (Nov.-Dec. 1969) she quickly signs up with I-Ching, a mystical blind man, who becomes her mentor, guide, and superior. Indeed, I-Ching constantly berates Wonder Woman for her failure to listen and obey, telling her such things as to be silent and to "not presume to instruct your instructor!" when she offers advice, (O'Neil, "The Wrath" 2), and curtly instructing her that she is "intelligent ... but, like the clay of the sculptor, unformed," (O'Neil, "A Death" 7), a condition I-Ching says he will fix for her. Even though she is an Amazon, a long time military intelligence officer, and a superhero with years of experience, Wonder Woman accepts these harsh judgments and dismissals and passively defers to I-Ching over and over.

Indeed, the new Wonder Woman is submissive to almost every man she meets. Time and again, she is saved by men, chastised by men, and defers to men. This is compounded by her singular ability to instantly fall in love with almost every man she meets, in spite of the fact that they inevitably betray her.

Right from the start of the new Wonder Woman she subordinates her desires to those of the men around her, giving up her superpowers and her connection with her mother and all her Amazonian sisters so that she can stay with and help her boyfriend Steve Trevor (O'Neil, "Wonder Woman's Last"). Meanwhile, Steve Trevor thinks nothing of embarking on a top-secret mission that requires the whole nation to believe he is a national traitor without telling Wonder Woman, his superhero girlfriend, what he is doing. She thinks of him, but he does not think of her.

Here again is the main theme of the series, Wonder Woman's need to please the men around her. So when Steve speculates about his desire to date her in her secret identity of Diana Prince even as he cuddles her as Wonder Woman, she does not get mad at him for being unfaithful and rude but instead says she needs to work harder to please him (O'Neil, "Wonder Woman's Rival").

Later when Steve is captured and being held hostage in some unknown location, Wonder Woman proceeds to fall for a private eye, Tim Trench, who is helping her track Steve down. They first meet when she notices Trench following her and she attacks him thinking he is a villain. As he easily tosses her aside, he growls, "You dumb chick — I wasn't gunnin' for you! I was trying to save you" (O'Neil, "A Death" 3). He then, in fact, proceeds to save her, the superhero, by throwing her down on the ground and standing protectively over her as he trades gunfire with a band of villains. Throughout this conflict, the supposed superhero Wonder Woman lays prone on the ground, not assisting, as he tells her, "Keep your pretty head down, lady!" (O'Neil, "A Death" 4). Hence, right from the start, the male private eye is established in the dominant role over Wonder Woman.

Nevertheless, Wonder Woman falls for him, telling him that "beneath your rough manners, I detect a heart of gold." (O'Neil, "A Death" 17). Her affection is met with betrayal as he turns criminal, abandoning her to an attack by her nemesis Dr. Cyber. Nevertheless, immediately upon escaping this attack, Wonder Woman falls in love with yet another seemingly random man who was driving past the scene of the attack. Letting this new man whisk her off to London, she swoons as he proposes to her only hours after meeting her, declaring, "Ohhh ... What's happening to me?" as she passionately kisses him (Sekowsky, "A Time" 13). Once again she is betrayed as the man turns out to be in league with Dr. Cyber.

In this pattern of actions, the purported central weakness of the new Wonder Woman is revealed to the reader: her emotionality. Again and again, the new Wonder Woman displays extremes of emotions and these emotional displays are almost invariably followed by a male critique stigmatizing the emotions.

For example, in addition to being repeatedly love sick and giddy over her own beauty, Wonder Woman is continuously breaking down in tears. She cries in five of the first seven issues of the new series and is shown dramatically crying on the third cover of the new series, *Wonder Woman* #180 (Jan.-Feb. 1969). These bouts of tears are inevitably critiqued by the male figures around her as a form of weakness.

The new Wonder Woman, despite her long history as a crime fighter, is also now exceedingly tentative and scared. A typical example of this new attitude occurs in *Wonder Woman* #180 (Jan.-Feb. 1969). As Wonder Woman enters an underground lair with Trench and I-Ching, Trench compares the lair to a tomb and Wonder Woman pleads, "I wish you wouldn't talk about things like that" (O'Neil, "A Death" 19). Later as I-Ching and Wonder Woman prepare to infiltrate Dr. Cyber's underwater base, Wonder Woman declares, "I'm scared" only to be chastised by I-Ching to "put fear away! Our cause is the cause of mankind! We must serve it bravely!" (O'Neil, "The Wrath" 6).

Similarly, in the very next issue, *Wonder Woman* #182 (May-Jun. 1969), as Wonder Woman and I-Ching face an attack from a group of hunter falcons, I-Ching springs to action yelling, "Diana! Defensive stance!" to which a cringing Wonder Woman declares, "W-What can we do?" (Sekowsky, "A Time"

4). I-Ching tells her to use her training and tells her specifically how to hit the birds and Wonder Woman replies, "I'll do my best ... but I have a feeling that my best won't be good enough" (Sekowsky, "A Time" 4).

In these and other similar exchanges, Wonder Woman is revealed as ineffectual and insecure in her own abilities. Even in those rare moments when Wonder Woman is being effective in the superhero role she negates her own part in favor of the men around her. For example, in *Wonder Woman* #181 (Mar.-Apr. 1969) as Wonder Woman subdues a group of thugs she thinks, "Ching's training continually amazes me! I'm never sure I can do a maneuver ... until I've done it" (O'Neil, "The Wrath" 20). This theme, that the abilities she possesses are less the result of her hard work, skills, training, and experience and more the result of an almost robotic programming from I-Ching, is recurrent throughout the issues of the new Wonder Woman. Indeed, Wonder Woman overtly acknowledges I-Ching as her superior declaring, "Ching fights better even though he's sightless" than she does, in spite of her vast years of Amazonian training and superhero experience (O'Neil, "The Wrath" 20).

Ching makes clear he also believes in her inferiority. Indeed, I-Ching constantly berates her for her ineffectualness, linking this ineffectualness to her emotional weakness, whether or not she takes on the superhero role. For example, when she does not act, I-Ching derides her, telling her she has "pity in [her] heart — pity for Steven Trevor and for yourself! This must stop! We have job to do! Soft emotions cloud intellect!" (O'Neil, "Wonder Woman's Last" 17). However, when she later gets mad and goes after Steve Trevor's killer I-Ching still criticizes her saying, "Diana stop! You behave as does a beast! There is no need for violence!" (O'Neil, "A Death" 22). From the perspective of I-Ching and the other men in her life, no matter what Wonder Woman does, whether she is passive or active, she is seen as being guided by emotion thus revealing her to be weak and ineffectual.

In this we see the ultimate problem with the new Wonder Woman. For all the creators' discussion of how they were creating a modern, feminist Wonder Woman their transformation of the character contained only the most superficial of empowering characteristics.

The new Wonder Woman starts a business but in a stereotypical feminized occupation, clothing boutique owner. Wonder Woman trains in martial arts and becomes a globe-trotting spy but only at the cost of seemingly losing all of her past knowledge, skills, and confidence. Moreover, even with this training she is only able to rise to the skill level of being a tentative apprentice to the more dynamic, powerful men around her. Wonder Woman embraces the culture of the sexual revolution with numerous romantic partners and modern clothing but she clings to the traditional gender roles that keep her desperate to win men's attention through her beauty and unable to take charge of her own sexuality or to gain credit and worth for her attributes beyond her looks.

Given such a depiction it is no surprise that feminists rejected the new Wonder Woman. As Gloria Steinem wrote speaking of the 1940s Wonder Woman that was being celebrated over the new Wonder Woman in *Wonder Woman*:

> Wonder Woman's final message to her sisters almost always contained one simple and unmistakable moral: self-reliance, be strong, earn your own living,. Don't depend on a man or any force outside yourself, not even a friendly Amazon. In Wonder Woman's own words, "You saved yourselves — I only showed you that you could" [42].

These feminist traits were in direction opposition to the supposedly feminist new Wonder Woman.

The creators of the new Wonder Woman said they were making her more modern, more human, more in touch with the real world but in making her 'human' they stripped Wonder Woman of the traits that had made her a symbol of female empowerment (Daniels 121). This did not have to be the case.

The new Wonder Woman's original writer Dennis O'Neil would make similar humanizing transformations with the superhero characters Green Lantern in 1970 and Superman in 1971. Just as he did with the new Wonder Woman, O'Neil stripped Green Lantern and Superman of their powers and made them confront the real world. However, where humanization of Wonder Woman meant giving up her strength, confidence, and sense of purpose and becoming instead an insecure, subordinate, stereotypical female character, for Green Lantern and Superman it meant deep introspection about the nature of power and how their role of superhero could be enacted in better, more socially beneficial ways. In this manner, humanizing the male characters meant expanding their core strengths and ennobling their role as superheroes while for Wonder Woman it meant mitigating her superhero role and undermining her core strengths and sense of purpose.

Hence, it is no surprise that feminists rejected the new Wonder Woman. For while the older Wonder Woman they embraced still had her own set of limitations and conflicts with feminist ideas she much more clearly embodied the idea that women could have power and strengths of intellect and body and be valued for the important social roles they fulfilled than the supposedly more modern new Wonder Woman of the late 1960s and early 1970s.

WORKS CITED

Daniels, Les. *Wonder Woman: The Complete History.* San Francisco: Chronicle, 2000.
Ferree, Myra Marx, and Beth B. Hess. *Controversy and Coalition: The New Feminist Revolution.* Boston: Twayne, 1985.
Johnson, Miriam M. "Functionalism and Feminism: Is Estrangement Necessary?" In *Theory*

on *Gender/Feminism on Theory*, edited by Paula England. New York: Aldine De Gruyter, 1993.

O'Neil, Dennis (w), and Mike Sekowsky (a). "A Death For Diana!" *Wonder Woman* Vol. 1 #180 (Jan.-Feb. 1969). New York: DC Comics.

_____. "Wonder Woman's Last Battle!" *Wonder Woman* Vol. 1 #179 (Nov.-Dec. 1968). New York: DC Comics.

_____. "Wonder Woman's Rival." *Wonder Woman* Vol. 1 #178 (Sep.-Oct. 1968). New York: DC Comics.

_____. "The Wrath of Dr. Cyber!" *Wonder Woman* Vol. 1 #181 (Mar.-Apr. 1969). New York: DC Comics.

Rosenberg, Rosalind. *Divided Lives: American Women in the Twentieth Century*. New York: Noonday, 1992.

Sekowsky, Mike (w) (a). "Detour." *Wonder Woman* Vol. 1 #190 (Sep.-Oct. 1970). New York: DC Comics.

_____. "Detour 2." *Wonder Woman* Vol. 1 #191 (Nov.-Dec. 1970). New York: DC Comics.

_____. "Earthquaker!" *Wonder Woman* Vol. 1 #187 (Mar.-Apr. 1970). New York: DC Comics.

_____. "A Time To Love, a Time To Die!" *Wonder Woman* Vol. 1 #182 (May-Jun. 1969). New York: DC Comics.

_____. "The Last Battle!" *Wonder Woman* Vol. 1 #184 (Sep.-Oct. 1969). New York: DC Comics.

_____. "Morgana the Witch!" *Wonder Woman* Vol. 1 #186 (Jan.-Feb. 1970). New York: DC Comics.

Steinem, Gloria, ed. *Wonder Woman*. New York: Bonanza, 1972.

Wonder Woman's Lib

Feminism and the
"New" Amazing Amazon

PAUL R. KOHL

Wonder Woman, William Moulton Marston and the Feminine Ideal

When William Moulton Marston, a psychologist by training, created Wonder Woman in 1941, he consciously designed a character that would serve as a female role model. Reflecting in a 1943 article in *The American Scholar*, Marston wrote, "not even girls want to be girls as long as their feminine stereotype lacks force ... strength" (1). Marston's goal was clear and so was his success. In Wonder Woman he crafted a hero who would stand the test of time and be a symbol for feminine strength and justice. No less a figure than Gloria Steinem recognized the power of Wonder Woman as a feminist icon and placed her on the cover of the first issue of *Ms.* magazine in 1972 under the banner "Wonder Woman For President."

Ironically, the iconic character image on that first *Ms.* cover was not the one that had been appearing in the pages of *Wonder Woman* since 1968. In that year the Amazing Amazon had been de-powered and de-costumed and reduced to plain old Diana Prince, Wonder Woman's alter-ego. Among others, Steinem was not happy with DC Comics' decision and used her own publishing powers to make it clear in an editorial appearing in that very same issue of *Ms.* DC had removed those qualities that made Wonder Woman a unique and powerful figure and replaced them with the characteristics of a more standard female character.

Diana Prince, Denny O'Neil and the "New" Wonder Woman

Steinem's displeasure may have come as a surprise to writer Denny O'Neil and writer/artist Mike Sekowsky. As architects of the change to the "New" Wonder Woman, they might have imagined that Steinem would be pleased at their attempt to update the character for the new feminist times. After all, the star-spangled costume left little to the imagination and could be seen as quite sexist, especially in the 1960s version, in which hot pants replaced the 1940s short skirt. There were also the matters of fetishism and bondage that early stories portrayed. Wonder Woman's strength and powers likewise came naturally to her and so didn't reflect the struggle of the average woman for equality. Remove those characteristics and you should have a new feminist role model. Or will you?

An examination of O'Neil and Sekowsky's new direction on Wonder Woman gives some indication that Steinem was right in her criticism. Removing her powers and costume may have made Diana Prince more human, but it also made her subject to the forces of a patriarchal society in a way she was not as Wonder Woman. However, there is evidence that O'Neil and Sekowsky may have consciously written a text that is itself a feminist critique. To truly understand the ramifications of O'Neil and Sekowsky's treatment of the New Wonder Woman, it is instructive to turn to the theories of two of the finest feminist scholars of the twentieth century, Simone de Beauvoir and Laura Mulvey.

Diana Prince, Simone de Beauvoir and *The Second Sex*

Simone de Beauvoir is probably the most significant feminist theorist of the twentieth century, and her 1949 magnum opus, *The Second Sex*, is the work that details her most important theories on the role of women in contemporary society. First and foremost is her argument that women's history has been man-made and that the term "woman" has always been defined by men. As she writes in her introduction to *The Second Sex*, women "have gained only what men have been willing to grant; they have taken nothing, they have only received" (xix).

De Beauvoir's theory is an extension of Existentialism, which posits that every consciousness has two possible states: the transcendent, observing ego, and the fixed, observed ego. The two are in a constant dialectic, with the observing ego needing the observed ego by which to measure and define itself. According to Josephine Donovan, "In Hegel's view self-consciousness forever needs or desires other people in order to prove or validate its existence, if only by the negative proof that it is not the other consciousness" (118).

Since the definition of the female is a product of male domination, woman is defined in opposition to the "dominant gender." Woman is defined as the Other. As de Beauvoir explains it, the male defines himself as the essential, a subject; the female, on the other hand, is inessential, an object (xvii). She is defined by what she lacks, the phallus.

Woman's presence as the Other, then, is determined by her existence in a world where she is defined by the dominant Male. William Moulton Marston's stroke of genius in creating Wonder Woman was having her "born" into a world where men did not exist. Feminist cartoonist and critic Trina Robbins reminds us of Wonder Woman's origin, noting that

> Wonder Woman's birth ... is an all-woman affair. In a feminist reversal of mythic hero birth stories, in which a virgin mother is magically impregnated by a male deity, the virginal amazon Queen Hippolyta, desiring a baby, is instructed by the goddess Athena to mold one from clay. Then Aphrodite bestows the gift of life upon the statue, who becomes the baby princess Diana. Thus ... Diana has two mommies [3].

Growing up on Paradise Island the young Diana has no experience with men until Steve Trevor's plane crashes offshore and he is brought to the island to be nursed back to health.

Marston, in creating Wonder Woman as a symbol of female empowerment, overturned the patriarchal equation that privileged male qualities such as physical strength and aggression. In his *American Scholar* essay he noted that "Women's strong qualities have become despised because of their weakness" (2). These "weak" qualities would be seen as strengths in "a new kind of superhero, one who would triumph not with fists or firepower, but with love."

It is this love for Steve Trevor that sends Wonder Woman to man's world. With her powers Wonder Woman is able to resist definition in her newfound home. Marston once more provided the perfect tool to make her immune to the false judgments of man's world, the Golden Lasso of Truth. Marston also provided the heroine with a weakness that Simone de Beauvoir would understand as a perfect metaphor for the male-female relationship. When Wonder Woman's bracelets are bound together by a man, she loses her powers. The symbolic chains and shackles of later feminist criticism are here made real. But of course, Wonder Woman is never bound for long and always regains her powers. That is, until 1968.

Diana Prince, Laura Mulvey and "The Male Gaze"

The year 1968 is noted for its earth-shattering political events, but the transformation of Wonder Woman from super-powered Amazing Amazon to de-powered Diana Prince is not one of them. The change was announced in a one-page announcement at the end of *Wonder Woman* #177 (Aug. 1968), her last Silver Age adventure in which she teams up with Supergirl. Wonder Woman appears out of costume, hair long and straight, and with back turned. The copy reads: "Can you believe you're looking at Diana Prince? In the next issue she'll turn around — and you won't believe your eyes! But the most startling change is yet to come — Yes, the really Big Change is coming to Wonder Woman!" *Wonder Woman* #178 (Oct. 1968) would be writer Denny O'Neil's first attempt at bringing a DC superhero to relevance in the changing times of the late 1960s. In the next two to three years he would do the same for Batman, Superman, and Green Lantern to much greater success and acclaim.

In *Wonder Woman* #178 (Oct. 1968) O'Neil and Sekowsky begin the big change by giving Diana Prince a major makeover. Feeling she has betrayed Steve Trevor in Wonder Woman's testimony as he is put on trial for murder, Diana attempts to find the real murderer in her Diana Prince guise. To do so, however, she trades in her military grays for the hip new fashions of the day.

Step one of the transformation complete, O'Neil and Sekowsky go for the big change in issue #179 (Dec. 1968), stranding Diana on Earth, powerless as the Amazons and Paradise Island travel to another dimension to rest and renew their powers. As Diana's mother, Queen Hippolyta, explains, "For ten thousand years, we have lived here, performing the mission assigned to us ... helping mankind find maturity! But now, our magic is exhausted!" (8). Diana refuses to accompany the Amazons and relinquishes her powers to stay with Steve Trevor. In the Amazon Rite of Renunciation she states "I hereby relinquish all mystic skills! I lay upon the sacred altar the glories of the Amazons and willingly condemn myself to the travails of mortals!" (9).

She returns to New York, as she puts it "truly alone ... an orphan ... without friends, without a home ... a stranger and alone" (9). As she begins her new life as an ordinary woman Diana Prince is unaware that for the first time in her life she will no longer be immune to the dreaded "male gaze."

The "male gaze" is a term coined by feminist film scholar Laura Mulvey in her 1975 essay "Visual Pleasure and Narrative Cinema." In it she theorizes that commercial cinema is built around a style that privileges the male point-of-view, giving them subjectivity in the vast majority of films. The female, on the other hand, becomes an object, the focus of the male gaze. As E. Deidre Pribram writes, "Mainstream cinema's contradictory/complementary representations of women as either idealized objects of desire or as threatening forces to be 'tamed' are not attempts to establish female subjectivity but rather reflect the search for male definition" (1). Or as Mulvey herself puts it more succinctly, "Unchallenged, mainstream film coded the erotic into the language of the dominant patriarchal order" (716).

In their new interpretation of Wonder Woman Denny O'Neil and Mike Sekowsky immersed Diana Prince in a milieu that accentuated the male gaze, a milieu epitomized by page 10 of issue #178, a full page montage of Diana excitedly trying on the newest fashions. On the first panel of the following page she walks into a hippie club, standing next to a psychedelic sign that reads "Love." Two hipsters stare at her, the first one, whom we see only from behind, exclaiming "Like wow, man! Like look!" (11). Through this faceless character, O'Neil and Sekowsky prompt the comic reading audience to gaze at the now powerless heroine. That gaze will continue to be invited during the course of The "New" Wonder Woman's adventures.

Diana Prince, Mike Sekowsky and Being Human

According to Gerard Jones and Will Jacobs in *The Comic Book Heroes*, Mike Sekowsky had once worked for Stan Lee in the late 1940s creating teenage girl humor comics. Twenty years later, after several years on DC's flagship book *Justice League of America*, he found himself directing the adventures of Diana Prince following O'Neil's departure. During his tenure "the amazing Amazon took over a boutique to sell mod clothes of Sekowsky's own bizarre design" (128). In issue #182 (Jun. 1969) Diana goes on her own shopping spree in swinging London, subsidized by Reginald Hyde-Whyte, one of a string of male admirers she gains during the Sekowsky run. On page 9, as Hyde-Whyte gazes on, Diana tries on a series of mod threads. Sekowsky's captions read: "Happiness for any healthy, red-blooded young gal, is bedecking herself in the latest fashion finery... And our Wonder Woman just happens to be a healthy, red-blooded young gal" (9). Diana's own response is a healthy, red-blooded "Wheeee! I'm a butterfly on the first day of spring" (9).

In accepting Hyde-Whyte's gifts and gaze Diana is also accepting her role as "the Other" in de Beauvoir's formulation, a situation made clearer on page 14 of issue #182 (Jun. 1969). As Diana and Reginald sit in his car, kissing, she thinks to herself "I've never felt this way before — but ... I hardly know him ... I ... I..." Having succumbed to Reginald's charms, she continues, "As an Amazon princess — as Wonder Woman — I had perfect control of my emotions! As plain Diana Prince, I'm human — too darn human!" (14). Reginald Hyde-Whyte is not the only male whose gaze captures Diana's heart during the O'Neil and Sekowsky runs. There is private eye Tim Trench, who, in his first appearance, in issue #180 (Feb. 1969), tails Diana and her new partner, I-Ching, referring to them as "A sharp lookin' chick and a blind oriental" (1). Two panels later we see Trench's reflected gaze in Diana's compact mirror.

Diana falls for Trench after Steve Trevor is killed. In issue #181 (Apr.

1969) she thinks to herself, "I'm becoming fond of Tim — Very fond! He's crusty ... but he's also strong, decisive ... a Man! At times he makes me forget Steve ... almost! I wonder if being human means being fickle!" (17). Diana's relationship to Trench, Hyde-Whyte, pilot Patrick McGuire, and private eye Jonny Double, is different from Wonder Woman's relationship to Steve Trevor. While Wonder Woman was clearly Trevor's superior and his protector, Diana Prince more often than not finds herself protected by her new men, including I-Ching.

Not that Diana is helpless. Thanks to the martial arts instruction of I-Ching she holds her own against an array of villains, most of which happen to be female, as well. At the head of the class is Dr. Cyber, a genius super-criminal who plans on ruling the world. Cyber's beautiful face is horribly scarred in battle with Diana in *Wonder Woman* #187 (Apr. 1970). She returns to seek revenge, masking her new visage. Her goal: to transfer her brain into Diana's still beautiful body.

Dr. Cyber's goal to regain her beauty in addition to conquering the planet affirms her acceptance of the role of object in the patriarchal order. Despite her desire to torture Diana by having her awake during the transference operation, she stops when the male doctor, Doctor Moon, warns her against it: "The woman should be unconscious! Else my scalpel might slip — and mar her features!" (O'Neil "The Beauty Hater").

Dr. Cyber's actions here are an example of what de Beauvoir terms "bad faith," defined by Josephine Donovan as "Women ... denying their potential as freely creative subjects and accepting their role as Other or object" (124). Dr. Cyber's quest for revenge for the marring of her feminine beauty detracts from her larger goal of world conquest. Appropriately enough, Cyber heeds the orders of Moon, seemingly the only male presence in her organization, leading of course to Diana's ultimate victory and Dr. Cyber's death.

Dr. Cyber's choice is indicative of what de Beauvoir sees as the existential choice of women, the rejection of their femininity. She states that "Woman's independent successes are in contradiction with her femininity, since the 'true woman' is required to make herself object, to be the Other" (246).

Diana as well, throughout the O'Neil-Sekowsky run chooses to maintain her femininity. For example, in issue #189 (Aug. 1970), after hiding out with I-Ching and Patrick McGuire in a Chinese rice field, Diana exclaims "Now, the first thing — before anything else — I need a bath! These rice paddies aren't exactly a field of roses!" (13). The following panel shows Diana, nude and bathing in a barrel. The caption reads "As Diana bathes, Patrick talks to the villagers." He exhorts the villagers they are trying to save from the Chinese military to "Hurry — load the boat with the guns and ammunition —." Meanwhile, Diana washes her hair.

Panel 2 of page 13 in *Wonder Woman* #189 is a perfect example of the male gaze, as Mulvey defines it. In this example, however, there is only the reader gazing upon the objectified naked figure of Diana Prince. Returning to Pribram's formulation, she is portrayed here as the "idealized object of desire." Elsewhere in the series there are prime examples of the second side of the woman as Other equation, the "threatening forces to be tamed."

Interestingly, there are an abundance of female villains in the O'Neil-Sekowsky issues of *Wonder Woman*. Wonder Woman has always had female villains, including her arch-enemy the Cheetah. Here Diana Prince faces not only Dr. Cyber and her all-woman team, but also Morgana the Witch, I-Ching's rogue daughter Lu Shan, the grotesque trio "Them," and the hero-villain Catwoman.

The most fascinating of these is "Them," who appear in issue #185 (Dec. 1969). A trio of mod dominatrixes, their femininity is covered by their androgynous clothing and appearance, thus coding them as male. In contrast to "Them," in the role of the Other is Cathy, a teen runaway who takes shelter in Diana's boutique. Cathy's status as object is shown on pages 7 and 8 of issue #185 as she is bathed and shampooed by Diana while telling her why she ran away from home:

> CATHY: My parents didn't understand me — I felt stifled at home... So I ran away — I wanted freedom — freedom to find myself — to think —
>
> DIANA: And did you find what you were looking for?
>
> CATHY: No — I found THEM!

Cathy's attempt to find freedom leads her instead to slavery, as the wicked trio has literally enslaved her as their servant and hopes to do the same to Diana. Hegel characterized the subject-object duality as a master-slave relationship. Cathy's recognition of herself as object precludes her ever being free. In fact by accepting the role of "Other" she engages in what Erich Fromm called an "escape from freedom" (quoted in Donovan 122).

What of Diana's relation to "Them," however? Diana refuses to be enslaved, suggesting she recognizes herself as a subject not an object. In physically defeating the trio and revealing them as criminals, she effectively destroys their ability to define the Other with the words "I'm going — to break the myth — that you run things around here!" (Sekowsky, "Them!") As Josephine Donovan notes, "The refusal to be object forces those who would see women as objects toward a recognition of their existence as subjects. Such an experience is radicalizing and forces the dynamics of relationship beyond what Hegel and others called the master-slave dialectic" (128). After the trio of female subjects is defeated Cathy becomes Diana's employee and later attempts to enlighten her on feminism (Delany). The story of Diana's defeat of "Them" suggests another way of looking at the O'Neil/Sekowsky storylines, a reading that is more in line with a feminist critique.

Diana Prince, I-Ching and the Possibility of Critique

One character yet to be discussed, and the most paradoxical, is the blind Asian mystic I-Ching, who takes the newly powerless Diana Prince under his wing and trains her in the physical and mental arts of the Orient. With his help Diana becomes nearly as adept as her Amazon persona. But what does I-Ching's blindness in a series that revels in the "male gaze" suggest?

To start with, I-Ching and Diana Prince first meet in issue #179 (Dec. 1968). As she first returns to New York without her powers, she witnesses a group of thugs attacking I-Ching, thinking he is a helpless blind man. Blind maybe, but not helpless as he effortlessly routs the three hoodlums. Diana is astonished as I-Ching announces that he knows who she is and seeks her help to find Dr. Cyber. He then proceeds to train her and accompany her on her adventures.

I-Ching's final appearance comes in issue #204 (Feb. 1973), the issue in which Wonder Woman finally regains her powers and becomes an Amazon princess once more. Interestingly, in the script by long-time Wonder Woman writer Robert Kanigher, I-Ching is killed by an assassin's bullet. As he dies in her arms he says "Farewell — daughter I never had — " (4). She returns with "Farewell ... father ... I never had." Later in the same issue Diana's powers are returned.

I-Ching's status in The "New" Wonder Woman series runs parallel to her time without powers, to her time as an object under the male gaze. But his own blindness leaves him with a purity, a parental purity, that cannot see the "daughter" as object. It is quite possible that I-Ching is a stand-in for O'Neil and Sekowsky, aware of whom their hero really is, giving her new skills, and disappearing as her old life is restored by the writer who guided it for so many years.

If I-Ching is really the alter-ego of the series' writers, what might this suggest about their intentions? Is The "New" Wonder Woman more of a feminist treatise than people like Gloria Steinem might have taken it for? Perhaps *Wonder Woman* 178–204 (Oct. 1968–Feb. 1973) can be compared to another text reviled for its attitudes towards women that has since been reclaimed as an important feminist text.

Diana Prince, Michael Powell and *Peeping Tom*

Michael Powell's 1960 film *Peeping Tom* virtually ended the career of one of Britain's greatest filmmakers, so great was the wrath of audiences and critics alike. Laura Mulvey gives some examples in her notes to the Criterion DVD edition of *Peeping Tom*, including "The sickest and filthiest film I remember seeing" and "The only really satisfactory way to dispose of *Peeping Tom* would be to shovel it up and flush it swiftly down the nearest sewer. Even then the stench would remain" (Mulvey, *Peeping Tom*).

Peeping Tom concerns a serial killer named Mark Lewis, who also happens to be a movie cameraman. His perverse method of killing women involves filming them with a special camera that has a spike attached to its front. As the spike pierces the throat, the camera captures the faces at the moment of death. Afterwards Mark watches the films for his pleasure.

Peeping Tom is a sadistic film which was all the more despised because of the sympathy it displayed towards Mark Lewis, himself a victim of a sadistic father and his ever-present film camera. But as Mulvey notes, "*Peeping Tom* is a film of many layers and masks." For one, it displays "Mechanisms of looking and the gender divide that separates the secret observer (male) from the object of his gaze (female)... It is this relentless exposure of cinematic conventions and assumptions that has attracted the interest of feminist film critics." In other words, *Peeping Tom* unmasks the process of the male gaze fifteen years before Mulvey's own theory. Interestingly, it does so with the help of a blind character, Mrs. Stephens, the mother of Mark's neighbor and love interest, who intuits something peculiar to Mark and unveils the male gaze.

I-Ching's character is even more important in intuiting the male gaze through his inability to display it. If he is indeed a stand-in for the book's authors, does he "turn a blind eye" to the presence of the male gaze in *Wonder Woman*? Or does his blindness suggest that he will not engage in it, but only reveal it? Is Denny O'Neil and Mike Sekowsky's *Wonder Woman*, like Powell's *Peeping Tom*, essentially a feminist text?

Wonder Woman, Gloria Steinem and Conclusions

When DC rebooted its entire universe in 2011 with the New 52, Gloria Steinem was one of the first to announce her displeasure with the character of the new Wonder Woman. According to artist-activist Linda Stein, Steinem noted that DC Comics was "Craziest for a) apparently not doing research with anyone who loves WW about the re-design, and b) eliminating Paradise Island, which was always a kind of celestial C-R (consciousness-raising) group she could return to." Stein herself added that DC "went for a replay of the typical male wish-list and the diminishment of women" (1).

The importance of Paradise Island and Wonder Woman's 1941 origin cannot be stressed enough. Having Diana born and grow up in a haven where men do not exist gives the Amazons of Paradise Island the opportunity to define themselves as subjects, not objects or "The Other" as they would be in man's world. The goal of women, according to de Beauvoir, should be self-definition, but, according to Stein, DC "passed on its opportunity to create the first non-objectified female superhero in contemporary pop culture" (1).

Over forty years ago, DC likewise changed Wonder Woman. She was made powerless and dropped fully into the male world of objectification and the "male gaze." She challenged but did not always succeed in defining herself in a world which consistently defined her as the "Other." Forty years ago, Gloria Steinem used her own power to bring the "real" Wonder Woman back. As a reward, it is possible Robert Kanigher had Steinem assassinated on the first page of issue #204 (Feb. 1973) in the guise of "Dottie Cottonman, Woman's Magazine, Editor..."[1] At the same time DC pulled the plug on the women's lib story that had begun in issue #203 (Dec. 1972). That issue's cover sported a "Special: Women's Lib Issue" logo and includes an infamous scene where Diana Prince refuses to join the Women's Lib movement because, she says, "In most cases, I don't even like women" (13). Issue #203 also sports one of several bondage covers in The "New" Wonder Woman that harkened back to the original Wonder Woman series of the 1940s.

What was going on here? The signals given off by DC and The "New" Wonder Woman were decidedly mixed. It could be read as the denigration of a powerful super-heroine, removed from her status as subject and dropped into a male-dominated world where she immediately becomes an object. Or it could be read as a feminist critique of the same.

All this should serve to remind us that popular texts are polysemic in nature, that is they can have more than one meaning. Either way, it is an important and often overlooked era in Wonder Woman's history, one which should not be forgotten by those who truly wish to create female characters who define themselves.

NOTE

1. Ruth McClelland-Nugent offers an alternative interpretation of this scene in her essay in this volume.

WORKS CITED

Beauvoir, Simone de. *The Second Sex* (1949). Translated by H. M. Parshley. New York: Knopf, 1971.

Delany, Samuel R. (w), and Dick Giordano (a). "The Grandee Caper." *Wonder Woman* #203 (Dec. 1972). New York: DC Comics.

Donovan, Josephine. *Feminist Theory: The Intellectual Traditions of American Feminism.* New York: Continuum, 1994.

Jones, Gerard, and Will Jacobs. *The Comic Book Heroes.* Rocklin, CA: Prima, 1997.

Kanigher, Robert (w), and Don Heck (a). "The Second Life of the Original Wonder Woman." *Wonder Woman* #204 (Feb. 1973). New York: DC Comics.

Marston, William Moulton. "Why 100,000,000 Americans Read Comics." *The American Scholar* (Winter 1943–44). Quoted in Philip Charles Crawford, "The Legacy of Wonder Woman: An Enlightening Look at the Feminist Ideals that Informed this American Icon." www.schoollibraryjournal.com/article/CA6417196.html. Retrieved Sep. 20, 2012.

Mulvey, Laura. "*Peeping Tom.*" Commentary, Criterion DVD, 1999.

_____. "Visual Pleasure and Narrative Cinema." In *Critical Visions in Film Theory*, edited by Timothy Corrigan and Patricia White. Boston: Bedford/St. Martin's, 2011.

O'Neil, Dennis (w), and Dick Giordano (a). "The Beauty Hater." *Wonder Woman* #200 (Jun. 1972). New York: DC Comics.

O'Neil, Dennis (w) and Mike Sekowsky (a). "A Death for Diana." *Wonder Woman* #180 (Feb. 1969). New York: DC Comics.

_____. "Wonder Woman's Last Battle." *Wonder Woman* #179 (Dec. 1968). New York: DC Comics.

_____. "Wonder Woman's Rival." *Wonder Woman* #178 (Oct. 1968). New York: DC Comics.

Pribram, E. Deidre. "Introduction." *Female Spectators: Looking at Film and Television*. London: Verso, 1988.

Robbins, Trina. "Wonder Woman: Lesbian or Dyke? Paradise Island as a Woman's Community." (2006) Girl-wonder.org/papers/robbins.html. Retrieved Oc. 25, 2012.

Sekowsky, Mike (w/a). "Red For Death." *Wonder Woman* #189 (Aug. 1970). New York: DC Comics.

_____. "Them!" *Wonder Woman* #185 (Dec. 1969). New York: DC Comics.

_____. "A Time to Love, a Time to Die." *Wonder Woman* #182 (Jun. 1969). New York: DC Comics.

Stein, Linda. "Wonder Woman Confronts a Makeover Moment: A Missed Chance." www.ontheissuesmagazine.com/cafe2/ article/104. Retrieved Oct. 25, 2012.

Steinem, Gloria. *Ms. Magazine,* Jul. 1972.

Not Quite Mod

The New Diana Prince, 1968–1973

PETER W. LEE[1]

In 1968, Wonder Woman was in trouble. She had lassoed the "Japanazis" into submission during the Second World War, retreated into domesticity to appease Cold War containment, and dodged Fredric Wertham's seductive accusations with innocents Wonder Girl and Wonder Tot. Now, in the late 1960s, her sensational comics were facing another identity crisis. To modernize Diana Prince during a time of cultural change, DC stripped her superpowers. The change was not altruistic; although historian Bradford Wright claims that *Wonder Woman* continually earned mediocre sales, DC disagreed (250; Daniels 125–129). As editor/writer/artist Mike Sekowsky told angry fans in *Wonder Woman* #187 (Mar.-Apr. 1970), "The Old Wonder Woman was a loser — she was a loser for so long the book was going to be dropped [but] the sales figures on the new Wonder Woman now make her a winner." The "mod" look lasted five years but was too radical: consumers, creators, and continuity could not break from a thirty-year history. The new *Wonder Woman* tried to link with the women's movement, but since feminists favored the old superheroine, DC returned Diana Prince to her starred shorts. As a role model, Prince's inability to join or lead the in-crowd indicated that she was not quite modern.

Female Empowerment: Forgetting the Old

In *Wonder Woman* #178 (Sep.-Oct. 1968), Wonder Woman accidentally sends boyfriend Steve Trevor to the slammer. While considering the predicament, the superheroine concludes that she "foolishly tried to lead *two* lives."

Setting aside her alter ego to help Trevor, Prince acquires a makeover, including flowing tresses and psychedelic dresses, to infiltrate a "hippie club." Writer Denny O'Neil treats the Prince's "mod" look — which originated in Britain — as synonymous with the American counter-culture; the mix-up was indicative of DC's attempt to update Prince without understanding the larger cultural milieu. Yet, for now, being different from the past was enough. An exonerated Trevor also reconsiders Prince with a faraway look and Wonder Woman realizes that she'll "lose him forever if I don't do *something* to keep him interested in *me*! Wonder Woman must change." Concerned with Trevor's roaming eye, her alteration will involve more than surface appearances (O'Neil, "Wonder Woman's Rival").

In issue #179 (Nov.-Dec. 1968), Queen Hippolyta informs her daughter that the Amazons must enter a new dimension "to rest and renew our powers!" Wonder Woman refuses to abandon Trevor, who "*desperately* needs me." To stay in Man's World, Prince surrenders her costume and powers. She hits the streets and meets I-Ching, a blind, elderly Chinese kung fu master. I-Ching warns her about "the evil of him who is called Doctor Cyber [who] must be destroyed!" Prince shrugs, "If *you* say so!" She masters the martial arts, but when Trevor is killed while trying to infiltrate Cyber's hideout, Prince displays another new talent: unchecked emotion. "Soft emotions cloud intellect!" I-Ching cautions. Prince fumes, "What I'm feeling isn't *soft*, I-Ching ... I *hate* Cyber!" Hard feelings mount when Cyber captures Tim Trench — a Sam Spade wannabe and a new love interest. Prince is not the only hot-headed woman around. She had assumed that Cyber was male, but learns that her nemesis is a "beautiful, wholly merciless *woman*!" (O'Neil, "Wonder Woman's Last").

Cyber was a mirror of Prince's new direction. Hardly a simpering sidekick for a more sinister man, Cyber and her female crew run a "world-wide radio-television network" that combines capital and capitols: "I have made world domination my life's goal! Soon the earth and all its treasures will be mine!" Her plots transcend traditional womanhood, and while her bared thighs may lure men's gazes, Cyber remains all business. In *Wonder Woman* #187 (Mar.-Apr. 1970), she levels Hong Kong with earthquakes, kills innumerable civilians, and threatens a repeat performance unless the international community "declare me *supreme ruler* of earth!" (Sekowsky, "Earthquaker!").

Having lost her mission to pacify a violent man's world, Prince meets this and other threats through violence. Her supporting cast urges her to exercise restraint rather than rashness, especially since Prince has discarded her unhip, cool-headed alter egos. In *Wonder Woman* #189 (Aug.-Sep. 1970) civilian Patrick McGuire meets and instructs the ex-intelligence officer Prince how to conduct an undercover operation. The former Major Prince's expertise far outstrips the World War II vet McGuire, yet she hangs on to his every word.

As civilian casualties mount, Prince grabs a machine gun, only to get injured herself. McGuire chides, "Well, if you're awake — let me show you how to use a gun with a kick like this" and he blasts the baddies (Sekowsky, "Red").

Prince's acquiescence to a male sidekick removes her agency. In *Wonder Woman* #185 (Nov.-Dec. 1969), Prince assists Cathy, a runaway who flees middle class comforts and falls in with outcasts called "Them." Prince saves the injudicious juvenile with help from a clean-cut neighbor, Tony. Cathy says that Them is "terrified of him — for some strange reason." With a combed coiffure and conservative duds, Tony signifies the establishment as he lives with a mom who cheerfully serves uninvited guests. He enlists his straight-arrow pals who "have just about *had it* with you creeps" and they end Them's social deviancy. Cathy's parents (mom in pearls and dad in a three-piece suit) thank Prince "for giving our Cathy back to us." Prince replies, "She never *really* left you" (O'Neil, "Them!"). She employs Cathy in her "Mod-ly Modern" boutique; despite her business marquee, Prince prefers conventionality. Her endorsement of a commercialized "mod" style rejects the counter-culture that advocated alternate lifestyles — "Them" or otherwise — of which DC's writers satirized as abusive misfits.

Wonder Woman supported traditionalism, but readers saw a potential for change. In *Wonder Woman* #194 (May-Jun. 1971), the letter page is renamed "Wonder Woman's Write-In," connoting activism. In *Wonder Woman* #195 (Jul.-Aug. 1971), one reader observed that "no other character in comicdom besides Diana Prince can claim to be dealing with life as it is today. [...] Diana is unique unto herself in dealing mainly with today's problems down on the streets where they happen" (O'Neil, "The Prisoner). *Wonder Woman* #199 (Mar.-Apr. 1972) hints at reform as writer Denny O'Neil, replacing a disgruntled Sekowsky, introduces Fellows Dill who recruits Prince for a bodyguard. Dill, a woman's clothes designer who believes in a minimalist approach, has a risky trade: "nuts are trying to *kill* me! Bunch of *fanatics* calling me the symbol of all that's wrong with America!" Prince takes the job but sides with Dill's foes, calling him "a symbol of sickness — you take feminine beauty and *pervert* it! You make your girls *objects*!" (O'Neil, "Tribunal").

DC's objective turns south when Prince and sidekick Johnny Double are captured by a cult who accuses them of aiding Dill "in his degrading of purity and holiness!" Double summarizes that "they're a herd of religious *nuts*!" Prince is silent; she condemns Dill, yet his critics are hardly paragons of virtue. In *Wonder Woman* #200 (May-Jun. 1972), Dill's dilemma dissipates as Prince encounters vandalized artwork of beautiful women. Keeping in mind Dill's peddling female flesh, Double observes that "we're getting close to *evil*— real *big* evil!" The culprit is Doctor Cyber, who, physically scarred after their last encounter, has an about face. She trades world conquest for an "anti-beauty kick" to "destroy all who trafficked in feminine *beauty*." Cyber claims responsibility for Dill's troubles, but she suggests that her crusade against him was nothing personal. She merely "despises loveliness because I was once *most* handsome" and Dill's business fit her agenda. With Prince imprisoned, Cyber now schemes to transfer "*my brain ... my identity* in a beautiful body" and selects Prince as a suitable host, but the issue ends in Cyber's apparent death. Her loss of face was more than skin deep as her unseen scar overcame the desire for domination. Double offers a masculine view that Prince "did her a *favor*! She was in *torment* ... a pitiable creature driven to deeds she surely *loathed*— she's finally ... at peace!" For Double, Cyber's physical blemish drove her batty; Cyber's short "anti-beauty kick" was an exercise in self-torture (O'Neil, "The Beauty Hater").

Cyber's fall from criminal mastermind to cosmetics misanthrope connotes Prince's uncertain commitment to social change. O'Neil decided to update the letter column's six issue-old herald. "Wonder Woman's Write-In? Yuch. Sounds like a protest demonstration for ball-point pen freaks." After mocking the alluded activism, he offered a prize for a new logo, an edition of his "No Evil Shall Escape My Sight" from *Green Lantern/Green Arrow*, an acclaimed critique of racial and class inequalities.[2] O'Neil's levity makes light of Wonder Woman as a reformist vehicle equal to Green Lantern's famed cross-country trip exploring the United States. Cyber's downfall and Double's analysis confirmed the superficiality of comic book feminism. For women rebelling against the "trafficking" of femininity, O'Neil hints that facelifts can solve all problems.

Wonder Woman did encounter the women's movement when writer Samuel Delany filled in for *Wonder Woman* #203 (Nov.-Dec. 1972), billed as a "women's lib issue." Prince is again unemployed, having sold Modl-ly Modern to a middle-aged, portly hipster and his "Lovey-puss." On the streets Prince encounters a gang of men making wolf calls. "What would *you* do?" the caption ponders. "When a problem presents itself as often as this ... what *can* you do?" Prince does plenty and beats them up, and Cathy, who attends a "women's lib" group, charges into the thick of it. Later, chauvinist Mike apologizes and offers Prince a job. Department store magnate Philip Grandee wants Prince to endorse a shopping hub for "the new *liberated woman*." The high salary, cool clothes, and television spots are, as the caption claims, the "dreams of an American princess." Prince accepts and the men share a private joke:

> MIKE: That *liberated woman* stuff you spouted, Mr. Grandee!? That's the first time I've ever heard you do anything but *laugh* at women's lib.
>
> GRANDEE: Grandee is for *anything* that puts money in Grandee's pocket ... and against everything that keeps it *out*. [Delany]

Cut to Cathy, who learns that Grandee pays below minimum wage. She labels his store as a repository of junk and the libbers plan to trash the joint. Prince admits that her boss is "a little *coarse*, but he's *for* the liberated woman!" As for Cathy's associates, Prince says, "I'm *not* a *joiner* and I wouldn't *fit* with your group. In most cases, I don't even *like* women...?" The interrogative punctuation gives an edge of uncertainty and Cathy's hair flares in anger: "*You* don't like *women*...? Well what do you think *you* are! What *you're* saying is ... you don't like *yourself!*" Prince turns to Double, but he flees after siding with Cathy. Prince muses, "Just like a *man*, to leave in an emotional situation!" More grounded are Cathy's hard feelings: "Perhaps I'm incompetent and unsure, but I'm *conscious* of it and enraged at anyone who says I must *stay* that way! *You're* a Wonder Woman! Skilled enough to *overcome* some of our problems, lucky enough to *avoid* others!" Cathy dares her to leave. Prince turns away in a five panel spread, but runs back into Cathy's arms. City Hall finally shuts Grandee's down due to safety violations, but Prince optimistically thinks that she's "*really* accomplished something for women's image!" An army of 250 angry women disagree; with Grandee's closed, these unemployed workers blame the movement for their misfortunes. Prince breaks the fourth wall and asks, "What do *you* say to *them* now? And will we have *time*? They look like they mean business!" Paralleling the opening panel, the closing caption queries, "What will Diana do now?" (Delany).

Prince's open query implies that the Grandee caper had no answers. DC provided an easy solution by sidestepping the plot with a series reboot. Writer Robert Kanigher, who had previously scripted the title, returns in *Wonder Woman* #204 (Jan.-Feb. 1973) and severs Prince's mod years from continuity. Kanigher picks up where he left off as I-Ching dies and Prince acquires amnesia: "It's all a *blank!*" Prince struggles to Paradise Island and soon awakens in costume with her worried mother hovering. Hippolyta utilizes selective shock therapy to restore her daughter's old mission: "to stop man from destroying himself and the *whole world!*" "Fate" draws her to the U.N. where she resumes a demure Diana Prince, complete with glasses, and lands a job as a translator. The interviewer is dismayed: "That *plain Jane* would be a universal linguist! Well — I suppose I could *lose* her among all the beautiful girls I'm going to hire who can *only* speak a *few* languages!" Like Dill and Grandee, the U.N. official shows that little has changed in *Wonder Woman*. The exploratory stance in the previous issue, of which Prince has no memory, disappears into comic book limbo, along with Cathy and Double. Prince muses, "I feel as if I've been *reborn!* I wonder what's going to happen to me — the second time around?" (Kanigher, "The Second"). It is actually Prince's third incarnation but, in any case, her mod self is rendered moot.

Compounding DC's contradictory direction for Wonder Woman were readers' mixed reactions that were printed in the letter columns. Readers rarely provided demographics, but both sexes hailed and hated the change. Some equated modernism with growth, while not necessarily connecting Prince to feminism. In *Wonder Woman* #181 (Mar.-Apr. 1969), Michael Reynolds approved, "She had become boring as the last remaining 'Golden Age' character." Stella Back agreed that a grown-up Prince was "far more believable than when she was a tot." In *Wonder Woman* #182 (May-Jun. 1969), Drury Morox analyzed that the old heroine was antiquated as "a symbol which perhaps we still need; but the need is not the same now as it was in the days of World War II." Sekwosky concurred in issue #189 (Jul.-Aug. 1970) that "too many of DC's stories are still being written and plotted for the year 1940 instead of 1970." In *Wonder Woman* #190 (Sep.-Oct. 1970), he assured fans that "you won't see any bug-eyed monsters or dinosaurs stomping around through the city, stepping on cars, wrecking buildings, etc.— nor will you see aliens from outer space trying to take over the world."

Despite this support, DC stayed on the defensive as other readers persistently clamored for the tiara and lasso. In *Wonder Woman* #184 (Sep.-Oct. 1969), Peggy Sarokin demanded, "Please bring Wonder Woman back and forget about that strange woman who had her book for the last two or three issues." Randall Way shouted, "*Forget* the new, *bring Back the old*!" DC was aghast: "You can't mean that! You mean you really want that *dowdy, grim, short, fat, square, frumpy* Wonder Woman back?" Kenneth Kraft reproached Way in *Wonder Woman* #186 (Jan.-Feb. 1970) because Prince now had "a realistic personality with *human* problems and emotions instead of the same old superhero characteristics." The letters page logo also changed from the activist-oriented "Wonder Woman's Write-In" to "Princessions" in the "women's lib issue," the last of Prince's mod period. Like Prince's open-ended legacy in the feminism, the herald was also ambiguous. An illustration featured the mod-garbed Prince, but the title also foreshadowed the superheroine's return in the next issue.

DC asserted that Wonder Woman's retrograde was a turn for the better: the banner "Super-Heroine Number One!" debuted on the cover of *Wonder Woman* #206 (Jun.-Jul. 1973). Still, Prince's mod era remained controversial among fans. In issue #216 (Feb.-Mar. 1975) Mary Jo Duffy asserted, "Every female, feminist, and comic book reader owes you a hearty thanks for what you have done and are continuing to do for Wonder Woman. After that discontinuity and menaces that couldn't threaten a nursery school, the Amazing Amazon is back in the real world!" Others were less happy. "DC's most original character is dead!" mourned one. Another fan lamented, "Now that both Steve and I-Ching have been killed off, Wonder Woman has no one" and complained that the superheroine was back "into her old rut." One reader found satisfaction that Prince regained her Amazonian invulnerability, since she was "susceptible to attempted plays upon her emotions. I am extremely glad to see her [as] an Amazon again!"

Hurt by the Ones She Loved: Mod and Men

Prince's vulnerable feelings concerned her fans, but such emotions, especially romance, was an integral part of her identity. When DC announced the big change, tongues wagged that Prince and Trevor may be tying the knot. In *Wonder Woman* #178 (Sep.-Oct. 1968) Bill Starret whet his lips: "I've tried to envision what possible changes you could possibly be planning? Turn W.W. into a homebody, married to Steve Trevor, with Wonder Tot kicking around the house? Or [...] Steve Trevor fighting alongside her, as a partner?" A beefed up role for Trevor was popular among readers, either as a super-man or a man of a house. Elaine Bridgeton complained that Wonder Woman "is still suffering over Steve, and is no closer to marriage than she ever was. Boy, if that happens to me, I think I'd fall apart." Lester Tracy chimed in that marriage "would revive a great deal of interest in this magazine." Peter Horton queried, "How long does she think she can get away with holding him off the way she does? If I were Steve I would have given up on the Amazon a long time ago." DC encouraged this approach: one ad in *Wonder Woman* #177 (Jul.-Aug. 1968) alluded that Prince was moving into matrimony as she saunters away in flashy garb. "Can you believe you're looking at Diana Prince? The most startling change is yet to come — yes, the really big change is coming to — Wonder Woman!" On Prince's finger is a prominent, sparkling, red ring, hinting that the "big change" might be a pressing engagement.

Wedding bells were not on the future once Trevor dies in *Wonder Woman* #195 (Jul.-Aug. 1971), Sekowsky dismisses Trevor as "dull and boring and I didn't like him so I disposed of him." Soon after, she meets gumshoe Tim Trench, a short-lived beau who sets a pattern. Throughout the mod run, Prince flirts with any suitor and her partners continually exploit her. *Wonder Woman* #181 (Mar.-Apr. 1969) finds Prince tossing about in bed, thinking, "I'm becoming fond of Tim — very fond! He's crusty ... but he's also strong ... decisive ... a man! At times he makes me forget *Steve ... almost!*" While Prince waffles, Trench steals a cache of jewels. As he makes a clean getaway, Reginald Hyde-Whyte saunters up and sweeps Prince off her feet: "*I love you*— I want you [...] more than anything in the world ! I want to marry you!" They smooch but I-Ching's interruption sobers her up ("As *Wonder Woman*— I had perfect control of my emotions! As plain Diana Prince, I'm *human*— too *darn* human!"). Whyte, too, is mortal: as Cyber's dupe, he covers the villainess's retreat but confesses to Prince that his feelings for her are genuine. Ditto for Prince: "You lied to me! You said you loved me!" *Pow! Krawm! Wap!* And Whyte faces the fury of a woman scorned. When I-Ching urges restraint, Prince shuts him up and runs away (O'Neil, "The Wrath"). After decades of superpowered steadfastness, the emotional trauma of a long-time boyfriend dead and his deadbeat replacements overwhelm her.

While some fans found Prince's vulnerability refreshing, others worried over her love life. In *Wonder Woman* #185 (Nov.-Dec. 1969), Larry L. Stout resented Prince's shallowness over Steve's death: "Didn't she attend his funeral? Doesn't she ever weep or mourn for him? After all, she did love him for 30 years. All of a sudden, no concern? Yet she weeps in issues #182 and #183 for a man she just met and thought she loved." In *Wonder Woman* #197 (Nov.-Dec. 1971) Carol Lynn Pagina fretted that Prince could not "wait until he was cold before she went flirting with every Tom, Dick, and Harry. Steve should come back and *haunt* her!" Others passed judgment on Prince's love life and in *Wonder Woman* #188 (May-Jun. 1970), one youth implored, "Please don't give her a steady boyfriend, because we boys need a girl we can call our own ... and why not Diana ... she's young and pretty... How about It?"

DC was happy to set hearts a flutter with a comic cavalcade of suitors. In *Wonder Woman* #187 (Mar.-Apr. 1970), a rowdy cargo pilot, Patrick McGuire, competes in a tug-of-war with a rigid British major over Prince's dating rights. Although Cyber devastated Hong Kong, all is well when both men take her to dinner as punishment for not possessing a passport. In *Wonder Woman* #194 (May-Jun. 1971), Prince vacations in a "tiny fairytale-like country" and is mistaken for Princess Fabiola. Circumstances force Prince to masquerade as royalty, and when she meets Fabiola's groom, the narrator notes, he is "a girl's dream of a prince — just like something out of a fairy tale." Prince coos, "Mmm — lucky Fabiola!" At the end, Prince watches the royal wedding and sighs, "There for the fate might go I!" (Sekowsky, "The Prisoner"). With Trevor gone, Prince is up for grabs by all and sundry, but never lands a man to call her own.

Even evildoers acknowledged that Prince was at risk to romance. In *Wonder Woman* #196 (Sep.-Oct. 1971), Prince saves Ambassador Anatole of Kolonia and he invites her to dinner. She patriotically accepts, adding that "he's awfully *good-looking!*" With international relations at stake, a general presses Prince back into service. "*You're back in—* and you're back in because we *need* you." They certainly do: when Anatole meets the President, Prince knocks the ambassador down and declares him a fake. "All those attempts on his life were cleverly staged affairs—*meant to be foiled!* And I was the *patsy* who fell for them!" She reveals that when he bent over, the edge of his mask showed. The general states, "We owe a lot to this young lady, Mr. President." While the officer's conclusion is correct, Anatole had wined and wooed her throughout, blinding the perceptive Prince. His faux face took advantage of her femininity and almost rendered her mission impossible. Prince attributes her last minute heroics to dumb luck: "Luckily I was *right*— or I certainly would have had a lot of explaining to do!" (Sekowsky, "Target").

Prince's last mod man was Dill's lackey, Johnny Double. Despite Prince's dubbing Double "the most *callous* man I've ever met," she insists on a first-name basis and he responds with an intimate moment "that seems to stretch an eternity." In *Wonder Woman* #201 (Jul.-Aug. 1972), Prince's relationship with Double becomes serious as she takes I-Ching to meet him. Prince admits that Double's "sort of a *loser* ... but he's *sweet*." Unfortunately, Double runs into trouble and Prince is conflicted. She's "tired of danger ... of battle — wandering the earth! I have no *reason* to involve myself in Johnny's problems — none — except that he's brave, decent, honorable, and I care for him!" (O'Neil, "Fist"). Just as Prince had relinquished everything for Steve Trevor; she would double dip for her latest boyfriend and sell her boutique.

Wonder Woman's continuity confirmed her romantic entanglements. In a backup story in *Wonder Woman* #200 (May-Jun. 1972) Prince opens her "memory album" from *Wonder Woman* #144 (Feb. 1964) and tells I-Ching about her "crush on *Mer-Boy* and at the *same* time I was getting involved with a bird-boy!" The flashback ends with Wonder Girl's heartstrings in a bind. "Whom would you choose, dear reader? Mer-Boy or Bird-Boy? Bird-Boy or Mer-Boy? I can't make up my mind!" The caption emphasizes the dilemma: "Whom? Whom? Whom?" and asks fans to follow Wonder Girl "in future issues of *Wonder Woman Magazine*!" (Kanigher, "Mer-Boy"). The coda was eight years old and false advertising: DC eliminated the backups after this issue. Wonder Girl's unresolved tryst highlights her past as a femme flirt for present-day readers, a tradition she carries with Trench, McGuire, Double, and other brave and bold men.

Love was a selling point beyond the narrative. While Prince was disillusioned with the opposite sex, DC encouraged readers to try the "new" Wonder Woman through conventional means. One ad for *Wonder Woman* #181 (Mar.-Apr. 1969) and #184 (Sep.-Oct. 1969) appeared in the romance title *Girls' Love Stories* #141 (Feb. 1969) and #145 (Aug. 1969), respectively, singing, "Girls! If you dig romance, and we know you *do*— you'll really flip for the new Wonder Woman!" Hyperbole followed: "Yes, romance ... plus intrigue, high adventure, and a brand-new kind of story that will bring you a brand-new kind of thrill!" Similarly, *Wonder Woman* #198 (Jan.-Feb. 1972) contained a teaser for Dill's storyline with a spicy enticement: "Coming ... new triumph ... new tragedy ... as Diana finds love in the midst of evil!" Love was not in Prince's uppermost thought, as readers see her chained, kneeling against a wall, with eyes wide and mouth agape as a masculine shadow hovers over her near-nude body. For the social-savvy Diana Prince wallowing in a midst of evil, love — and a touch of sex — sold her title.

No Place Like Home: Paradise Found

With the contentions between Prince's mod lifestyle, the larger counter-culture, and her Amazon past, Wonder Woman found her heritage as a refuge from the human experience. *Wonder Woman* #183 (Jul.-Aug. 1969) begins with Prince running away from Reginald Hyde-Whyte's Jekyll-Hyde revelation. "This being *a human hurts!*" Her trauma is cut short when an Amazon materializes and requests aid. Prince's return home is more than a rebound from Whyte as her roots reassert her heritage. With her mother incapacitated by Ares (Prince's grandfather), Prince is left in charge. The God of War demands that Prince reveal the gateway to Man's World. The depowered Prince waffles at first, but when her unconscious mother clasps her hand, they pool their strength and Prince balls her fists: "You will *not* take my mother!" (Sekowsky, "Return"). Her human vulnerability, raw and open in the splash page, is closed by a defiance of the gods.

Prince prepares for war in *Wonder Woman* #184 (Sep.-Oct. 1969), but the Amazons need help. Prince decides to enlist Roland, El Cid, Siegfried, Lancelot, Arthur, and other heroes. She reasons, "I shall ask for their help. And being the kind of men they are — *they'll come!*" The men refuse, citing a lack of benefits and preference for retirement. Prince's plea that heroism is its own reward falls on deaf ears, save for a group of Valkyries. The female front cannot hold, but at the critical moment, the song of Roland bursts through as the men arrive. Ares, stunned by his granddaughter's assembled all-stars, respectfully withdraws and the knights dub their leader a hero. Prince experiences hardship in Man's World, but when she trades American gender roles for Amazonian power does she regain an agency that eludes her anywhere else on earth.

Prince's excursions into a mythological past allow her to flourish without I-Ching or a wisecracking sidekick. In *Wonder Woman* #190 (Sep.-Oct. 1970), after McGuire shows the ex-intelligence officer how to use a gun, Prince takes a detour in another dimension where freedom fighters are battling an evil queen. Prince meets a fugitive prince but forgets rank and romance as she takes charge. While McGuire had to sweep Prince from harm's way, in *Wonder Woman* #192 (Jan.-Feb. 1971) she fashions cannons from trees, mixes gun powder, and leads the charge, dragging the explosives to a bang up finale. Her mother arrives and admires her daughter's handiwork. Even in this land of female despots and Prince's single-handed victory, chauvinism surfaces as one rebel is skeptical about women warriors: "I don't believe it!" An Amazon clobbers the unbeliever, as they do not put up with putdowns.

Even Paradise Island was not a safe haven for female empowerment. Of the many who invaded the sanctuary home, none made such inroads as Jerry Lewis in *The Adventures of Jerry Lewis* #117 (Mar.-Apr. 1970). Lewis's series falls out of DC's continuity, but his funny-book was taken seriously by newsstands, fans, and creators who teamed the Amazon Princess with the King of Comedy. Lewis realizes "his lifelong ambition," and comes "face to face with the girl of his dreams" when he and his nephew, Renfrew, find her on a curb, perturbed by a puddle. When Prince pulls a tendon trying to cross it, she worries that "criminals in this city might learn about my injury and take advantage of my helplessness!" She hurries to Paradise Island to see "Dr. Bratwurst," whose flowing white beard covers a lack of pants and his medical quackery (Unknown).

While Bratwurst bandages Prince's leg, they learn that the evil Zodor holds Queen Hippolyta captive. An immobilized Prince deduces that "the Amazons need a new leader! [...] Somebody who inspires courage and bold leadership!" She chooses Lewis and dons him in Hercules's lion skin (ignoring that Hercules' subjugation of Hippolyta drove the Amazons to Paradise Island as refugees). When this fails, Prince disguises Lewis as herself with a busty armor and wig to rally the troops ("He'll do — he'll *have* to!"). Other Amazons, with their hair in curlers and wearing bath towels, would rather meet beauticians than rescue their queen, but they submit on the condition that they have time to finish house chores. Nephew Renfrew gives the Amazons a thumb's down, grimacing, "Dames! *Phooey!*" and defeats Zodor with a slingshot. Prince kisses Lewis and the dizzy comedian wonders, "How could my dream girl give me such a nightmare?" Prince, who found empowerment only at Paradise Island, may have had similar thoughts (Unknown).

The DC Universe: The Mod and the Mighty

Jerry Lewis was not the only DC superstar to subvert Prince's agency. Scholar Tom Donaldson has shown that DC's stable of superstars resisted feminism, and in this traditional environment, Wonder Woman disassociated herself from her peers (Donaldson). In *Wonder Woman* #190 (Sep.-Oct. 1970), Sekowsky explained that guest stars would be "kind of difficult because so few of the other characters would really *fit* with the new Wonder Woman." In *Justice League of America* #69 (Feb. 1969), Prince divulges to the Justice League of America her secret identity. She adds, "I've lost my *Amazon powers* [and] my main reason for coming here is to ... *resign*! I've no more than an ordinary mortal now ... much as I admire the Justice League, I feel I no longer have a place in it!" The League has ordinary men like Green Arrow—who remains silent—but they readily let her go. Superman allows for the possibility of a return and softens her resignation to a "leave of absence." The Flash is pessimistic, feeling that Prince lost her purpose: "I've always felt that some day *Superman* might marry her ... now they've lost each other!"

The Flash's woe over Prince's wedding bells proved premature. No superhero guest-starred in the new *Wonder Woman*, but Prince's appearances in other comics reaffirmed that she still inhabited a woman's sphere within a man's world. In *World's Finest Comics* #204 (Aug. 1971), Clark Kent applies for a computer dating service on assignment and I-Ching encourages Prince to do the same: "I realize your romantic life has been fraught with *woe* ... but this should not deter you!" The two meet and Kent stammers, "Oh no ... I don't *believe* it! You—*Diana Prince*—? You're my ... *date*?!" He suspects she is on a rebound: "Poor Diana! Must be *tough*, being an ordinary gal after being *Wonder Woman* for so many years!" When Prince trounces some muggers, the incognito Man of Steel is pleased: "The lass doesn't *need* superpowers!" Later, they enter an inhospitable future and Superman takes charge when the same muggers menace Prince, who admits, "I'm not sure could've handled that alone!" She ignores the surrounding holocaust to create fireworks. "Funny ... we've been acquaintances for years—yet we've never really gotten to be *friends*! Maybe we should *do* something about that!" She puckers up but Superman backs down: "In another second or so, I'll feel like kissing you—and we both know I *shouldn't*." Prince reluctantly agrees, "Right you are—darn it!" (O'Neil, "Journey"). Although Prince remains doubtful about the future, settling down with a super-man is on her mind.

Readers had another opportunity to see Prince and Superman in action. *Superman's Girl Friend, Lois Lane* #93 (Jul. 1969) featured a catfight cover when Prince muscles in on Lane's dream as Superman's bride. Lane is initially thrilled that Prince is powerless. After dreading the Amazon wedding Superman, the girl reporter takes heart that Wonder Woman is now "an *ordinary mortal* ... without her *Amazon* powers! Now *Superman* won't marry her—for the same reason he won't marry *me*!" When Superman assists Prince in a charity, the crowd goes wild: "He should marry her! *Kiss her Superman! Kiss Wonder Woman!*" (Kanigher, "The Superman"). Superman obeys and Lane's nightmares return, first showing love, then marriage, then a super-baby that needs no carriage.

Lane soon decides to fight for her man. Prince agrees: "We can't go on like this, with *both* of us wanting him! We might as well have it out *right now*!" After a flip and a slap, a floored Lane is down and out. Superman grins and flies off with the winner. In the end, though, Lane worries for nothing when Superman affirms his bachelorhood, stating, "I care too much for you, Lois!" Prince confirms, "Much as I admire *Superman*, I hope you didn't think *I'd* ever be a competitor of yours for his love, Lois!" Lane grins that she had "a few bad moments! But it's all over now!" (Kanigher, "The Superman"). Yet the issue was full of bad moments as she — and readers — witnessed Prince falling hard for the Man of Steel. As house ads reminded fans, she consistently swooned over handsome faces since Trevor's death.

Superman was not Prince's only eligible super bachelor. In *Brave and the Bold* #87 (Dec. 1969-Jan. 1970), she runs into Bruce Wayne at a racing track, who is building a new reputation as "playboy *no more!*" When a racing fiend menaces Wayne, Prince defends him while he feigns helplessness lest someone, including an unsuspecting Prince, sees him "doing any of my *Batman* stuff!" He soon decides to flex his muscles: "This *whole bit* is *getting* to me! I *can't* let a *woman* and a *blind* man rescue me — my *male* ego won't let me!" When Wayne is clobbered, Prince offers to race in his stead. His male ego will not allow her to best him in vigilantism and velocity and he arranges for Batman to take his place. While the Dark Knight streaks down the course, Prince commandeers a car to make sure everything stays legit and the owner demands her arrest (Sekowsky, "The Widow-Maker").

The police handcuff Prince, but Batman intercedes with an urgent message: "Bruce wants to know if you'll have dinner with him tonight." Apparently, Wayne's racing victory has restored his male ego, so he takes advantage of Prince's legal troubles and offers her a night on the town rather than one in jail in lieu of his pledge. She takes the unspoken cue: "Tell him *okay*—if he'll go [pay] my *bail!*" As the officers escort her, Prince muses, "What will the old *JLA* members think when they find out an ex-member's got a *police record?*" Prince need not worry, as the League treated her more as date material for its most prominent members (Sekowsky, "The Widow-Maker").

Prince's place in the DC Universe reaffirmed traditional femininity as a romantic foil for the world's finest heroes and her role as a boutique owner meshed well with superheroines. In *Adventure Comics* #397 (Sep. 1970), Supergirl is bored: "When a girl feels this way — some *new* clothes are in order!" The Maid of Steel shops for a "groovy" look and spots Prince. "In a way, I envy her," Supergirl sighs. The fashion crisis continues when she asks Prince to locate the sorceress Morgana. Prince does so and then volunteers as a consultant: "Neither of you can go out dressed *that* way!" In *Wonder Woman* #198 (Jan.-Feb. 1972), one fan had stressed that since Prince was "relevant to today's society [with] the costumed super hero is almost out of place." Prince herself disagrees as she dresses them in new outfits, free of charge. Her work is done as the superheroes engage in fisticuffs while the martial artist watches. At the end, Supergirl thanks Prince for her new threads (Sekowsky, "Now"). *Wonder Woman* had the potential to showcase the development of the modern woman, but Prince finds fulfillment as a gal pal for the Man of Steel and the World's Greatest Detective, a clothes guru for the Maid of Might, and a gag for Jerry Lewis.

Conclusion: The New Original Wonder Woman

Given DC's inconsistent stance towards Diana Prince, feminists preferred the original Wonder Woman. Feminists have used the Amazon princess as a champion for her fellow sisters ("Sister"; Daniels 131). Wonder Woman appeared on the cover on *Ms.* #1 (Jul. 1972), lassoing the establishment into submission. The magazine's founder, Gloria Steinem, concluded that Prince's mod life was "discouraging [...] a mere mortal who walked about in boutique clothes and took advice from a male mastermind" (Steinem, np). *Ms.* editor Joanne Edgar agreed that modernism and Prince made a poor combination, but she hoped that Wonder Woman's revival would "return our heroine to the feminism of her birth. And maybe to politics too?" (55).

Edgar might have been disappointed that Prince earns a job as a U.N. interpreter at the cost of her mod self. The United Nations is far from the street level of everyday feminists like Cathy. While Wonder Woman encountered civil rights activists — *Wonder Woman* #206 (Jun.-Jul. 1973) features women marching on the U.N. — the demure Prince does not challenge the status quo. When men advance on the "hippie traitors," the women defend themselves with the Amazon's assist; Prince herself ceased to have agency for everyday change.

One letter in that issue summarized the new old *Wonder Woman* as a "significant advance backward." DC editor Allan Asherman explained that "no radical change is taking place in *Wonder Woman*. We are merely returning her to her first and foremost plane of reference ... her Amazon heritage." Her heritage had resisted modernization: Prince's boutique flopped as did her liberated love life. Dr. Cyber died for physical perfection, not global governance, the "women's lib" story ended unfinished, and Prince's peers saw her as a companion for fun evenings sans crime. Fans still saw the potential for change. One group felt that they were "being shaped by someone or something outside ourselves [...] in other words, to accept the place we have been given in the world of men" (Bread and Roses). The new *Wonder Woman* had an opportunity to address those concerns in Man's World and the results mirrored the uncertain social discourse as Americans questioned their gender roles. The mod Prince vanished from DC's continuity, but Wonder Woman remained an affirmation of female strength. That readers and creators openly debated Prince's purpose was itself empowering.

NOTES

1. The author would like to thank Mr. Osgood Peabody for assistance in researching DC's *Wonder Woman* house ads.

2. O'Neil was apparently tired of *Wonder Woman*. He acknowledged a missed opportunity to celebrate *Wonder Woman's* two hundredth issue. In that issue's letter column, he writes, "Oh, sorry, sorrier, sorriest! [...] We should have done something special. A two-parter featuring both old and new Wonder Woman, or a reprint of the first-ever Wonder Woman adventure, or some blessed thing. Well, we didn't."

WORKS CITED

Advertisement. *Girls' Love Stories* Vol. 1 #141 (Feb. 1969). New York: DC Comics.

Advertisement. *Girls' Love Stories* Vol. 1 #145 (Aug. 1969). New York: DC Comics.

Bates, Cary (w), and Don Heck (a). "War of the Wonder Women!" *Wonder Woman* Vol. 1 #206 (Jun.-Jul. 1973). New York: DC Comics.

Bread and Roses. "Outreach Leaflet," [1970]. In *Dear Sisters: Dispatches from the Women's Liberation Movement*, edited by Rosalyn Baxandall and Linda Gordon. New York: Basic, 2000.

Daniels, Les. *Wonder Woman: The Complete History.* San Francisco: Chronicle, 2000.

Delany, Samuel R. (w), and Dick Giordano (a). "The Grandee Caper." *Wonder Woman* Vol. 1 #203 (Nov.-Dec. 1972). New York: DC Comics.

Donaldson, Thomas C. "The Inflexible Girls of Steel: Subverting Second Wave Feminism in the Extended Superman Franchise." In *The Ages of Superman: Essays on the Man of Steel in Changing Times*, edited by Joseph J. Darowski. Jefferson, NC: McFarland, 2012.

Edgar, Joanne. "Wonder Woman Revisited." *Ms.* #1 (Jul. 1972): 52–55.

Finger, Bill (w), and Win Mortimer (a). "Wonder Woman and Supergirl vs. the Planetary Conqueror." *Wonder Woman* Vol. 1 #177 (Jul.-Aug. 1968). New York: DC Comics.

Kanigher, Robert (w), and Ross Andru (a). "Mer-Boy vs. Bird-Boy!" *Wonder Woman* Vol. 1 #144 (Feb. 1964). New York: DC Comics.

Kanigher, Robert (w), and Don Heck (a). "The Second Life of the Original Wonder Woman." *Wonder Woman* Vol. 1 #204 (Jan.-Feb. 1973). New York: DC Comics.

Kanigher, Robert (w), and Irv Novick (a). "The Superman-Wonder Woman Team!" *Superman's Girlfriend, Lois Lane* Vol. 1 #93 (Jul. 1969). New York: DC Comics.

Maggin, Elliot S. (w), and John Rosenberger (a). "Paradise in Peril!" *Wonder Woman* Vol. 1 #216 (Feb.-Mar. 1975). New York: DC Comics.

O'Neil, Denny (w), and Dick Dillin (a). "Journey to the End of Hope!" *World's Finest Comics* Vol. 1 #204 (Aug. 1971). New York: DC Comics.

_____. "A Matter of Menace!" *Justice League of America* Vol. 1 #69 (Feb. 1969). New York: DC Comics.

O'Neil, Denny (w), and Dick Giordano (a). "The Beauty Hater." *Wonder Woman* Vol. 1 #200 (May-Jun. 1972). New York: DC Comics.

_____. "The Fist of Flame." *Wonder Woman* Vol. 1 #201 (Jul.-Aug. 1972). New York: DC Comics.

O'Neil, Denny (w), and Don Heck (a). "Tribunal of Fear" *Wonder Woman* Vol. 1 #199 (Mar.-Apr. 1972). New York: DC Comics.

O'Neil, Denny (w), and Mike Sekowsky (a). "A Death for Diana." *Wonder Woman* Vol. 1 #180 (Jan.-Feb. 1969). New York: DC Comics.

_____. "Wonder Woman's Last Battle." *Wonder Woman* Vol. 1 #179 (Nov.-Dec. 1968). New York: DC Comics.

_____. "Wonder Woman's Rival." *Wonder Woman* Vol. 1 #178 (Sep.-Oct. 1968). New York: DC Comics.

_____. "The Wrath of Dr. Cyber." *Wonder Woman* Vol. 1 #181 (Mar.-Apr. 1969). New York: DC Comics.

_____. "The Wrath of Dr. Cyber." *Wonder Woman* Vol. 1 #197 (Nov.-Dec. 1971). New York: DC Comics.

Sekowsky, Mike (w) and (a). "Assault on Castle Skull." *Wonder Woman* Vol. 1 #192 (Jan.-Feb. 1971). New York: DC Comics.

_____. "Cyber's Revenge!" *Wonder Woman* Vol. 1 #188 (May-Jun. 1970). New York: DC Comics.

_____. "Detour." *Wonder Woman* Vol. 1 #190 (Jul.-Aug. 1970). New York: DC Comics.

_____. "Earthquaker!" *Wonder Woman* Vol. 1 #187 (Mar.-Apr. 1970). New York: DC Comics.

_____. "The House that Wasn't." *Wonder Woman* Vol. 1 #195 (Jul.-Aug. 1971). New York: DC Comics.

_____. "The Last Battle!" *Wonder Woman* Vol. 1 #184 (Sep.-Oct. 1969). New York: DC Comics.

_____. "Morgana the Witch!" *Wonder Woman* Vol. 1 #186 (Jan.-Feb. 1970). New York: DC Comics.

_____. "Now ... Comes Zord." *Adventure Comics* Vol. 1 #397 (Sep. 1970). New York: DC Comics.

_____. "The Prisoner." *Wonder Woman* Vol. 1 #194 (May-Jun. 1971). New York: DC Comics.

_____. "Red for Death!" *Wonder Woman* Vol. 1 #189 (May-Jun. 1970). New York: DC Comics.

_____. "Return to Paradise Island!" *Wonder Woman* Vol. 1 #183 (Jul.-Aug. 1969). New York: DC Comics.

_____. "Return to Paradise Island!" *Wonder Woman* Vol. 1 #198 (Jan.-Feb. 1972). New York: DC Comics.

_____. "Target for Today?" *Wonder Woman* Vol. 1 #196 (Jul.-Aug. 1971). New York: DC Comics.

_____. "Them!" *Wonder Woman* Vol. 1 #185 (Nov.-Dec. 1969). New York: DC Comics.

_____. "A Time to Love, a Time to Die!" *Wonder Woman* Vol. 1 #182 (May-Jun. 1969). New York: DC Comics.

_____. "The Widow-Maker!" *The Brave and the Bold* Vol. 1 #87 (Dec. 1969-Jan. 1970). New York: DC Comics.

"Sister." In *Dear Sisters: Dispatches from the Women's Liberation Movement*, edited by Rosalyn Baxandall and Linda Gordon, 123. New York: Basic, 2000.

Steinem, Gloria. "Introduction." *Wonder Woman.* New York: Holt, Rhinehart and Winston, 1972.

Unknown (w) and (a). "Jerry Meets Wonder Woman." *The Adventures of Jerry Lewis* #117 (Mar.-Apr. 1970). New York: DC Comics.

Wright, Bradford. *Comic Book Nation: The Transformation of Youth Culture in America.* Baltimore: Johns Hopkins University Press, 2001.

The Near-Awakening
of Diana Prince

W. C. BAMBERGER

In 1972 novelist/essayist/critic Samuel R. Delany wrote the scripts for a multiple-issue feminist story arc for *Wonder Woman*. Paradoxically, the contemporary rise of feminism as a social and commercial phenomenon intervened to squelch this updated story arc and send an injured Diana Prince hurtling back to an earlier incarnation of herself.

Delany at this time was a well-known author, particularly in science fiction circles. He had published his first novel in 1962, when he was just twenty. By 1972 he had published nine science fiction titles. Delany had been a lifelong reader and advocate of comic books, and was friends with Denny O'Neil, a writer and editor for DC comics.

Delany's recollection is that he met O'Neil in 1967. The middle sixties, as Delany characterized them in a 1980 interview, saw "the explosion of D.C.'s 'relevant comics,' of which Denny and Neal Adams were both the cutting edge and the popular front" (Delany, 89). The attempt at creating a more "relevant" Wonder Woman character had prompted drastic changes in both Diana Prince's clothing and her powers. In 1968, with O'Neil participating in the change of direction, Diana had surrendered her powers so as to be able to remain in this dimension, while her fellow Amazons departed to another. Gone were Wonder Woman's star-spangled suit and her golden lasso. She began to wear white outfits, tight pants suits or short skirts, meant to suggest a *gi*, a karate training uniform, and she makes her living operating a small boutique. In keeping with the martial arts theme, she learns from and often travels in the company of a Chinese martial arts master, I-Ching, named for the ancient Chinese divination text. I-Ching is blind, but his other senses are so finely tuned that he has little trouble navigating his way through the world. At times he offers Diana bits of aphoristic advice: "Wise men liken

117

beauty to the flame — pleasing to the eye but perilous to the touch," for example.

But the Wonder Woman character was having a rocky time of it. As Delany tells it,

> They'd been trying to do the relevant bit with a number of standard titles: *Green Lantern* (with Green Arrow) was, of course, the great success. But now they were trying the same thing with *Wonder Woman*. Only it wasn't working. Mainly that was because the people they had writing it didn't have much of a feel for the woman's movement. Short of getting a woman writer for the series (Don't ask me why they didn't put some energy in *that* direction!), nobody could come up with anything. So at one point I said to Denny: "I think I have more of a sense of this thing. Why don't you let me do a couple?" So I *did* [Delany, 89–90].

The first of these issues, #202, appeared in October 1972. It picked up a storyline O'Neil had been writing. O'Neil's story begins with Diana and I-Ching going to the office of Jonny Double, a private investigator with whom Diana is romantically involved. The office is a shambles and two Asian assassins appear and try to kill Diana and I-Ching. The assassins kill themselves rather than let Diana take them alive. Using his knowledge of dialects, I-Ching puzzles out their country of origin (Tibet) and that they are involved with a group that worships a giant ruby which has a curse on it. In a rare moment of existential exhaustion, Diana hesitates to take up the chase, thinking, "Weary ... so weary! ... Tired of danger ... of battle — of wandering the earth!" (O'Neil and Giordano, 60). Wonder Woman does this while wearing a diaphanous nightie.

In the end, Diana sells her boutique to finance a trip for herself and I-Ching: they fly to Tibet to search for Jonny. There they find a kind of criminals' Shangri-La — a beautiful, temperate valley hidden in the snowy Tibetan mountains. In a cave there they find the hypnotic gem, "The Fist of Flame," and engage in a battle for its possession, with both a Tibetan cult and with a familiar Wonder Woman nemesis, Catwoman, who is also intent on stealing the gem. Outnumbered by the cult warriors, the trio join forces to make good their escape. Averting their eyes, they put the hypnotic gem into a carrying bag and run through the cave in search of an escape route. As the issue nears its cliffhanger close, we are told that I-Ching's evil daughter Lu Shan, who also covets the powerful gem, is holding Jonny Double prisoner. In the last two panels, the trio is suddenly and inexplicably transported to another world. The following issue, the first part of Delany's story arc, titled "Fangs of Fire," picks up at this moment.

The world the trio land in, we are told, is known as "Nehwon." This is "nowhen" spelled backward, a suggestion that this is a world outside of time.

The name is certainly a nod to Samuel Butler's famous utopian satire *Erewhon* — "nowhere" spelled backward, more or less — but it more immediately points to the origin of the two fantastic characters that stand over the dazed trio. These two men, Fafhrd (a seven-foot barbarian) and his diminutive partner The Gray Mouser, as well as the name of their world are borrowings from the fantasy works of Fritz Lieber (1910–1992). Lieber was one of the first to write "Sword and Sorcery" stories, and it was in fact he who coined the term. Lieber had begun writing stories about this adventurous pair in the 1930s, and was still actively writing them when Delany wrote "Fangs of Fire."

As a follow-up to this issue, the first appearance of Lieber's pair in a comic book, Denny O'Neil would, in 1973, launch *Sword and Sorcery*, a short-lived comic series with the pair as its stars. As these were licensed characters, it seems very likely that O'Neil, as editor of Delany's issues, directed him to include Fafhrd and the Gray Mouser as a way of introducing them to the comics-buying public in advance of their own premier issue. They appear in the last panel of "The Fist of Flame" — and fervid comic art fans will immediately notice that Fafhrd loses his headband and grows an impressive red moustache in the few seconds that transpire between the end of this issue and the first page of the next, Delany's "Fangs of Fire."

Diana's first thought bubble in "Fangs of Fire" acknowledges the sexual tension always present as part of Wonder Woman's adventures fighting men: Fafhrd, a giant of a man, is reaching for Diana and she thinks "What he's reaching for probably isn't what I want to give!" (Delany and Giorando, Oct. 1979). While this issue does not yet feature any overt feminist elements, there is a subtle change in the panel art. Delany's layout instructions to the artist, Dick Giordano, were very detailed (Delany, 118–119), and whereas the previous issue, also drawn by Giordano, had featured a number of upskirt drawings and some derriere-centric angles as well as sheer nightie art, this issue includes nothing of the sort. Employing her mastery of judo, Diana knocks Fafhrd to the ground and is about to interrogate him, when she is stopped by the Gray Mouser who is holding a sword to Catwoman's throat.

I-Ching pulls The Fist of Flame from the carrying bag, but instead of reacting to the giant ruby with the expected unbridled greed, the barbarian pair are unexpectedly amused. "There's irony for you, Mouser!" Fafhrd says. They had been looking for a giant sapphire called The Eye of the Ocean: "We've been hunting one jewel ... and now we've found another!" I-Ching tells the group that, "according to ancient texts the Fist of Flame and the Eye of the Ocean are in strange occult conjunction! Gazing into one, you can see what is before the other!" (Delany and Giordano, Oct. 1983). Diana looks into the Fist of Flame and sees Jonny — on earth, a captive of Lu Shan. At this point, Delany begins setting up pairs: In frustration, Lu Shan casts the

Eye of the Ocean sapphire aside because she needs both jewels to operate her "Dimensional Energy Transfer Matrix Machine," which will make transfer from one world to the other reliable rather than haphazard; moments later, equally frustrated, Diana throws the Fist of Flame ruby from her, and we also learn that a sorcerer named Gawron has a Dimensional Energy machine of his own on Nehwon; each machine needs both jewels to work. Diana and her ragged band set off to find Gawron's machine.

They soon find Gawron's well-guarded cave headquarters and decide to enter. Delany here introduces a bit of humor into the action, humor specific to the names of two of the characters. The Gray Mouser and Catwoman are teamed in a search for a back way in. I-Ching discovers a white mouse and says, "My Squeaky friend, you, if anyone, know this cave's back door! Show my confused companions the way, for they who would reach the heights must often follow the lowly." The caption for the next panel reads, "How could our two cat people resist" (89–90). So intent are they on their pursuit of the mouse that they barely notice that they have indeed entered Gawron's lair. (To compound the joke a step further, a black cat living in the cave appears and pursues the mouse out of sight.) Meanwhile, Diana and Fafhrd fight their way in through the front entrance. The white mouse returns to I-Ching and leads him inside, as well. As all the principals enter the main chamber, a random jump of the Eye of the Ocean brings Jonny, Lu Shan and her gang from their world into Nehwon, directly into Gawron's cave. A melee breaks out: Diana frees Jonny, I-Ching gathers up both gems and hurries to the Dimensional Energy machine. He holds a jewel within the jaws of each of the two carved serpents on the sides of the machine's entrance and Diana's group is able to escape through it back to their own world. At the last moment, the Gray Mouser grabs the Fist of Flame as he passes through the gateway of the machine.

Back in their own world, the earthborn trio breathe sighs of relief, but, curious about this new world, Fafhrd and the Gray Mouser immediately venture out into the streets. In another humorous episode, construction workers take them for "hippies." Finding the noise, smells and confusion of the modern world overwhelming to their barbarian senses, the pair runs back to the safety of Diana's group but they suddenly vanish, returning to Nehwon by way of one of the Fist of Flame's random leaps. I-Ching has the last word in this issue: "I sense an adventure ahead — a kind that is a bit more down to the earth we know" (102).

I-Ching was, of course, correct. Having dutifully wound up the previous storyline (and assisted in the introduction of two new characters to the DC comics universe), Delany was now free to delve into the feminist and other themes that interested him. The following issue, which appeared in December of 1972, was titled "The Grandee Caper." The cover also brandished the words "Special Women's Lib Issue" above the title. The new storyline begins with Diana walking down a sidewalk, followed by a group of six men making sexist comments. She tries ignoring them but finally whirls and says, sounding rather pedantic considering the situation, "I'm not a side of beef! If you thought you'd get anywhere coming on to me like that, there'd be an excuse! But you don't think you will any more than I do!" (Delany and Giordano, 130). Before the situation can be fully resolved, "a figure, all speed and spunk," a young blonde woman, runs out of an alley and attacks the men, using some amateurish judo moves that don't have much effect. Diana finds herself drawn into the fight. After the men are run off, Diana realizes the young woman is Cathy Perkins, who used to work at Diana's boutique. Cathy says she has just come from a woman's lib meeting. She finds a note one of the men dropped. The note, on Grandee's Department Store stationary, directs someone to "Get W. W. for me!" Diana dismisses the note as unimportant, but Cathy is worried that someone is after Wonder Woman.

Now without a job, having sold her boutique, and without a place to live, Diana accepts Cathy's invitation to stay temporarily at her place. Upstairs from Cathy's apartment the two friends can hear a married couple that argues all the time. The wife is timid, and the husband is verbally abusive. One of the men who had been harassing Diana on the sidewalk comes to the apartment looking for Wonder Woman, bringing the offer of a job from the owner of Grandee's. When he realizes who Diana is he begins stuttering: "I didn't realize last night when I ... You're a woman I really respect and I ... I thought you were just some ordinary...." But for Diana, "The pedestal bit is as bad as last night's routine" (130).

Grandee offers Diana an exorbitant salary and a free luxury apartment to endorse his in-house clothing lines. He tells her he wants to use her strong image to reach "that newest factor in the American economic scene, the new liberated woman!" (135). In the middle of the meeting Grandee's office is invaded by a trio of vicious guard dogs. Diana saves the men from the dogs, and then accepts Grandee's offer. Even after she has saved him from the dogs, Grandee continues to speak to Diana in a condescending manner, telling her that she should go and wait for them downstairs because they have things to discuss, "man to man." At this point, Diana finds nothing problematic in Grandee's attitude. She is only thinking of how the arrangement will enhance the material facts of her life and his condescension doesn't register. What the two men discuss is that Diana has been fooled; Grandee is only interested in women's lib ideas and Wonder Woman's independent image for the money he might be able to pocket by using them.

When Diana and Jonny Double return to Cathy's apartment, Cathy tells them that she has learned that Grandee is paying his female sales help twenty-five cents an hour below minimum wage. Diana knows that this is only legal if he isn't involved in interstate commerce and Cathy says that Grandee sells cheap, locally made goods in order to circumvent the law. Diana defends Grandee, and Cathy insists that Diana come to one of her group's meetings. Diana is dismissive of the idea; she responds by saying she's for equal wages, but that she doesn't join groups. She then goes on to say, "In most cases I don't even like women...." Astonished, Cathy responds with, "What you're saying is ... you don't like yourself!" Jonny leaves after siding with Cathy. Cathy then explodes at Diana,

> I never asked to be denied what's denied me because I'm a woman! I'm told to be a whole person, but never fight, build or envision — only to respond! Perhaps I'm incompetent and unsure, but I'm conscious of it and enraged at anyone who says I must stay that way!
> You're a Wonder Woman! — skilled enough to overcome some of the problems, lucky enough to avoid others! But you know what all of them are! [141–142].

This outburst begins to awaken Diana's feminist side via her sense of justice. She realizes that Grandee preys on women, and decides to accompany Cathy to the storefront meeting of her women's lib group. There she meets a number of independent women, including the woman who owns the kennel from which Grandee rents his guard dogs, a black belt karate instructor, and a woman who is doing a wide-ranging study of women's problems. The group has been picketing Grandee's store but are now meeting to plan a new action. The meeting is suddenly invaded by a group of Grandee's thugs. Diana is not the only woman who fights back, and the men are outfought — but they drag Cathy along with them as they escape. Diana, the kennel owner, and the woman who has a black belt track the thugs to Grandee's Department Store.

As the trio is sneaking into the store, Diana is shown looking at the ceiling of a shadowy storeroom and telling herself, "I think I've got the final dope on Grandee!" The caption below this panel addresses the reader directly: "Can you see what Diana sees? Wonder Woman is wonderously observant! What about you?" (149). (The misspelling "wonderously" is surely deliberate.) The trio breaks in on Grandee and his thugs and frees Cathy. Diana takes Grandee by his shirt front and announces, "You have no legal sprinkler system in your store rooms! Nor do you have sufficient fire exits!" (151). This is the "final dope" that ultimately gets Grandee's store shut down by the mayor.

At the next women's group meeting where they are discussing the good news — and Diana is thinking, "Now I feel I've really accomplished something for women's image"— the meeting hall is invaded yet again. This time the invaders are a group of angry women. They accuse Diana and Cathy's group of having deprived 250 women of employment by having the store closed down. In the last panel Diana says, "What do you say to them now? And will we have time? They look like they mean business!" And the caption beneath this last panel asks, "What will Diana do now?" (152).

These last two panels offer a suggestion of some of the directions in which Delany had planned to take the story of Diana's enlightenment. Delany's clash of groups of women trying to empower themselves reminds us how movements toward social change often encounter unanticipated consequences. At times some of these are negative, as here. In a paradoxical situation the model of which can often be found in the real world, the shutting down of Grandee's, a business that took advantage of the relative powerlessness of women, threatens to further impoverish and disenfranchise women who have already been victimized. Comments Delany made later suggest he had planned for the women to join together as a cooperative to aid their financial independence (Delany, 118–119).

As noted above, Delany's published comments on the experience of writing these two issues make it clear that he meticulously described to the artist what he wanted to see in the panel art. So, it is likely significant that all of the women seen in the invading group are African American (as is Delany himself). The women's liberation group, on the other hand, is a mixture of races, with whites appearing to be slightly in the majority. Clashes along the line of race and class divisions were not unknown in the women's liberation movement of the 1970s, and it may well be that Delany planned to introduce at least a suggestion of this theme, as well.

The contrast between the subject matter in the two issues Delany wrote is great, but the emotional and dramatic arcs are similar. In the first, Diana fights caped men with swords to capture a gem and save her male friend and make her way back to her own world. In the second, she fights unarmed thugs and a few guard dogs to save the dignity and prevent economic victimization of some female friends. There are plot similarities, as well. Both episodes begin with Diana entering into combat with men in conjunction with another, less powerful woman; there is a modesty to the climaxes of both. In neither is Diana the sole heroine, someone who saves the day singlehandedly: in the first it is I-Ching who leads the group out of danger on Nehwon; in "The Grandee Caper," several other women are involved in the triumph — it is very much a cooperative, group victory. Despite these similarities, the shift in focus involves a shift in scale: in the more traditional comic book story, Diana jumps from world to world, pursues a magical gem, fights for her life and the lives of others, while in the second, Diana moves from apartment to department store, and fights for equal pay and against sexist attitudes. This shift may not have satisfied all long-time *Wonder Woman* readers. They may have wondered, as the last caption in the comic asks, "What will Diana do now?" The answer, as it turned out, was taken out of Delany's hands.

In an ironic plot twist, some aspects of feminist thought in the real world clashed with the feminist and relevancy elements in the comics. There had been complaints that the most famous female superhero had been rendered powerless at a time when women were actively seeking equality with men. In July 1972, six months before "The Grandee Caper" appeared, Gloria Steinem had published the first issue of *Ms.* magazine.

Citing Gloria Steinem's championing of the star-spangled, braceleted image, and undoubtedly hoping to take advantage of this free publicity, DC Comics made the decision to restore Diana to her previous Wonder Woman image, which meant, as Delany put it, that they chose to

> throw out all of Wonder Woman's concerns for women's real, social problems. Instead of a believable woman, working for other women, fighting corrupt department store moguls and crusading for food cooperatives against supermarket monopolies ... she got back all her super [...] powers and went off to battle the Green meanies from Mars [Delany, 90].

The issue that followed "The Grandee Caper" was titled "The Second Life of the Original Wonder Woman." It was written by Robert Kanigher, who had been writing comic books since the mid–1940s, and had been one of those responsible for the character's first modernization in 1958. Kanigher slashed away everything that had come into Diana's life since 1968: there was no mention or reference to where Delany's story arc had been broken off, or to feminism. The story begins abruptly with a sniper firing shots from high atop a building. One shot kills a pair of newlyweds in a car, which crashes into a restaurant where Diana and I-Ching are sitting down to lunch. The next shot kills I-Ching. Diana hitches a ride on a rope ladder dangling from a helicopter and attacks the sniper. She falls from the building, lands on a stone gargoyle a few stories down and awakens with amnesia — all in the first five pages. Driven by some mysterious compulsion (her doctor likens it to the migratory impulses of birds and fish), Diana steals a military jet, is shot down, crashes in the sea and fights a shark, is rescued by a passing Amazon vessel, and has her memory, her powers and her former costume restored. After an intra–Amazon competition, she returns to the U.S. where she quickly gets a job as a translator at the UN.

In the last panel Diana thinks, "I feel as if I have been reborn." Her brief foray as a feminist activist has been, literally, forgotten.

WORKS CITED

Delany, Samuel R. *Silent Interviews* (Hanover and London: Wesleyan University Press/ University Press of New England, 1994).

Delany, Samuel R. (w), and Dick Giordano (a). "Fangs of Fire." *Wonder Woman* #202 (Oct. 1972). New York: D.C. Comics. Reprinted in *Diana Prince: Wonder Woman* (Volume 4) (New York: D. C. Comics, 2008), 79–102. Page citations refer to the reprint edition.

_____. "The Grandee Caper." *Wonder Woman* #203 (Dec. 1972). New York: D. C. Comics. Reprinted in *Diana Prince: Wonder Woman* (Volume 4) (New York: D. C. Comics, 2008), 129–152.

Kanigher, Robert (w), and Don Heck/Dick Giordano (a). "The Second Life of the Original Wonder Woman." *Wonder Woman* #204 (Feb. 1973). New York: D. C. Comics. Reprinted in *Diana Prince: Wonder Woman* (Volume 4) (New York: D. C. Comics, 2008), 153–175.

O'Neil, Denny (w), and Dick Giordano (a). "The Fist of Flame." *Wonder Woman* #201 (Aug. 1972). New York: D.C. Comics. Reprinted in *Diana Prince: Wonder Woman* (Volume 4) (New York: D. C. Comics, 2008), 55–78.

"I No Longer Deserve to Belong"

The Justice League, Wonder Woman and The Twelve Labors

JOSEPH J. DAROWSKI

In her 1942 origin story, Wonder Woman had to win a competition among her Amazonian sisters in order to enter the man's world as Paradise Island's champion, proving she was suited for the role of superhero. More than thirty years later, after regaining her previously lost powers, Wonder Woman again had to prove her worth, this time before being readmitted to the superhero team, the Justice League.

In 1974, DC Comics began a multi-part storyline that ran for two years and has since been referred to as *The Twelve Labors*. In this tale, Wonder Woman has regained her Amazonian powers after spending a period of time as a normal human. When de-powered, Wonder Woman had not served as a member of the Justice League. Wonder Woman feels compelled to complete twelve labors, just as Hercules did in Greek mythology, in order to prove that she deserves a spot on the Justice League's roster.

The story began in *Wonder Woman* #212 (Jul. 1974) and concluded in *Wonder Woman* #222 (Mar. 1976). At the time, *Wonder Woman* was published bi-monthly by DC Comics. These eleven issues published across two years, which included a double-sized *Wonder Woman* #218 (Jul. 1975) containing two stories, covered twelve battles. In each story, a different member of the Justice League observes Wonder Woman and narrates the story. The issues were written by Len Wein, Cary Bates, Elliot S. Maggin, and Martin Pasko, and drawn by Curt Swan, Irv Novick, John Rosenberger, Dick Dillin, Kurt Schaffenberger, Dick Giordano, and Jose Delbo.

Comic book historian Les Daniels explains that editor Julius Schwartz encouraged this new storyline and the role of the Justice League as observers when he was brought on as the new editor for the monthly *Wonder Woman* comic book. Schwartz had previously been brought on as an editor to revive other DC superhero titles, including Flash, Green Lantern, Superman, and Batman. Daniels quotes Schwartz describing his decision to edit *Wonder Woman*:

> I agreed to do it, but only on a limited basis, to get it going again [...] I never particularly cared for Wonder Woman, so I came up with the gimmick of having the Justice League spy on her, so to speak, to see whether she was worthy of being readmitted. It gave me the opportunity to do a series of issues in which I could have a guest star featured, and it did well in the sales department [134].

Interestingly, the Justice League insist that Wonder Woman does not need to prove that she is worthy of inclusion, but Wonder Woman herself insists she engage in this elaborate test. As she explains it, "I will rejoin if I prove worthy! If—like Hercules–I succeed in twelve labors!" (Wein 15).

The eleven issues were reprinted in a trade paperback collection, *Wonder Woman: The Twelve Labors*, in 2012. This collection includes a disclaimer at the bottom of the "Contents" page, "The comic in this volume were produced in a time when racism played a larger role in society and popular culture, both consciously and unconsciously. They are reprinted here without alteration for historical accuracy" (6). It seems as though this may be a generic disclaimer that is placed on all DC trade paperbacks that collect stories from earlier eras. There are no obviously racist characterizations or language used in these stories. Unsurprisingly, there is largely a homogenous whiteness to the featured characters and the background figures, which would align more with what Beverly Daniels Tatum refers to as "passive racism" rather than any "active racism" that the disclaimer seems to be warning readers about. Notably, gender issues are brought to the forefront of the narrative, but no disclaimer is provided on that topic.

A Women's Lib Adventure

In 1975, the same year many of the issues in this storyline were published, Catherine E. Potkay, Charles R. Potkay, Gregory J. Boynton, and Julie A. Klingbell conducted a study that had subjects describe the traits of comic strip characters they were shown. In addition, to newspaper comic strip characters, subjects were shown images of Superman and Wonder Woman in the course of this study. In the study,

> Superman had been described as *strong* (by 75% of the subjects) and as *intelligent* (25%), *helpful* (15%); *kind* (13%), *smart*, *superhuman*, and *brave*.

Wonder Woman was also described primarily as *strong* (52% of the subjects) and as *sexy* (25%), *intelligent* (12%), *smart* (12%), *beautiful* (12%), *brave, powerful, helpful,* and *women's libber* [190].

The women's libber label is unsurprising. As the researchers note, "data for the study were gathered in 1975 at a time when the women's movement was having high public and collegiate impact, including symbolic uses of the Wonder Woman character" (191). The editors of the feminist publication *Ms.* magazine "obtained permission to adapt the 1940s version of Wonder Woman for the magazine's inaugural cover" and also used images from Golden Age *Wonder Woman* comics to illustrate an article in the same issue (Robinson 82). To some degree Wonder Woman had indeed been adopted as a symbol of the feminist movement.

However, besides this larger cultural appropriation of Wonder Woman by the feminist movement, when reading Wonder Woman comics from this period one encounters both overt and subtle efforts to explore gender roles and promote the feminist movement. At times, these efforts are problematic in their clumsiness, but they are clearly evident. There would have likely been a cultural association with Wonder Woman as a women's libber to non-comic book reader, but a reader from that period may also have used that label to describe Wonder Woman even if they were unaware of the movement's appropriation of the character.

In *The Twelve Labors*, not all of the stories address issues of the feminist movement head on, but those that do leave little to subtext. The first issue of the storyline, *Wonder Woman* #212 (Jul. 1974) entitled "The Man Who Mastered Women," includes a villain named the Cavalier and his efforts to gain control of Indira Gamal, the female prime minister of the fictional nation Pamanasia. Superman has been assigned by the Justice League to monitor Wonder Woman and judge if she succeeds in completing one labor, after which another member of the Justice League will take a turn to essentially babysit the Amazon Princess. No explicit mention is made of the Prime Minister's gender in relation to her role as a world leader, though very overt exclamations about other gender roles do come on the very next page.

Masked "gunmen" (so identified by Clark Kent) parachute in and attack but almost all are defeated by Wonder Woman. One lone, masked figure who has not yet been dispatched is taking aim at Wonder Woman's back when "Morgan Tracy, the U.N.'s trouble-shooter diplomat" enters the scene with a flying tackle, incapacitating this final attacker. Wonder Woman thanks Tracy for his aid, but says, "I knew she was behind me!" This statement confuses Tracy, who says, "'She'? What are you talking about, Wonder Woman? This punk is a ... a girl!?! I don't understand! Why would a woman be a part of..." (Wein, 10). Morgan cannot seem to process the idea that a female would be a villainous would-be assassin.

As Judith Lorber explains, "Gender is such a familiar part of daily life that it usually takes a deliberate disruption of our expectations of how women and men are supposed to act to pay attention to how it is produced. Gender signs and signals are so ubiquitous that we usually fail to note them unless they are missing or ambiguous" (54). For Morgan, a female in the role of villain completely disrupts his expectations of gender roles and it takes him some time to adjust what he is seeing.

Later, attention to traditional gender roles is again raised when Morgan Tracy offers Diana Prince, Wonder Woman's civilian alter ego, a job. He asks, "Would you consider leaving your guide job for a position as my assistant... No, my associate" (Wein 11) Tracy initially offers the stereotypical role, what Lorber refers to as a role with "less power, prestige, and economic reward" due to "structured inequality" that women face in society (61). Tracy corrects himself, offering a position that would be seen as more equal, the position he is likely to have offered a male colleague.

The villain in this first issue is the Cavalier, who has a group of barely clothed henchwomen do his dirty work for him. What appears to be a coloring error makes one of the women appear more scandalously attired than the publisher was likely to intend, as her brassiere-style top is colored the same way as her skin. The Cavalier is a swashbuckler who uses his "chemically heightened sensual attraction" to force women to do his bidding (Wein 23). Wonder Woman is able to quickly dispatch the henchwomen and is able to resist the Cavalier's powers. Making the already fairly clear gender issues even more blatant, Wonder Woman accuses the Cavalier of being a chauvinist, to which he indignantly responds "Chauvinist? You offend me! I don't merely believe in man's superiority — I'm convinced of it!" (Wein 25). After this statement Cavalier is immediately overpowered and defeated by his former henchwomen, who have been freed from the influence of his heightened sensual attraction.

This issue was Wonder Woman's first solo adventure in her quest to regain membership in the Justice League. The issue ends with Superman giving his report to Batman, Green Lantern, and the Flash. Superman clearly approves of Wonder Woman's efforts, though her success is partially undermined in the close of the issue. While providing his report, Superman reveals that at a key moment he used his "superventriloquism" to influence Wonder Woman's actions. During the earlier narrative, Wonder Woman ascribes her decision to "woman's intuition," but it was apparently Superman offering her a suggestion from a distance. Superman had been trying to watch Wonder Woman without interfering, but became a participant in the story when he felt it necessary to influence the outcome.

Of all the issues to directly address the feminist movement, the most problematic is *Wonder Woman* #219 (Sep. 1975), "World of Enslaved Women."

This issue, written by Martin Pasko and drawn by Curt Swan, sees the Elongated Man take a turn to watch over Wonder Woman. In this story, the male leaders of a world from an alternate dimension are kidnapping feminist leaders from Earth. One of the feminists who disappears is Betty Jo Kane, a tennis player who is having a match against "a chauvinist hustler name Willy Wrigley," clearly analogues for Billy Jean King and Bobby Riggs, who faced off on the tennis court in "The Battle of the Sexes" in 1973 (Pasko 157). Betty Jo Kane disappears in the middle of this match, seemingly disappearing into thin air, which causes the outraged women who were watching the game to begin attacking the men around them in the crowd. Or, as the Elongated Man's narration explains, "Betty Jo's fans began proving just how militant angry feminists can be" (Pasko 158).

It seems from the themes of this issue that Pasko is attempting a profeminist story, but references to "militant angry feminists" undermine the effort. Bradford W. Wright explains that in comic books from this period the modern feminist movement was often addressed with "ambivalence" as "writers seemed to regard 'women's lib' with the same bemusement and dismissiveness that others in the media did" (250). While it is very difficult to infer authorial intent, it does not appear that Plasko or other writers of this epic are being deliberately dismissive of the women's movement, but there are moments where the narrative tone belies a lack of understanding of the movement's objectives. The writer and artist seem to fall back on stereotypes of feminists, as being angry and anti-male, rather than attempting a nuanced portrayal of the issues.

The issue continues with Wonder Woman finding a clue that leads her to conclude the world's feminist leaders are transported away after visiting "Consciousness III Salon," a "beauty salon for the liberated woman" (Pasko 158). The reader is shown this is a salon for "liberated" women when Wonder Woman first enters one and a worker is overheard saying, "It's not important what your husband wants, only what you want" (Plasko 159). The leaders of the alternate dimension's world run this salon and apply a shampoo with interdimensional transportation abilities, the shampoo activates when the women become emotionally agitated. Besides the use of a beauty salon in order to entrap women, the feminist agenda of the story is further troubled by the creators employing the "emotional woman" stereotype as a key plot point.

Why are the leaders of this other planet, called Xro, kidnapping Earth's leading feminists? Because when women, but not men, are transported from one dimension to the other their emotions are reversed. The men of this other world are kidnapping the women campaigning for equality on Earth so that when they come to Xro, they will tell the women to remain docile and subservient. Wonder Woman is able to return Earth's citizens to the correct dimension, though what exactly happens to the sexist rulers of Xro is not explicitly shown. As Wonder Woman is leaving, the women have formed a mob and are declaring "Death to the male oppressors!" so some sort of future revolution is implied (167).

Lillian S. Robinson, in writing about comic books from the 1970s, explains that "the principle manifestation of" the feminist movement is battles with "caricatures of overt machismo [...] combined with a rejection of male violence and male 'evil' (86). This issue clearly fits Robinson's description. The threat is absurdly sexist, old stereotypes of women are used, including an obsession with beauty salons, while new stereotypes of militant feminists are shown on Earth and spread to Xro. Robinson continues, "feminism, in these comics, often means just being anti-male, [...] paying no attention to any concrete issue raised by women's liberation beyond the crudest battle of sexist polarities" (86). The stories written by Pasko are particularly clumsy in their handing of feminism and their portrayal of feminists, often implying that feminists are simply man-haters.

Not all of the issues in this storyline deal with feminism as overtly as the two listed above. For example, *Wonder Woman* #214 (Nov. 1974) has a storyline that is essentially a mash up of Doctor Strangelove and the classic Twilight Zone episode "Time Enough," with no comically misogynist villains or exaggerated feminist demonstrations in sight. However, there is a random aside by Green Lantern, the narrator for this issue, when he sees Diana open a car door for a man he comments, "That's our Wonder Woman alright, the women's libber opening a door for a gentleman!" (Maggin, "Wish," 52)

Two issues also written by Martin Pasko have brief commentaries that acknowledge gender issues, but the plot does not address the theme as obviously as occurred in "World of Enslaved Women." "Revolt of the Wonder Weapons," the first of two stories in the double-sized *Wonder Woman* #218 (Jul. 1975), concludes with Red Tornado saying, "One should never underestimate the power of a woman, especially a Wonder Woman" (143). *Wonder Woman* #220 (Nov. 1975), "The Man Who Wiped Out Time," features the Atom watching Wonder Woman's adventure. In the Atom's narration there is a moment when he considers intervening in Wonder Woman's behalf, but after seeing her successfully save herself he comments, "Imagine — thinking Wonder Woman needed me to save her. Talk about chauvinism!" (Pasko 181). Much like "World of Enslaved Women," this adventure is a bit uneven in its portrayal of women. In the same panel as Atom is accusing himself of being a chauvinist for thinking of helping out, Wonder Woman is self-congratulatory about pulling off a feat "without even mussing my hair!" (181). Wonder Woman is more concerned about her appearance and coiffure, stereotypically female concerns, than most male superheroes would be shown to be in moments of crisis.

Wonder Woman #221 (Jan. 1976), "The Fiend with the Face of Glass," was also written by Pasko and addresses issues of women's identities and self-worth being tied inseparably to their physical appearances. The story involves older women, referred to by Wonder Woman as "aging beauties," being tricked into using a product which is a "facelift in a jar," though the plot diverges into several strange directions from there (196). Significantly, the mastermind behind this trap is a villain named Dr. Cyber whose face was scarred in a previous battle, and now her primary motivation in life is a desire to steal Wonder Woman's beautiful face and have it surgically placed onto her own head.

The Male Gaze

While it is clear that the creators were attempting to deal with feminist issues and promote gender equality in several of the issues, there are two significant aspects of the storyline which undermine their intent. First, the framing device which accompanies each issue problematizes Wonder Woman's role as the lead in her own comic book. Second, the need to prove herself worthy of being considered a hero is an old theme in Wonder Woman comic books that is rarely found in male superhero comic books.

Each issue of this storyline features a framing device of another superhero beginning a report on Wonder Woman's adventures and closes with the conclusion of their report. This character also provides first person narration for the entirety of the issue. For eleven of the twelve issues, the narrator is a male superhero, the sole exception being *Wonder Woman* #216 (Mar. 1975), which features Black Canary as Wonder Woman's secret supervisor.

The character that follows Wonder Woman and files the report in each issue is featured prominently on the cover, often larger than Wonder Woman. In order of appearance, the guest stars are Superman, the Flash, Green Lantern, Aquaman, Black Canary, Green Arrow, Red Tornado, The Phantom Stranger, the Elongated Man, the Atom, Hawkman, and Batman. Because of the prominence of these characters on the covers, the framing device which opens and closes each issue featuring the guest star, and the first person narration, Wonder Woman becomes a secondary character in her own monthly comic book. She is no longer the protagonist driving the action, she is an observed figure. Or put another way, readers are given less Wonder Woman in this Wonder Woman story.

Male gaze was a theory introduced to critique cinema, attempting to "unmask the power of patriarchy in Hollywood cinema" (Manlove 83). The male gaze critiques the tendency in film to assume a male viewer and treat female characters as objects in stories rather than subjects of stories. The female characters are acted upon, rather than acting for themselves. In film theory the male gaze is an implicit issue, in this storyline for eleven of the twelve stories it is an explicit reality.

Furthermore, because the Justice Leaguers have promised to observe Wonder Woman secretly, an element of voyeurism is added to the storylines. Though undoubtedly unintended, this casts the male members of the Justice League into somewhat creepy roles. Some of the superheroes use their powers to observe from a distance, Superman uses his x-ray vision to track Wonder Woman's progress from the sky (Wein 23), Red Tornado hovers outside her window (Pasko, "Revolt," 135), Aquaman watches her fly overhead as he swims along in a river (Bates 73). Other images take on more of an air of stalking, as Green Arrow watches her walk down a hallway (Maggin, "The Day," 114), Green Lantern peeks out at her from behind pillars (Maggin, "Wish," 52), and Batman spies on her from a janitor's closet (Pasko, "Will," 215). Elongated Man goes so far as to videotape her the entire time he is watching her (Pasko, "World, 187). Perhaps the most uncomfortable panel shows Atom, shrunk down until he is only a couple of inches tall, peeking from around a telephone to watch Diana Prince change into her Wonder Woman costume. Because Wonder Woman uses a pseudo-science/magic involving her magic lasso to change her civilian clothes into her superhero costume she does not disrobe, but there is an undeniable peeping tom aspect as Atom watches Diana Prince change her clothes (Pasko, "The Man," 176).

Proving Herself Again

In the essay "The Wonder Woman Precendent: Female (Super) Heroism on Trial," Julie D. O'Reilly explains that because Wonder Woman's origin involves her proving herself in combat before becoming a superhero as opposed to Superman who simply put on the cape and tights and was a superhero, "Wonder Woman's legacy is one of deference, or at least, limited agency; Superman's is one of assumed authority" (274). O'Reilly further explains, "Central to Wonder Woman's legend, then, is the questioning of her status as a hero because she is subject to the approval or disapproval of Amazon mother and sisters" (275). In this case, it is her own approval Wonder Woman is seeking, as the other members of the Justice League have argued that she can join the League immediately, but she demurs until she has proven herself. In this story, it is more an issue of self-doubt than the external pressures that existed in Wonder Woman's origin story.

O'Reilly argues that there is a tradition in writing the origins of female superheroes, rather than a tale of female empowerment too often there is "submission to and acceptance of a series of trials put forth by those who would sanction their position as heroes (275). This tendency demonstrates that "female superheroes operate according to a different code of heroism than their male counterparts, a code with built-in limitations" (275). *The Twelve Labors*, which essentially reintegrates Wonder Woman into the larger DC universe and serves as a pseudo-origin story for the newly re-empowered Wonder Woman, contains many of the troublesome tropes O'Reilly identified with the character's original origin.

While the Twelve Labors are meant to prove Wonder Woman's status as hero, the fact that the status is questioned at all undermines some of the profeminist intent of the story. It seems clear that the creators were attempting to embrace or at least acknowledge the feminist movement, but an imperfect execution and a problematic narrative structure prevents Wonder Woman from standing on her own as an empowered female character.

WORKS CITED

Bates, Cary (w), and Irv Novick (a). "The War-No-More Machine." *Wonder Woman* #213 (Sep. 1974). Reprinted in *Wonder Woman: The Twelve Labors*. New York: DC Comics, 2012.

Bates, Cary (w), and John Rosenberger (a). "Amazon Attack Against Atlantis." *Wonder Woman* #215 (Jan. 1975). Reprinted in *Wonder Woman: The Twelve Labors*. New York: DC Comics, 2012.

"Contents." Wildman, Robin, ed. *Wonder Woman: The Twelve Labors*. New York: DC Comics, 2012.

Daniels, Les. *Wonder Woman: The Complete History*. San Francisco: Chronicle, 2000.

Lorber, Judith. "'Night to His Day': The Social Construction of Gender." In *Race, Class, and Gender in the United States: An Integrated Study*, edited by Paula S. Rothenberg, 54–65. New York: Worth, 2004.

Maggin, Elliot S. (w), and Curt Swan (a). "Wish Upon a Star." *Wonder Woman* #214. Nov. 1974. Reprinted in *Wonder Woman: The Twelve Labors*. New York: DC Comics, 2012.

Maggin, Elliot S. (w), and Dick Dillin (a). "The Day Time Broke Loose." *Wonder Woman* #217 (May 1975). Reprinted in *Wonder Woman: The Twelve Labors*. New York: DC Comics, 2012.

Maggin, Elliot S. (w), and John Rosenberger (a). "Paradise in Peril." *Wonder Woman* #216 (Mar. 1975). Reprinted in *Wonder Woman: The Twelve Labors*. New York: DC Comics, 2012.

Manlove, Clifford T. "Visual 'Drive' and Cinema Narrative: Reading Gaze Theory in Lacan, Hitchcock, and Mulvey." *Cinema Journal* 46.3 (Spring 2007): 83–108. Jan. 4, 2013.

O'Reilly, Julie D. "The Wonder Woman Precedent: Female (Super) Heroism on Trial." *The Journal of American Culture* 28.3 (2005): 273–283. Jan. 4, 2013.

Pasko, Martin (w), and Curt Swan (a). "The Fiend with a Face of Ice." *Wonder Woman* #221 (Jan. 1976). Reprinted in *Wonder Woman: The Twelve Labors*. New York: DC Comics, 2012.

_____. "World of Enslaved Women." *Wonder Woman* #219 (Sep. 1975). Reprinted in *Wonder Woman: The Twelve Labors*. New York: DC Comics, 2012.

Pasko, Martin (w), and Dick Giordano (a). "The Man Who Wiped Out Time." *Wonder Woman* #220 (Nov. 1975). Reprinted in *Wonder Woman: The Twelve Labors*. New York: DC Comics, 2012.

Pasko, Martin (w), and Jose Delbo (a). "Will the Real Wonder Woman Please ... Drop Dead!" *Wonder Woman* #222 (Mar. 1976). Reprinted in *Wonder Woman: The Twelve Labors*. New York: DC Comics, 2012.

Pasko, Martin (w), and Kurt Schaffenberger (a). "Give Her Liberty — and Give Her Death." *Wonder Woman* #218 (Jul. 1975). Reprinted in *Wonder Woman: The Twelve Labors*. New York: DC Comics, 2012.

_____."Revolt of the Wonder Weapons." *Wonder Woman* #218 (Jul. 1975). Reprinted in *Wonder Woman: The Twelve Labors*. New York: DC Comics, 2012.

Potkay, Catherine E., Charles R. Potkay, Gregory J. Boynton, and Julie A. Klingbell. "Perceptions of Male and Female Comic Strip Characters Using the Adjective Generation Technique." *Sex Roles* 8.2 (1982): 185–200. Jan. 4, 2013

Robinson, Lillian S. *Wonder Women: Feminisms and Superheroes*. New York: Routledge, 2004.

Tatum, Beverly Daniels. "Defining Racism: 'Can We Talk?'" *Race, Class, and Gender in the United States: An Integrated Study*. Ed. Paula S. Rothenberg. New York: Worth, 2004. 124–31. Print.

Wein, Len (w), and Curt Swan (a). "The Man Who Mastered Women." *Wonder Woman* #212 (Jul. 1974). Reprinted in *Wonder Woman: The Twelve Labors*. New York: DC Comics, 2012.

Wright, Bradford W. *Comic Book Nation: The Transformation of Youth Culture*. Baltimore: Johns Hopkins University Press, 2001.

"Steve Trevor, Equal?"

Wonder Woman *in an Era of* *Second Wave Feminist Critique*

Ruth McClelland-Nugent

When feminist editor Gloria Steinem published the first issue of *Ms.* magazine in 1972, she chose a beloved childhood icon for many feminists of her generation to grace the cover. Powerful and self-reliant, hailing from a peaceful, female-centered society, she represented many values that deeply resonated with Second Wave feminism. In response to the critiques and praises of feminist fans, *Wonder Woman*'s writers and editors began including some identifiably liberal feminist themes in the comic in the early 1970s: equal treatment in the workplace, condemnation of appearance-based discrimination, and sisterhood among women. Perhaps no topic provoked more divided responses on the letter pages than storylines revolving around the search for an egalitarian heterosexual relationship between Wonder Woman and her boyfriend Steve Trevor, twice killed and resurrected in this period. Although the storylines of the comic and the sentiments of its letter pages were clearly influenced by feminism in 1970s, this focus was in discernible decline by the 1980s, reflecting a wider anti-feminist backlash in the in the U.S. media.

Second Wave feminism, so-called in contrast to the first wave of women's right's activism that centered around achieving women's suffrage, grew out of widespread dissatisfaction with gender roles in the Cold War world. Routinely denied admission to higher education, paid less than men for the same work, and ineligible for many bank loans and credit cards, feminists challenged not only individual acts of sexism, but an entire social system that underlay discrimination (Rosen 196–226). Feminist theorist Kate Millet identified the problem as global:

> Our society, like all other historical civilisations, is a patriarchy. The fact is evident at once if one recalls that the military, industry, technology, universities, science, political office, and finance — in short, every avenue of power within the society, including the coercive force of the police, is entirely in male hands [Millet 25].

There could hardly be a clearer alternative to this patriarchy than Wonder Woman's home, the all-female society of Paradise Island. Growing up in a world where traditionally feminine qualities were valued as much or more than masculine qualities, Wonder Woman was an attractive figure for feminists seeking a pop culture analog for their values, particularly in her original 1940s incarnation. In the introduction to a 1972 reprint of Golden Age *Wonder Woman* issues, Gloria Steinem praised the title character for her promotion of feminine cooperation and nonviolence (Steinem). An accompanying essay by Phyllis Chesler celebrated Wonder Woman's potential as a role model in a world that still judged female competence harshly, and where relationships are expected to revolve around male dominance:

> As futuristic as the comic strip is, it is nonetheless grounded in reality. It clearly portrays the fact that women have to be better and stronger than men to be given a chance in a man's world ... the comic also underlined the importance of successful female role models in teaching women strength and confidence. And, as a corollary, the comic depicts as 'natural' the love of a strong woman for a man who, in *macho* terms, is "weaker" than herself. In all these ways, Wonder Woman is ahead of her time [Chesler].

Feminists were aware of the character's imperfections and idiosyncrasies. Writing in the inaugural issue of *Ms.*, Joanne Edgar took critical note of the compulsive heterosexuality of Marston's creation: "Wonder Woman in love, as if lassoed back into conventionality, became the simpering romantic maiden, willing to relinquish her Amazonian birthright to a man." Yet she still praised the character's "peacefulness and revulsion towards killing that have culturally distinguished women from men" (Edgar 55).

Like many Golden Age superheroes, however, Diana had changed. In her case, the changes sapped some of the feminist spirit form the comic. Her Amazon sisters had departed to another dimension, while Diana chose to remain with her boyfriend, Steve Trevor, thereby losing her superpowers. Unfortunately, Steve's death in the same issue, *Wonder Woman* #179 (Nov. 1968), left her quite alone. Wielding martial arts and wearing a white catsuit, she became what Joanne Edgar called "a female James Bond, but without his sexual exploits" (Edgar 55). Far from promoting sisterhood, this Wonder Woman is "ashamed to be a woman" (O'Neil, "The Wrath"). Although she lives an independent and action-filled life, writer Denny O'Neill described her as unhappy in #199 (Jul.-Aug. 1972), because she has no man to fulfill her:

...Once, she was an Amazon princess, strong and swift and immortal — a goddess. She exchanged her immortality for a human existence, with all its pain and sorrow, to be near a man she loved. And then she saw him spill his blood on cold stones, held his hand as a final sigh whispered through lips already dead. Diana can't forget Steve Trevor; she wonders if his memory must deny her ever loving another mortal. She wants to love, she wants it desperately. She can't — not now.... So she fills her days with adventure and learning and skills, waiting, and hoping, and wanting. She's Diana Prince. Envy her, and pity her ["Princessions"].

Some fans spotted sexism in this description. Using the language of feminist critics in #201 (Jul.-Aug. 1972), Mrs. Elizabeth Bleau wrote to the letter page: "The editorial did it. 'Pity her, envy her.' Ugh and ick. Your male chauvinism is showing. I could say something nastier but I won't. I believe in quiet, well-mannered commitment to the cause of liberation" ("Wonder Woman's Write-In"). Such critiques clearly hit a nerve; issue #203 (Nov. 1972) explicitly turned the mod Diana into a feminist. Billed as "Special Women's Lib Issue!" on the cover, the very first pages showed Diana taking on the problem of street harassment: "Here we go again! If I smile and try to be a good sport, they follow me and come on stronger! If I ignore them, and walk on by, I get — static!" The rest of the issue revolved around pay discrimination against women in a local department store. Diana, upon learning more about the plot, is concerned, but initially eschews involvement in a feminist organization, explaining to her feminist friend, Cathy that "[i]n most cases, I don't even like women..." Her friend Cathy responds: "What you're saying is ... you don't like yourself!" Diana realizes the truth of Cathy's statement, and for the first time, identifies as a feminist (Nov.-Dec. 1972). On the "Princessions" letters page, Denny O'Neil lavished praise on the story:

> I think Chip's tale is a small but nonetheless solidly polished milestone; it sets Diana solidly into women's liberation. In the story, Di and her friends echo the sentiments of millions of women who are ... well, sick of being second-class citizens. If you missed that particular aspect of this yarn, read it again. And think about it.

O'Neill's pro-liberation statements notwithstanding, the transition to feminism was not without hiccups. The storyline introduced in issue #203 (Nov. 1972) was never continued. A female editor, Dorothy Woolfolk (who had previously worked on the Golden Age comic as Dorothy Roubincek), was announced, but left abruptly (Hanley). Instead, Robert Kanigher, who had succeeded Marston as writer-editor in the 1940s, resumed duties in issue #204 (Feb. 1973). His script suggested some hostility towards Woolfolk's editorship; in the first page of issue #204 (Feb. 1973), a sniper haunting DC kills "Dottie Cottonman," a women's magazine editor.[1] The brutal murder of a fictionalized female colleague did not exactly signal support for feminist causes, but if Kanigher felt some ambivalence toward the comic's feminist turn, he was in good company. As Susan Faludi notes in *Backlash*, antifeminist hostility was common in newsmedia of the day: "At *Newsday*, a male editor assigned reporter Marilyn Goldstein a story on the women's movement with these instructions: 'Get out there and find an authority who'll say this is all of crock of shit'" (Faludi 75–76). Advertisers preferred to focus on empowerment as a matter of consumption, forcing often-incongruous connections between their products and liberation, such as Hanes pantyhose hiring a former NOW spokeswoman to peddle the "liberating" qualities of their product (Faludi 76).

By comparison, the return of Wonder Woman to her feminist roots and Golden Age costume struck her fans as genuinely empowering and feminist-friendly. Reader Tom Purchase, writing in #212 (Jun. 1974), praised a recent issue as "[sounding] like something NOW would put out — and I don't think that is bad at all! ... I wonder if your commix mag can help slow down this sexism... Women's Lib is human Lib (sorry for the cliché); young boys need liberation as much as girls do." Anne Forfreedom cited Wonder Woman as an exemplar of the peaceful pre-historic matriarchy:

> Wonder Woman is an important symbol to me, since we contemporary women are now beginning to realize our great matriarchal Amazonian heritage. For that reason, I'm glad your writers and illustrators are showing the peace-loving and tender aspects, as well as the military successes, of the Amazons. Our real foremothers combined many characteristics, which is precisely why patriarchs could not accept the continued existence of such all-female societies. Thank you again for your hard work in maintaining accuracy and interest in Wonder Woman. Her feminist sisters salute Wonder Woman, the Amazon Princess!

The commitment to pursuing feminism within the comic apparently strengthened when Julius Schwartz took over editing in 1974; editorial assistant Martin Pasko explicitly re-affirmed the comic's dedication to battling "gender stereotypes" ("Wonder Words"). Under Schwartz's leadership, dialogue featured more explicitly feminist vocabulary. In #214 (Oct.-Nov. 1974), for example, Wonder Woman's colleague Green Lantern calls her "The Women's Libber opening doors for gentleman!" and Wonder Woman herself employs feminist language, calling villain "The Cavalier" a "male chauvinist" and apologizing to women she must incapacitate with "Forgive me, my sisters!" (Maggin, "Wish"). Wonder Woman also identified thinly disguised versions of real-life feminists whom that she rescued in #219 (Aug.-Sep. 1975): Bernadette Devlin ("Bonita Doolin") Golde Meier ("Minna Golden") and Billie Jean King ("Betty Jo Kane") (Pasko, "World").

Writers also frequently found ways to show the respect Wonder Woman garnered in her professional life, equal to and respected by male colleagues. Fellow superhero the Atom was impressed with her wits in #220 (Oct.-Nov. 1975): "I've never seen anyone think that fast — before I knew what was happening, the Amazing Amazon had doped out a plan" (Pasko, "The Man"). Green Lantern mused on her courage: "If you think the Batman's got guts, you've never seen Wonder Woman run into a hail of lead, playing bullets and bracelets!" (Maggin, "Wish") Even in the non-super persona of Diana Prince, she attracted praise for acts like fending off a dog attack with her judo skills. A male observer notes in #215 (Dec. 1974-Jan. 1975) that "Miss Prince handled herself like a true champion! Not even Wonder Woman could have fared any better against those curs!" (Bates). Respect in the workplace included respect amongst women. Female colleagues are shown cooperating, rather than competing out of stereotypical jealousy. As Wonder Woman's only female super-colleague in the JLA, Black Canary shows feminine solidarity with her in #216 (Feb.-Mar. 1975), leaving a page out of her report that would reveal a key Amazon secret to male members. She reasons: "there are some things that must be known to no man — not even the men of the Justice League of America!" (Maggin, "A Paradise").

Not every reader was enthralled with this direction. Scott R. Taylor complained about making Wonder Woman a "super women's-right's fighter." But more praise than pans filled the letters pages. Margie Spears wrote: "The Wonder Woman you presented in issue #212 is wonderful ... still feminine with room enough left over for the feminist! A very attractive balance." Elizabeth Harlee enthused, "I was hoping that when the 'real' WW returned to her loyal fans she would come in all her glory. By all means keep it up! Remember, 'Big Sister' is watching!" Bob Robinson, who otherwise disliked issue #220, praised a scene wherein "the woman is being awakened to go to work by her husband, instead of the reverse ... nice touch!" The associate editor responded that "yours truly found nothing so startling about the man waking up his wife in order to send her off to work. It happens all the time in the home of Laurie and — BOB ROZAKIS" (Feb.-Mar. 1976). Some readers liked the feminism, but felt the comic could do better. An anonymous reader published in #221 noted that the "Planet of Enslaved Women" story, while feminist on the surface, was undermined by sexually exploitive cover art and a negative picture of feminists:

> I would like to register my disgust with Wonder Woman 219. The cover features the Amazon in a compromising pose, tied by her own magic rope, and proclaiming to a number of armed men, "I've made myself helpless! Now kill me!" This is an invitation to any male sexist to buy the issue. What is worse, inside the issue angry feminists erupt against innocent males when their tennis star disappears, and there is constant warring between the

sexes with Wonder Woman as the chief protagonist. What the world needs is reconciliation between the sexes and a basis for new understanding and growth [Dec. 1974-Jan. 1975].

But no area of change garnered as much argument as the possible resurrection of Steve Trevor. Well before the plotline was introduced, some readers expressed anxiety about this development. In a letter published in issue #214, Betsy Morse asked, "couldn't we leave Steve Trevor ... the pretty, colorless, boyfriend at rest?" While the Schwartz-led team did indeed resurrect Steve in 1976, they altered him greatly from his last published incarnation in 1968. Gone was the Silver Age trickster constantly pressuring Wonder Woman to marry him, and oblivious to his secretary Diana Prince. Such portrayals would have been inconsistent with popular media associations of feminism, singlehood, and women's fulfillment. The *New York Times* in 1974 described single women as "self-assured, confident, and secure," concluding that "The [women's] movement, apparently, is catching on" (Faludi 96).

In this context, it is not surprising that Steve Trevor (resurrected in *Wonder Woman* #223) seeks a relationship premised on trust, but not necessarily on marriage. This Steve is aware of Diana's secret identity from the beginning, implying trust and intimacy. There is implied physical intimacy as well; after Diana helps Steve check into a hotel, he asks her not to go: "Please don't go ... yet! It's been so long since we've been together ... we have to ... well ... get to know each other all over again!" Diana responds: "No, Steve ... I've been on the go non-stop since my vacation from the U.N. started ... and it's late ... and — corny though it sounds — I'm getting a headache!"(Pasko, "Wonder Woman Versus"). The physical closeness of the couple is reaffirmed at the end of the comic, as they watch television together, with Steve's head in Diana's lap. The issue ends with a passionate kiss. As (literally) a man of the past, Steve has trouble adjusting: "I feel out-of-place in 1976! The world's so strange and new to me that I might as well be on Mars." Yet Steve becomes Diana's partner, helping her bring down super-villain "Emperor Maximus" and signing up for the organization "Spy on Spy." He disguises himself as "Steve Howard," bringing him momentarily closer to Diana as they laugh over the difficulties of secret identities (Maggin, "Maximus").

Most letters were positive about the new Steve. Tony Edwards wrote that "...in his new incarnation he has really become an asset to the comic. He's independent without being foolhardy or chauvinistic." In the same page, Bob Rodi raved "THIS is Steve Trevor? Steve was one of the most irritating, annoying, nerve-grating characters in DC's history, but death and the knowledge gained while in that state must have changed him. He is a gentle, devoted, maybe over-amorous companion for Di." In the next issue, Rodi enthused that "...the romance that was so rancid between Wonder Woman and Major

Trevor works beautifully between just-plain Diana and just-plain Steve... Steve's personality has changed, but though he's no longer obnoxious or egotistical, he's still the same man — a mover, a doer, a man who thinks on his feet."

These promising developments were abruptly interrupted by a change of setting from the contemporary Earth-1 to the Earth-2 of World War II. An unsigned editorial comment in #233 (Jul. 1977) explained this as a commercial decision, driven by a desire to make the comics version compatible with the television incarnation. Some readers hated to see the more modern version of the Steve-Diana relationship abandoned. Carol Strickland wrote in #235 (Sep. 1977): "You have reduced the symbol of modern womanhood to a tried and true 1950s-1960s version: that of being the perpetual Steve Trevor rescuer." Robin Smith was more conciliatory in #237 (Nov. 1977), writing

> it's nice to see the original Amazon Princess of the television show resurrected, but the Wonder Woman of Earth-1 was just getting interesting... She was a heroine of OUR time... Long live Princess Diana! The symbol of independent womanhood, crusader of human rights, champion of justice, model of mercy, tower of strength, and fountain of kindness.

Although the World War II stories certainly backed away from the contemporary feminism of the previous years, they were not without glimmers of sisterhood. The Golden Age setting allowed for the re-introduction of Wonder Woman's friend Etta Candy as a roommate and work buddy. The rhetoric of feminist Amazonian philosophy re-appeared with veteran writer Gerry Conway, who took up scripting duties in 1977. In his version, Wonder Woman is given to exclamations like "in the name of womanhood!" in issue #233 (Jul. 1977) (Conway, "Seadeath") and dealing with openly expressed sexism from none of other than General McArthur in #237 (Nov. 1977) (Conway, "The Secret"). If not exactly a Second Wave feminist, she was at least recognizably the Golden Age proto-feminist that Steinem *et al* had praised in 1972. And the editorial staff were still willing to defend their feminism from accusations of misandry. When fan Mark Rogers, writing in issue #240, referred to Wonder Woman's "man-hating tendencies," the letter column editor was quick to correct him:

> One thing that we have dwelled upon is that the AMAZING AMAZON does NOT hate men! None of the Amazons do and their culture is not based on that at all. Actually the Amazons (and Wonder Woman) hate the VIOLENCE perpetuated by men and their wars. It is the love of mankind (or HUMANKIND) if you will) that prompted the Amazons to send PRINCESS DIANA to the outside world in the first place! [Feb. 1978].

When the comic book returned to present-day storylines in 1978, some readers hoped to see more of the egalitarian Steve. As Harvey Walker asked in April 1978: "...when (and where?) are we going to learn the fate of such things as Steve Trevor Howard's identity problem and Diana Prince's relationship with her brought-back-to-life boyfriend?" But it was not to be. Reintroduced in issue #245, in issue #248 the modern Steve was abruptly kidnapped, tortured, and murdered via the draining of the mystic power Aphrodite had used to resurrect him. A note on the letters page told readers "we're pretty confident that we'll not see him here again" (Harris, "The Crypt"). A follow-up story in *Adventure Comics* #460 made it clear this was final; after a trip to the land of the dead, Diana learns that Steve's soul is not there, but has been placed "among the stars" as a tribute from the gods (Harris, "The Quest").

The comic also turned away from the mid–70s emphasis on sisterhood. In issue #250 (Dec. 1978), a reader asked about an all-female super hero team; the editorial response explained "we could hardly expect her to join an American organization that excluded men." It was an odd conclusion to reach about a character who was accustomed to life on an all-female island. But then again, the Amazons as depicted in the late 1970s were hardly paragons of sisterhood. A multi-issue story arc undertaken under editor Ross Andru showed the Amazons jealous of each other's power (#250–251) and going mad *(#252–253)*, less sisterly feminists than stereotypically "crazy" and "jealous" women. The Amazon-centric stories, which portrayed the ancient warriors in chainmail bras and diaphanous skirts that revealed their buttocks and breasts, led M. L. Fennessy to ask in issue #252 (Feb. 1978) whether the point was sexual titillation: "it seemed that [artist] Mr. Whitman and his friends have this thing for skimpy and see-through clothing ... that seemed to be the main purpose behind the whole story." Or, as Sarah Finnegan noted in issue #256 (Jun. 1979): "Those practically bare battle outfits may look revealing and sexy, but personally I'd be wary of wearing an outfit that did not give full protection." Even the title character was not immune to increasingly blatant sexual objectification; issue #251 (Jan. 1979)'s opening panel was a full-page, close-up illustration of Wonder Woman's star-spangled buttocks.

But it was not yet the end for feminist themes in Wonder Woman. When Gerry Conway returned to the comic in issue #259 (Sep. 1979), he undertook a multi-issue story arc that re-established the old Marston paradigm of the Amazons as peace-loving servants of Aphrodite, battling the strife set out by the god Mars. Although his Diana is restless, rejecting a would-be suitor and unhappy at her work in the UN, he attributes this not to loneliness, but to an increasingly sharp values conflict with "Man's World"; it is not that she is a complete pacifist, but that she has "reflexes and instincts born on Paradise Island ... where skill is everything and brute force always a last resort!"(Conway, "A Power"). Echoing the feminist ideal described by Joanna Edgar's 1972

Ms. editorial, Conway described an Amazon in #264 (Feb. 1980) as "many things, but at the core, she is a woman triumphant. A woman free of society's limiting expectations, a woman totally fulfilled in her womanhood."

Conway even brought back Steve Trevor, thanks to DC's infinite "alternate dimensions." A Steve Trevor from one of these alternate worlds crash-landed on Paradise Island just after Diana lost her previous memories of Steve, thanks to the mysterious "mists of Nephilim." Even for comic book readers, this was a little contrived. Robert L. Hoffman, II, asked on the letters page of #276 (Feb. 1981): "Could you do me a favor and lend me the mists of Napalm or whatever you call them so I could forget Wonder Woman #271?" This Steve Trevor, an Air Force colonel once again, does not know Wonder Woman's secret identity as his colleague, Air Force Major Diana Prince; this dynamic, with Steve as Diana's superior officer and unaware of her secret identity, negated some of the egalitarian possibilities in their relationship. But the Air Force setting allowed Conway to re-introduce Etta Candy as a female friend, one whom Diana supports in the feminist goal of accepting herself as she is, rather than on "externals" (Conway, "Seek"). Conway also revived Golden Age character General Darnell, who in the 1940s had an unrequited crush on Diana Prince; re-interpreted through a modern lens, this became sexual harassment, unwelcome in the modern workplace (Conway, "The Strange"). Conway's Steve Trevor begins by feeling openly inferior to Wonder Woman, but finally comes a very modern conclusion about his feelings: "[it's] my problem, not yours. I love you, Angel. I never want to lose you. If that means I have to change, then I guess I'll change" (Conway, "Dragon").

Some fans responded with enthusiasm to this self-reflective Steve Trevor. Of the four letters published in April 1982's issue, three praised the dialogue in #285. Fred Grandinetti thought the romance was "finally progressing realistically, with both presenting honest emotions concerning 'who protects who.' And I was glad to see Steve help Wonder Woman." As Starla Ryan put it: "They work well together, functioning as a team" (*Wonder Woman* #290 Apr. 1982). *Wonder Woman's* readership was not uniformly positive about Conway's feminism, however. Reader Dan Beck reacted to Conway's re-assertion of feminist themes with extraordinary hostility:

> I have been reading WONDER WOMAN since the late '50s and I am sick and tired of her moaning and whining about men and her self-righteous belief that women are superior. Does Gerry Conway really believe what he wrote in 278? ... I don't mind a writer using her to make statements about equality for women, as long as the statements are not asinine, militant, or extremist in nature....Wonder Woman's inability or lack of desire to see life from a male point of view, or at least try to understand it, makes her the personification of all the inequalities of males and females. She is an exam-

ple of what neither sex should be like. But over the years, and especially in the past few, she seems to state (and teach young people?) that the female point of view is the only one to consider and the only one to contain any elements of sanity.

Beck's anti-feminist letter, which also defended General Darnell's sexual harassment, must have been discouraging for those supportive of the comic's direction. But Beck was not alone; in fact, the politics and culture of the United States were being caught up in a significant backlash against feminism as the 1970s turned into the 1980s. As Susan Faludi writes:

> Just when the "gender gap" surfaced in the voting booth in 1980, and women in politics began to talk of capitalizing on it, the Republican party elevated Ronald Reagan and both political parties began to shut women's rights off their platforms. Just when support for feminism and the Equal Rights Amendment reached a record high in 1981, the amendment was defeated the following year. Just when women were starting to mobilize against battering and sexual assaults, the federal government stalled funding for battered-women's programs, defeated bills to fund shelters, and shut down its Office of Domestic Violence — only two years after opening it in 1979 [Faludi xix].

The backlash became increasingly visible in *Wonder Woman.* Roy Thomas, who took over writing duties in 1981, toned down Conway's feminist-inspired re-interpretations of the Golden Age. Thomas was not hostile to women's advancement; his wife, Dann, co-wrote *Wonder Woman* #300 (Feb. 1983) and became the first woman to receive a writing credit on the comic (Thomas 1999). He also scripted *Wonder Woman* #288 (Feb. 1982) in which Wonder Woman changed her costume to include a W as a symbol for all women, in aid of the real-life Wonder Woman foundation charity for women. But Thomas' scripts tended to accept rather than challenge the dynamics of the 1940s. Under Thomas, Diana also helped Etta police her weight, rather than encourage healthier self-esteem in *Wonder Woman* #291 (May 1982). And General Darnell's unwanted attention to Diana became nothing more than a nuisance to be smiled at in *Wonder Woman* #294 (Aug. 1982).

Perhaps the peak of this ambivalence came in 1983, with Wonder Woman's 300th issue. Co-scripted by Roy and Dann, the multi-chaptered story centered around Wonder Woman finally accepting Steve Trevor's marriage proposal, but dreaming of various "alternate" histories for herself. Significantly, in none of these does Wonder Woman exist without a love interest. Perhaps equally significantly, even in her real-life timeline, she is never honest with Steve about her double identity; this causes Steve to leave her at the altar, explaining that he has unexamined feelings for Diana Prince. While love and marriage are certainly compatible with feminism, it seems significant that all of the stories in this landmark issue revolved around her relationship rather than her heroism. Importantly, 1983 also saw the beginnings of the popular American news media's obsession with the alleged miseries of single women. As Susan Faludi puts it, "The headlines spoke bleakly of THE SAD PLIGHT OF SINGLE WOMEN, THE TERMINALLY SINGLE WOMAN, and SINGLE SHOCK. To be unwed and female was to succumb to an illness with only one known cure: marriage" (Faludi 97).

For Wonder Woman, the alternative scenarios in #300 where she ends up single are bleak indeed; she is either evil (one story), or unhappy (two stories). Marriage is not easy either. One alternative dreamworld presents her in a presumably equal marriage to Superman in which both are aware of the other's secret identity. It ends in failure, as the pressures of their mutual careers doom their relationship. The Sandman also appears as a super-powered hero who is aware of Diana's secrets, but he is revealed to have been stalking her in her dreams. He admits that his predation was not "decent," and it hardly stands as a model of a healthy egalitarian relationship. On the other hand, the honest and open marriage of Earth-2 Wonder Woman and Steve Trevor, is clearly portrayed as a happy match (and one in which Steve cooks); whether the main timeline's Steve and Diana can ever achieve such openness is left unresolved at the end of the comic.

The ambivalence towards feminist perspectives continued in the Dan Mishkin-penned #301 and #302 as jealous Amazons battled each other over long-dead secrets. But ambivalence turned to outright hostility under the editorship of Ernie Colon, who took over the book in #304 (Jun. 1983). Although claiming to be "awed" by Diana in the first issue he edited, he also wrote long editorial comments openly hostile to the radical gender ideas of her creator, selectively quoting Marston in his "Thought for the Day" in order to argue with a strawman representation of Marston's gender theories: "I'm sorry, Doctor, but women are not superior to men." He continued this practice of choosing nominally feminist "Thoughts for the Day" only to knock them down, calling Susan B. Anthony "trite" in #308 and panning Ibsen in #306 (Oct. 1983):

> I don't buy it. Men and Women understand each other perfectly. But, like brothers or sisters, they insist on their own individuality, and well they should. This works just fine — with men and women of good will. Not every woman is fair game for the Advance, the move. I call women my sisters, and try to treat them as such. It certainly simplifies things for me. And women should help their brothers to be better men. What is a better man? Who has to ask that of a caring brother or father?

Colon's re-framing of sexism as a matter for individuals to work out, rather than a systemic problem to be addressed by social means, completely rejected the previous decade of the comics' engagement with patriarchy. But it was most definitely in tune with fan letters like Francis Herzberg's in #313 (Mar. 1984), who, apparently encouraged by Colon's antifeminist backlash, argued that "[a]nti-male propaganda is everywhere. Now is not the time to force it down children's throats, to indoctrinate them as they read. You, Mr. Colon, I know are very aware of the harm... A recent editorial showed you were not in favor of the current sex war... I am asking you that emphasis is moved away from antimale statements..."

While the letters to the letter page do not represent any kind of scientific sample, they certainly provide a look at how the editorial teams chose to represent reader opinion. By this measure, it is striking how much pro-feminist letters waxed in the early 1970s as Wonder Woman gained attention from prominent Second Wave feminists, and waned in the early 1980s, supplanted by letters openly hostile to feminism. Similarly, storylines fluctuated, embracing feminist critiques of patriarchal patterns in the mid–1970s, but abandoning those critiques in the early 1980s. Diana's relationship to the frequently-resurrected Steve Trevor, with its shifting portrayals of heterosexual egalitarianism, provides one of the most obvious measures of this changing feminist perspective. The inconsistency of Bronze Age *Wonder Woman* reflects a wider struggle in the media between the traditions of American patriarchy and the feminist promise of Paradise Island.

NOTE

1. For another interpretation of this event, see Paul R. Kohl's essay in this collection.

WORKS CITED

Bates, Cary (w), and John Rosenberger (p) and Vince Colletta (i). "Amazon Attack Against Atlantis." *Wonder Woman* Vol. 1 #215 (Dec.-Jan. 1974/75). New York: National Periodical Publications.

Beck, Dan. Letter. "Wonder Words." *Wonder Woman* Vol. 1 #284 (Oct. 1979). New York: DC Comics.

Bleau, Mrs. Elizabeth. Letter. "Wonder Woman's Write-In." *Wonder Woman* Vol. 1 #201 (Jul.-Aug. 1972). New York: National Periodical Publications.

Chesler, Phyllis. Interpretive Essay. Introduction. *Wonder Woman.* By William Moulton Marston (w) and Harry G. Peter (a). New York: Bonanza, 1972.

Colon, Ernie. Column. "Wonder Words." *Wonder Woman* Vol. 1 #304 (Jun. 1984). New York: DC Comics.

Colon, Ernie. Column. "Wonder Words." *Wonder Woman* Vol. 1 #306 (Aug. 1984). New York: DC Comics.

Colon, Ernie. Column. "Wonder Words." *Wonder Woman* Vol. 1 #308 (Oct. 1984). New York: DC Comics.

Conway, Gerry (w), and Don Heck and Vince Coletta (a). "Seadeath!" *Wonder Woman* Vol. 1 #233 (Jul. 1977). New York: DC Comics.

Conway, Gerry (w), and Jose Delbo (p) and Dave Hunt (i). "Dragon Hunt." *Wonder Woman* Vol. 1 # 285 (Nov. 1981). New York: DC Comics.

_____. "The Strange Disappearance of Etta Candy." *Wonder Woman* Vol. 1 #279 (May 1981). New York: DC Comics.

Conway, Gerry (w), and Jose Delbo and Joe Gielle (a). "Seek the Serpent, Find Death." *Wonder Woman* Vol. 1 #276 (Feb. 1981). New York: DC Comics.

Conway, Gerry (w), and Jose Delbo and Vince Coletta (a). "A Bomb in the Bird is Worth Two in the Band." *Wonder Woman* Vol. 1 #264 (Feb. 1980). New York: DC Comics.

_____. "A Power Gone Mad." *Wonder Woman* Vol. 1 #259 (Sep. 1979). New York: DC Comics. Print.

_____. "The Secret Origin of Wonder Woman." *Wonder Woman* Vol. 1 #237 (Nov. 1977). New York: DC Comics.

Delaney, Samuel R. (w), and Dick Giordano (a). "The Grandee Caper." *Wonder Woman* Vol. 1 #203 (Nov.-Dec. 1972). New York: National Periodical.

Edgar, Joanne. "'Wonder Woman' Revisited." *Ms.*, Jul. 1, 1972, 52–55.

Edwards, Tony. Letter. "Wonder Words." *Wonder Woman* Vol. 1 #226 (Oct.-Nov. 1976). New York: National Periodical.

Faludi, Susan. *Backlash: The Undeclared War Against American Women.* New York and London: Anchor/Doubleday, 1991.

Fennessy, M. L. Letter. "Wonder Words." *Wonder Woman* Vol. 1 #252 (Feb. 1979). New York: DC Comics.

Finnegan, Sarah. Letter. "Wonder Words." *Wonder Woman* Vol. 1 #256 (Jun. 1979). New York: DC Comics.

Forfreedom, Ann. Letter. "Wonder Words." *Wonder Woman* Vol. 1 #212 (Jun.-Jul. 1974). New York: National Periodical.

Grandinetti, Frank. Letter. "Wonder Words." *Wonder Woman* #290 (Apr. 1982). New York: DC Comics.

Hanley, Tim. "The Women Behind Wonder Woman." DC Women Kicking Ass. Jun. 20, 2012. Oct. 5, 2012. http://dcwomenkickingass.tumblr.com/.

Harlee, Elizabeth. Letter. "Wonder Words." *Wonder Woman* Vol. 1 #214 (Oct.-Nov. 1974). New York: National Periodical.

Harris, Jack C. (w), and Jack Abel (a). "The Quest for the Stolen Soul." *Adventure Comics* #460 (Nov.-Dec. 1978). New York: DC Comics.

Harris, Jack C. (w), and Jose Delbo (p) and Frank Chiaramonte (i). "Spirit of Silver ... Soul of Gold." *Wonder Woman* Vol. 1 #253 (Mar. 1979). New York: DC Comics.

Harris, Jack C. (w), and Jose Delbo and Joe Giella (a). "The Crypt of the Dark Commander." *Wonder Woman* Vol. 1 #248 (Oct. 1978). New York: DC Comics.

Harris, Jack C. (w), and Jose Delbo and Joe Giella (a). "The Empress of the Silver Snake." *Wonder Woman* Vol. 1 #252 (Feb. 1979). New York: DC Comics.

Harris, Jack C. (w), and Jose Delbo and Joe Giella (a). "Tournament." *Wonder Woman* Vol. 1 #250 (Dec. 1978). New York: DC Comics.

Harris, Jack C. (w), and Jose Delbo and Vince Colletta (a). "The Name Is Wonder Woman!" *Wonder Woman* Vol. 1 #251 (Jan. 1979). New York: DC Comics.

Harris, Jack C. (w), Jose Delbo (p) and Vince Coletta (i). "Vengeance from Ice and Fire." *Wonder Woman* Vol. 1 #245 (Jul. 1978). New York: DC Comics.

Herzberg, Francis. Letter. "Wonder Words." *Wonder Woman* #313 (Mar. 1984). New York: DC Comics.

Hoffman, Robert II. Letter. "Wonder Words." *Wonder Woman* #276 (Feb. 1981). New York: DC Comics.

Kanigher, Robert (w), and Don Heck and Bob Oksner (a). "Target Wonder Woman." *Wonder Woman* Vol. 1 #205 (Mar.-Apr. 1973). New York: National Periodical.

Letter. "Wonder Words." *Wonder Woman* Vol. 1 #221 (Dec. 1975-Jan. 1976). New York: National Periodical.

Maggin, Eliot S. (w), and Curt Swan and Phil Zupa (a). "Wish Upon a Star." *Wonder Woman* Vol. 1 #214 (Oct.-Nov. 1974). New York: National Periodical.

Maggin, Elliot S. (w), John Rosenberger (p), and Vince Colletta (i). "A Paradise in Peril." *Wonder Woman* Vol. 1 #216 (Feb.-Mar. 1975). New York: National Periodical.

Maggin, Elliot S. (w), Jose Delbo (p) and Vince Colletta (i). "Maximus, Emperor of Hollow Mountain." *Wonder Woman* Vol. 1 # 225 (Aug.-Sep. 1976). New York: National Periodical.

Millett, Kate. *Sexual Politics*. Champaign: University of Illinois Press, 1970.

Mishkin, Dan (w), Gene Colon (p) and Frank McLaughlin (i). "Dark Challenger." *Wonder Woman* Vol. 1 #301 (Mar. 1983). New York: DC Comics.

_____. "Victory!" *Wonder Woman* Vol. 1 #302 (Apr. 1983). New York: DC Comics.

Morse, Betsy. Letter. "Wonder Words." *Wonder Woman* Vol. 1. #206 (Oct.-Nov. 1974). New York: National Periodical.

O'Neill, Dennis. Column. "Wonder Woman's Write-In." *Wonder Woman* Vol. 1 #199 (Jul.-Aug. 1972). New York: National Periodical.

O'Neill, Dennis. Comment. "Princessions." *Wonder Woma*n Vol. 1 #203 (Nov.-Dec. 1972). New York: National Periodical.

O'Neill, Dennis (w), Mike Sekowsky (p) and Dick Gordiano (i). "Wonder Woman's Last Battle." *Wonder Woman* Vol. 1 #179 (Nov. 1968). New York: National Periodical.

_____. "The Wrath of Dr. Cyber." *Wonder Woman* Vol. 1 #197 (Dec. 1971). New York: National Periodical.

Pasko, Martin. Column. "Wonder Words." *Wonder Woman* Vol. 1 #212 (Jun.-Jul. 1974). New York: National Periodical.

Pasko, Martin (w), Curt Swan and Vince Collette (a). "The Fiend with the Face of Glass." *Wonder Woman* Vol. 1 #221 (Jan. 1976). New York: National Periodical.

_____. "World of Enslaved Women." *Wonder Woman* Vol. 1 #219 (Aug.-Sep. 1975). New York: National Periodical.

_____. "Wonder Woman vs. the United States." *Wonder Woman* Vol. 1 #224 (Jun.-Jul. 1976). New York: National Periodical.

Pasko, Martin (w), and Dick Gordano (a). "The Man Who Wiped Out Time." *Wonder Woman* Vol. 1 #220 (Oct.-Nov. 1975). New York: National Periodical.

Pignataro, Anthony J. Letter. "Wonder Words." *Wonder Woman* Vol. 1 #251 (Jan. 1979). New York: DC Comics.

Purchase, Tom. Letter. "Wonder Words." *Wonder Woman* Vol. 1. 212 (Jun.-Jul. 1974). New York: National Periodical.

Robinson, Bob. Letter. "Wonder Words." *Wonder Woman* Vol. 1 #222 (Feb.-Mar. 1976). New York: National Periodical.

Rodi, Bob. Letter. "Wonder Words." *Wonder Woman* Vol. 1 #226 (Oct.-Nov. 1976). New York: National Periodical.

_____. Letter. "Wonder Words." *Wonder Woman* Vol. 1 #227 (Dec. 1976-Jan. 1977). New York: National Periodical.

Rosen, Ruth. *The World Split Open: How the Modern Woman's Movement Changed America*. New York: Penguin, 2001.

Rozakis, Bob. Comment. "Wonder Words." *Wonder Woman* Vol. 1 #222 (Feb.-Mar. 1976). New York: National Periodical.

_____. Column. "Wonder Words." *Wonder Woman* Vol. 1 #225 (Aug.-Sep. 1976). New York: National Periodical.

Ryan, Stella. Letter. "Wonder Words." *Wonder Woman* #290 (Apr. 1982). New York: DC Comics.

Schowdowski, Victoria. Letter. "Wonder Words." *Wonder Woman* #264 (Feb. 1980). New York: DC Comics.

Spears, Margie. Letter. "Wonder Words." *Wonder Woman* Vol. 1 #214 (Oct.-Nov. 1974). New York: National Periodical.

Smith, Robin. Letter. "Wonder Words." *Wonder Woman* #237 (Nov. 1977). New York: DC Comics.

Steinem, Gloria. Introduction. *Wonder Woman.* By William Moulton Marston (w) and Harry G. Peter (a). New York: Bonanza, 1972.

Strickland, Carol. Letter. "Wonder Words." *Wonder Woman* Vol. 1 #235 (Sep. 1977). New York: DC Comics.

Thomas, Dann, and Roy Thomas (w) and Ross Andru, Rich Buckler, Gene Colon, Jan Duuserma, Dick Giordano, Larry Mahlstadt, Tom Mandrake, Frank McLaughlin and Keith Pollard (a). "Beautiful Dreamer, Death Unto Thee!" *Wonder Woman* Vol. 1 #300 (Feb. 1983). New York: DC Comics.

Thomas, Roy. "The Secret Origins of Infinity, Inc." *Alter Ego* Vol. 3 #1 (Summer 1999). Raleigh, NC: TwoMorrows.

Thomas, Roy (w), Gene Colon (p) and Frank McLaughlin (i). "Rampage." *Wonder Woman* Vol. 1 #292 (Aug. 1982). New York: DC Comics.

Thomas, Roy (w), Gene Colon (p) and Romeo Tanghal (i). "Swan Song." *Wonder Woman* Vol. 1 #288 (Feb. 1982). New York: DC Comics.

Taylor, Scott R. Letter. "Wonder Words." *Wonder Woman* Vol. 1 #222 (Mar. 1976). New York: National Periodical.

Walker, Harvey. Letter. "Wonder Words." *Wonder Woman* Vol. 1 #242 (Apr. 1978). New York: National Periodical.

Wein, Len (w), Curt Swan (p) and Tex Blaisdell (i). "The Man Who Mastered Women." *Wonder Woman* Vol. 1 #212 (Jun.-Jul. 1974). New York: National Periodical.

"Wonder Words." *Wonder Woman* Vol. 1 # 233 (Jul. 1977). New York: DC Comics.

"Wonder Words." *Wonder Woman* Vol. 1 #240 (Feb. 1978). New York: DC Comics.

"Wonder Words." *Wonder Woman* Vol. 1 #249 (Nov. 1978). New York: DC Comics.

"Wonder Words." *Wonder Woman* Vol. 1 #250 (Dec. 1978). New York: DC Comics.

Working Girl

Diana Prince and the
Crisis of Career Moves

MATTHEW J. SMITH

Although a succession of comic book creators have helped define Wonder Woman as the pre-eminent super-heroine, these men and women have struggled to cast her alter ego of Diana Prince in a consistently meaningful career. While Clark Kent works for the news media in each iteration of the Superman mythos and Bruce Wayne is portrayed as a wealthy playboy ruse for the Batman, Wonder Woman's alter ego has struggled to chart a consistent career path through her seven decades of publication. She has, for example, had positions as a military officer and a diplomat as well truly off beat roles as a fashion boutique owner and a fast food server. Her job hopping — especially in comparison to the stability of her peers in DC's "Trinity" — begs the question: Why has DC Comics struggled to settle Diana into a vocation when her male counterparts seem so content in theirs?

This chapter will survey changes from across Diana's spotty resume, from her first career moves (from princess to nurse to secretary — all within the first three issues of *Sensation Comics*) to her most recent role as an agent for the Department of Metahuman Affairs. Particular scrutiny will be applied to one transition in Diana's struggle, namely her brief stint as an astronaut trainee in 1979. This move came on the heels of the real world announcement from the National Aeronautics and Space Administration (NASA) in 1978 that a group of female astronauts would be training for the space program. This career choice, like most of Diana's jobs, involves some connection to government service (often, but not always the United States government), and this connection invites some deeper probing. Of course, at issue here are fundamental questions about female representation in the media, particularly with the depiction of how women identify, maintain, and succeed at careers outside the domestic sphere.

"I've Been ... Trying to Find a *New Reason* for Remaining in Man's World"[1]

As a member of DC Comics' A-List "Trinity," Wonder Woman is certainly a high profile figure, and yet the most inconsistent of the three in terms of career commitment. Superman, in his alter ego of Clark Kent, is perennially cast as a reporter. Any change is his employment typically isn't a change in his career, though. For example, after Kent had served as a reporter for great metropolitan newspapers for more than three decades, writer Dennis O'Neil looked to shake up Superman's status quo by transitioning him from working as a reporter in print at the Daily Planet to broadcasting for WGBS-TV ("Superman"). Another, more recent high profile split from the Daily Planet has landed with Kent working as a freelance blogger — but still reporting (Lobdell)! As a member of the fourth estate, Kent is a watchdog for abuses of those in power, a role that is entirely consistent with the vision laid out by his creators, Jerry Siegel and Joe Shuster.

The Batman is almost as consistent in his role as Bruce Wayne. Although depicted as a foppish playboy for much of his career, in recent years Wayne has been depicted as taking a more actively role in the management of the philanthropic Wayne Foundation and the corporate Wayne Enterprises. Certainly, this involvement reaches its pinnacle when Wayne publicly launches the Batman, Inc. initiative, acknowledging his role in funding the Batman's crime fighting mission (Morrison). Batman is the opposite of Superman; Wayne is in the elite compared to Kent's working class, the dark to his light. Their shared dichotomy leaves open an undefined role for the third member of the troika. And so, while Diana has demonstrated the ability to secure and hold on to a job — sometime for decades at a time — she has not demonstrated the same consistency and devotion to one career in her alter ego as her peers over the span of her adventures. Quite the contrary, the career choices made by Diana have sometimes been mercurial, problematizing her status as a role model for women readers. And the crux of this line of analysis lies in the presumption that what a hero does for a living — besides being a hero — matters. And it must, for all of the choices our heroes make speak to their character and values. Their vocation is an indication of their virtue and itself an inspiration. Hence, I would assert writers cannot leave Bruce Wayne an indolent playboy as creator Bob Kane had originally envisioned — for the temptation to make him a double do-gooder is just too strong to ignore. What, then, do Wonder Woman's career choices say about her?

Arguably, besides her role as a superhero, Wonder Woman has been consistent in one other role, that of princess of the Amazons. However, while princess may be her title, it is rarely depicted as her vocation. Save perhaps for those occasions where she dutifully leads armies of her fellow Amazons into battle, the adult Diana shies away from royal matters, most especially any that demand presiding over court. That precedent is firmly established by Wonder Woman's creator, Dr. William Moulton Marston, who writes at the conclusion of her very first story in *Sensation Comics* #1 (Jan. 1942): "And so Diana, the Wonder Woman, giving up her heritage, and her right to eternal life, leaves Paradise Island to take the man she loves back to America — the land she learns to love and protect, and adopts as her own!" (Moulton, "Wonder Woman" 9). I have previously examined the issue of cultural assimilation reflected in this statement elsewhere (Smith), but the point I wish to make here is that this statement directs the character away from a "heritage" of royalty and towards America, a land known for opening opportunity for the self-made individual. The question for Diana, then, is what to make of herself.

"Diana Prince Has an *Unusual* Record"[2]

While Clark Kent and Bruce Wayne have remained rooted in their original positions, Diana Prince has adopted careers that more readily reflect the times and challenges of a given period of history. For the first quarter century of publication, Diana maintains a rather stable association with the military, although in more than one role. Upon arriving in the outside world in *Sensation Comics* #1 (Jan. 1942), Diana purchases the credentials and role of army nurse Diana Prince in order to be near to a convalescing Steve Trevor. Nursing was certainly a credible position for women to occupy at the time, but just two issues later she is already making her next career move. As Steve returns full time to military intelligence, Diana begs to remain near to him. He capitulates by recommending her for a new position with his boss, Colonel Darnell, to serve as his secretary and assistant throughout the Golden Age and beyond. Diana's second career is also in keeping with expectations for women at the time, and her penchant for secretarial work also lands Wonder Woman a position of secretary with her allies in the Justice Society of America. At the dawn of the Silver Age, writer Robert Kanigher cast Diana as military officer in her own right, having earned a commission as a lieutenant and conveniently assigned to be Steve Trevor's assistant (*Wonder Woman* Vol. 1 #99 Jul. 1958). Although Kanigher's promotion may have come more than a decade after the Women's Armed Services Integration Act of 1948 allowed women to enlist in the military, it did punctuate that more significant opportunities had opened for women.

In all, Diana's initial military association lasted from 1942 until 1968, a period of time accounting for World War II and the Cold War when the military's role in defense of the nation was perceived highly favorably. To have a patriotically-garbed heroine like Wonder Woman affiliated with defense forces affirmed her legitimacy as a defender of the status quo. Of course, a role in the highly regimented military was also somewhat consistent with certain tenants of Marston's own philosophical ideas. He held unorthodox views about submission to "loving authority" where men would abdicate to women (Daniels). The patriarchal military certainly wasn't a model for that, but it did have a brand of authoritarian structure that resonated with Marston's own vision of following orders.

But even as the nation's confidence in its militant mission shuttered under the strain of the Vietnam Conflict, Diana's affiliation with the military also retreated. In *Wonder Woman* #178 (Sep.-Oct. 1968), she discards her military uniform and in the next issue takes ownership of a fashion boutique. The issue after that Steve Trevor's murder completes Diana's separation from the military (*Wonder Woman* Vol. 1 #180 Jan.-Feb. 1969). Writer Dennis O'Neil believed he was liberating Diana from a subservient role in the military by transforming her into an independent entrepreneur (Greenberger), abandoning both costume and superpowers to make Diana an "everywoman" who could be the *wonder* in *Wonder Woman* herself. Yet the so-called "mod" era proved to be an experience that last just four years.

Wonder Woman would maintain distance from the military in her next career move but re-allied herself with a governing entity, seeking employment at the United Nations beginning in *Wonder Woman* #204 (Jan.-Feb. 1973). Using her mastery of languages, Diana is first employed as a tour guide at the U.N. Building and then shortly thereafter recruited to serve in a more exciting role with the "U.N. Crisis Bureau," a trouble-shooting agency of the peacekeeping organization in *Wonder Woman* #212 (Jun.-Jul. 1974). Diana eventually steps back from that role to be reassigned to work on the U.N.'s public relations in *Wonder Woman* #225 (Aug.-Sep. 1976). She resigns from the U.N. altogether in *Wonder Woman* #248 (Oct. 1978). In the post–Vietnam era, Diana's choice to join the world's premiere peacekeeping organization reflected a tepid attitude towards the U.S. government and military. However, the constant change in that affiliation suggests that writers could not quite find a proper fit for such a patriotically potent icon in a multi-national organization. After all, Wonder Woman was back to wearing the stars and stripes throughout this period.

Diana's next career turn maintained a distance from the military, although it moved her back into a connection with the United States, as she joined the government-financed NASA as a civilian astronaut trainee in *Wonder Woman*

#251 (Jan. 1979). This would prove to be one of Diana's briefest career moves, as she resigned just six issues later in *Wonder Woman* #256 (Jun. 1979). Diana's next two career moves would oddly see her retrace her previous career steps. First she briefly returned to the U.N. working for a relief office, though quickly abandoned that position within a year. Then in the most surprising reversal of all, she returned to the military. However, this time she was a captain in the United State Air Force, working for the "Special Assignments Branch" within the Pentagon under Colonel Steve Trevor and General Phillip Darnell in *Wonder Woman* #272 (Oct. 1980). The move presaged Ronald Reagan's 1980 election as president and the return to prominence of American military respectability. Reagan was a military hawk who backed an expanded military, particularly to face down America's communist Cold War adversaries, and advocated renewed pride in America after the bruising experience of Vietnam. Coincidentally, Diana would remain in the military well into the Reagan era, continuing on for the next five years until the first volume of her comic book series would draw to a conclusion in early 1986.

When the second volume of Wonder Woman's adventures was launched in 1987, Diana back story was revamped and she was recast in the role of her people's ambassador to the outside world. In the rebooted continuity, Diana aimed for peace even though she was a trained warrior. As emissary to "patriarch's world," she was charged by her gods to spread Amazon virtues of peaceful co-existence. She would maintain this ambassadorial role as her primary occupation over the next two decades until her second volume concluded in 2006. Storylines sometime dictated that she take on additional jobs, such as working as a food service employee at a Taco Whiz to help raise rent money in *Wonder Woman* Vol. 2 #76 (Apr. 1993) or using her knowledge of Greco-Roman mythology as a lecturer at the Gateway City Museum of Cultural Antiquities in *Wonder Woman* Vol. 2 #105 (Jan. 1996). For a time, beginning in *Wonder Woman* Vol. 2 #127 (Nov. 1997), Diana was even transfigured into the Goddess of Truth and took a role in the Greek Pantheon before surrendering her godhood and returning to her mission among mortals in *Wonder Woman* Vol. 2 #139 (Dec. 1998). Diana's role as a diplomat reflected a wider acknowledgment of geopolitics, something particularly pertinent in the wake of the Soviet Union's collapse and the rise of America as the world's sole superpower. The post–9/11 world, however, called the unassailability of that superpower status into question.

Eventually, Diana stepped out of her role as public peacemaker and turned once more to the world of intelligence. At the launch of her third volume of adventures, Diana took another government job, working as an agent in the Department of Metahuman Affairs beginning with *Wonder Woman* Vol. 3 #2 (Sep. 2006). Although coming a bit later than the reorganization of U.S.

security interests under the Department of Homeland Security in the real world in 2002, the persistent issues associated with the post–9/11 bureaucracy are reflected in this move. With two wars abroad, America seemed no less certain about its security in a second term under President George W. Bush, and making the preeminent super-heroine deal with domestic security issues seemed quite timely. The focus of Diana's adventures devoted less attention to her career by the time the third volume finished. With the fourth and latest volume launched in 2011, Diana does not even seem to have any additional occupation beyond her roles as a princess to her people and a superhero in the outside world.

As Diana Prince's faux resume indicates, Diana is most often affiliated with a role with the state, be that working for intelligence in the United States' government or representing her island nation of Themyscira. Given the comparative brevity with which she occupied other positions, we could simply discount them as frustrated attempts by writers to find a distinguishing niche for Diana (Greenberger). However, to do so would ignore that fact that these efforts reflect concerns of their times (e.g., the eras of Vietnam, post–9/11). Because it directly paralleled contemporary events, Diana's brief foray into the space program would serve as a case study of the value of deeper reflection on these career shifts.

"We've ... Processed You for Acceptance as Our Newest *Astronaut*"[3]

On January 17, 1978, NASA announced that its latest class of astronaut trainees would include six women, the first women inducted into the space program since its inception eighteen years earlier (Lyons). That class would include Sally Ride, who would go on to become the first American woman in space. This progressive move by the administration must have really caught the fancy of DC Comics' editorial team, because within a year comic books featuring Diana Prince as a female astronaut recruit would be hitting newsstands across the country.

And so, shortly after separating from the U.N. at the end of 1978, Diana receives first a letter and then a follow-up visit from NASA officials responding to her application to join the astronaut trainee program. In *Wonder Woman* #252 (Feb. 1979) Diana reports for training at the Lyndon B. Johnson Space Center in Houston, Texas. There she meets her fellow trainees, a class that includes another woman, and begins training that includes briefings and physical conditioning. As Wonder Woman, she finds herself drawn into battle with Astarte, the Empress of the Silver Snake, who attacks a NASA space capsule and then a space shuttle in Earth orbit. In this issue and the next, writer Jack C. Harris makes it clear that Wonder Woman's invisible jet can reach space

Diana Prince
Themyscira House
New York, NY 10016
princess1@paradise.island

Objective

To serve and represent the state honestly and forcefully when needed

Work Experience

Nurse   December 1941–March 1942
United States Army

Secretary   March 1942–April 1958
United States Intelligence Service

Lieutenant   July 1958–October 1968
United States Military Intelligence

Owner/Operator   December 1968–August 1972
Di Prince's Boutique

Tour Guide   Feb. 1973–July 1974
United Nations Building

Special Agent   July 1974–September 1976
United Nations Crisis Bureau

Public Relations Officer   September 1976–October 1978
United Nations Special Services

Astronaut Trainee   Feb. 1980–June 1980
National Aeronautics and Space Administration

Aide Officer   July 1979–July 1980
United Nations

Captain, United States Air Force   October 1980–December 1985
Special Assignments Branch, The Pentagon

Ambassador   August 1987–March 2006
The Embassy of Themyscira

Special Agent   August 2006–January 2009
Department of Metahuman Affairs

References

General Phillip Darnell, Special Assignments Branch, The Pentagon
Dr. Helena Sandsmark, Curator, Gateway City Museum of Cultural Antiquities
Sarge Steel, Director, Department of Metahuman Affairs

and travel to the moon. Indeed, the Amazons seem to have a much more advanced space program than NASA, as a fleet of attack craft and a large transport vehicle appear (*Wonder Woman* Vol. 1 #253 Mar. 1979). Why, then, does Diana feel drawn to the more primitive work of NASA? As she explains in the next issue:

> Traveling in space is so easy for a wonder woman with a magical plane ... but I've grown to love the outside world as a *normal* woman as well — I want to succeed as Diana Prince as I would have as Wonder Woman — it's *important* to me —! [Harris, "The Angle" 8].

Even so, it takes Wonder Woman to foil the attempt of her old nemesis the Angle Man, aided by the god of war, Mars, and his cronies, from stealing and ransoming the space shuttle. New series writer Paul Levitz then has Diana attend a conference at the U.N. with her NASA superiors in *Wonder Woman* #255 (May 1979), before she returns to Houston to resume her training. Upon her return though, Wonder Woman must foil the attempt of the Royal Flush Gang from stealing secrets from NASA. In the process, though, she discovers that her fellow trainee, Mike Bailey, is a member of the gang. In frustration, she resigns from the program and returns to New York in *Wonder Woman* #256 (Jun. 1979).

And so after returning to work for the U.N. in New York, it would seem that Diana's career with NASA would be over; however, writer Gerry Conway pens "An Untold Story of *Wonder Woman's* Days with *NASA!*" appearing in *Wonder Woman* #265 (Mar. 1980) and #266 (Apr. 1980). In this two-part story Diana is assigned to pilot a shuttle mission, although, curiously, when Diana resigned from NASA she had only been a trainee. Her mission is interrupted, though, when the shuttle is abducted in mid-flight by a race of aliens who crash landed in the Rocky Mountains and want to study the shuttle in hopes of arranging their escape from Earth. Interestingly, then, the space shuttle factors prominently in three of the NASA storylines. It even launches in two separate stories well before the actual historical program began to send up space shuttles a year later on April 12, 1981.

Diana's move to the space program came at one of the historical high points in America's thinking about space exploration. Not only was NASA making the progressive move in gender representation by recruiting female astronauts, but the space shuttle program was on the eve of beginning its three decade odyssey. In popular culture, *Star Wars* (1977) had begun to dominate the popular imagination, and so moving the Amazing Amazon's adventures into this setting would seem to be rife with possibilities for imaginative storytelling. However, given that most of the published stories dealt repeatedly with abducting the space shuttle, not a lot of those possibilities seem to have materialized. In an interview for this essay, writer Paul Levitz agreed with the limitations and explained the quick move back to New York, "trying to get her to a place where more things were happening."

Although Diana Prince struggles to find any lasting vocation, she does seem to be attracted to working for agencies of state. And while it is understandable that Diana would be attracted to NASA as a government-sponsored program, her status there as a civilian trainee lacked the sense of authority that comes with her being a military officer or a nation's ambassador. Diana thrives best when acting as a representative of the state and not just in its employ. Perhaps that is why her roles at the U.N. changed so often and why her tenure at NASA was so brief.

"Agent Prince *Is* Good ... but She's No Wonder Woman"[4]

In seven decades of publication history, it is difficult to identify any lengthy era in which Superman does not regularly zip back into a news building to don a pair of glasses or Batman does not return to a mansion to doff his cowl, and yet Wonder Woman's refuge from the world of superheroics is far less consistent. (Even when Wonder Woman was adapted for television, she managed to have two different careers across three seasons.) This is not to take away anything from Wonder Woman's significance as a feminist icon; indeed, Diana's inability to establish a fixed career probably says more about the difficulty creators have in figuring her out than in any flaw in the character herself.

A certain dramatic tension from the contrast of their heroic persona from their alter ego seems to serve the other characters of DC's Trinity effectively. As a reporter, Clark Kent observes from an objective distance, but Superman inserts himself directly into any struggle. Kent reports the news but Superman makes the news. Meanwhile, Bruce Wayne luxuriates in a mansion at the edge of the city or in a penthouse high above, but the Batman delivers justice to the mean streets of Gotham. In her initial roles, first as a nurse and then as a secretary, Diana also provides a stark contrast to her superhero persona. Diana's initial roles call upon her to provide aid and comfort to men, but Wonder Woman kicks saboteurs' butts. As a nurse and secretary, her work exists to support Steve Trevor, but Wonder Woman is more dominant, saving Steve from getting in over his head time and again. Even when Diana settles into her role as ambassador for Themyscira for a period of time, the contrast works narratively. As ambassador she must address issues with the power of her words, but Wonder Woman is called to address conflicts with actions.

This idea also helps to explain why Diana's career with NASA was so brief. Astronauts are perceived as heroic roles in American society. Getting suited up to pilot a space shuttle is not just another day at the office. It is

nowhere near as common as being a secretary, a reporter, or even a philan-
thropist. The contrast fails because Diana doesn't need to be a hero-in-train-
ing, she already is one many times over. Compounding this lack of contrast
is author Jack C. Harris' decision to have Wonder Woman travel into space
under her own power — multiple times — in the very first storyline after joining
NASA in *Wonder Woman* #252–253 (Feb.-Mar. 1979). Such scenes undercut
the viability of what Diana might ever achieve as an astronaut, for sure, but
even if Diana were regularly scheduled for space missions, she would not be
doing anything much different from Wonder Woman. The lack of dramatic
tension doomed this career placement from the start.

The brevity of several of Diana's other positions also suffer in this way.
Working for agencies named Crisis Bureau or Department of Metahuman
Affairs would seem to offer opportunities for exciting story development, situations where Diana can get into enough trouble to justify Wonder Woman's
appearance to save the day. Yet again in these organizations what an Agent
Prince does isn't all that different from what a Wonder Woman does. After
leading a team from Department of Metahuman Affairs into a disastrous battle
against the villainous Genocide in *Wonder Woman* Vol. 3 #26 (Jan. 2009),
Diana does not return to her secret identity, even when offered the chance to
re-up by Steve Trevor in *Wonder Woman* Vol. 3 #42 (May 2010). In fact, the
succeeding two series writers do not even suggest Diana has any other job,
first in J. Michael Straczynski's year-long "Odyssey" storyline (2010–2011)
and then again in Brian Azzarello's "New 52" re-launch for *Wonder Woman*
Vol. 4 (2011-present). In fact, as of this writing in 2013, Diana hasn't been
depicted as employed since 2009. This is probably more than a symbolic nod
to the high unemployment associated with the "Great Recession," since Diana
does not seem to suffer any visible economic hardship. And it's too easy to
say that men are at fault since Diana gave up her last job — and didn't seem
all that committed to returning to it — under the guidance of long-term female
author Gail Simone.

Given her status quo as full-time hero since 2009, perhaps we should
conclude that alter egos are a trope of comics' past. Recent writers may have
concluded that rather than try yet another career for Diana — or retroactively
restore her to a subservient role in the military hierarchy — perhaps it is best
to leave the mundane behind. However, the very idea of the alter ego might
have been presented as a means to help the hero fit into society, to find a place
to belong. But it is also about the reader finding access to the hero through
their more modest connection to the rest of us. Without this everyman connection, Diana seems more distant. The continued primacy of heroes like
Superman, Batman, and even Marvel Comics' Spider-Man may be found at
least in part to their accessibility to the common reader through their alter

egos. And maybe like many other young women finding the right career path requires the exploration and experimentation that comes from trying on many jobs to find the right fit.

NOTES

1. So confesses Wonder Woman as she returns to New York and a job at the United Nations after leaving behind her role as an astronaut trainee in *Wonder Woman* Vol. 1 #257 (Jul. 1979) (Levitz 2).

2. Undersecretary Wagner, a U.N. official, explains that he has no qualms for rehiring Diana despite her uneven employment history in *Wonder Woman* Vol. 1 #257 (Jul. 1979) (Levitz, "The Case" 7).

3. Conrad Starfield from NASA welcomes Diana to the space program in *Wonder Woman* Vol. 1 #251 (Jan. 1979) (Harris, "The Empress" 7).

4. Agent Tom Tresser, Diana's partner in the Department of Metahuman Affairs, fails to connect fully the similarities between Diana and Wonder Woman in *Wonder Woman Annual* Vol. 2 #1 (Nov. 2007) (Heinberg, n.p.).

WORKS CITED

Byrne, John (w, a). "Lifelines Part One." *Wonder Woman* Vol. 2 #105 (Jan. 1996). New York: DC Comics.

_____. "Transfiguration." *Wonder Woman*. Vol. 2 #127 (Nov. 1997). New York: DC Comics.

Conway, Gerry (w), Jose Delbo (p), and Dave Hunt (i). "The Man with All the Angles." *Wonder Woman* Vol. 1 #272 (Oct. 1980). New York: DC Comics.

Conway, Gerry (w), Jose Delbo (p), and Joe Giella (i). "Land of the Scaled Gods." *Wonder Woman* Vol. 1 #265 (Mar. 1980). New York: DC Comics.

Conway, Gerry (w), Jose Delbo (p), and Vince Colletta (i). "The Uninvited." *Wonder Woman* Vol. 1 #266 (Apr. 1980). New York: DC Comics.

Daniels, Les. *Wonder Woman: The Complete History.* San Francisco: Chronicle, 2000.

Greenberger, Robert. *Wonder Woman: Amazon, Hero, Icon.* New York: Universe, 2010.

Harris, Jack C. (w), Jose Delbo (p), and Frank Chiaramonte (i). "Spirit of Silver ... Soul of Gold." *Wonder Woman* Vol. 1 #253 (Mar. 1979). New York: DC Comics.

Harris, Jack C. (w), Jose Delbo (p), and Joe Giella (i). "The Angle in the Stars." *Wonder Woman* Vol. 1 #254 (Apr. 1979). New York: DC Comics.

_____. "The Crypt of the Dark Commander." *Wonder Woman* Vol. 1 #248 (Oct. 1978). New York: DC Comics.

_____. "The Empress of the Silver Snake!" *Wonder Woman* Vol. 1 #252 (Feb. 1979). New York: DC Comics.

Harris, Jack C. (w), Jose Delbo (p), and Vince Colletta (i). "The Name is Wonder Woman!" *Wonder Woman* Vol. 1 #251 (Jan. 1979). New York: DC Comics.

Heinberg, Allan (w), Gary Frank (p), and Jon Sibal (i). "Backstory." *Wonder Woman Annual* Vol. 2 #1 (Nov. 2007). New York: DC Comics.

Heinberg, Allan (w), Terry Dodson (p), and Rachel Dodson (i). "Who Is Wonder Woman? Part Two." *Wonder Woman* Vol. 3 #2 (Sep. 2006). New York: DC Comics.

Kanigher, Robert (w), Don Heck (p), and Vince Colletta (i). "The Second Life of the Original Wonder Woman." *Wonder Woman* Vol. 1 #204 (Jan.-Feb. 1973). New York: DC Comics.

Kanigher, Robert (w), Ross Andru (p), and Mike Esposito (i). "Top Secret!" *Wonder Woman* Vol. 1 #99 (Jul. 1958). New York: DC Comics.

Levitz, Paul (w), Jose Delbo (p), and Vince Colletta (i). "The Case of the Impossible Crimes." *Wonder Woman* Vol. 1 #257 (Jul. 1979). New York: DC Comics.

_____. "Menace of the Mental Murderer." *Wonder Woman* Vol. 1 #255 (May 1979). New York: DC Comics.

_____. "The Return of the Royal Flush Gang." *Wonder Woman* Vol. 1 #256 (Jun. 1979). New York: DC Comics.

Lobdell, Scott (w), and Kenneth Rocafort (a). "They Will Join You in the Sun." *Superman* Vol. 3 #13 (Dec. 2012). New York: DC Comics.

Luke, Eric (w), Yanick Paquette (p), and Bob McLeod (i). "Gods and Monsters." *Wonder Woman* Vol. 2 #139 (Dec. 1998). New York: DC Comics.

Lyons, Richard D. "35 Chosen Astronaut Candidates: Six Are Women and Three Blacks: Group Picked from 8,079 Applicants to Start Two-Year Training in July for Orbital Missions Women's Movement Credited." *New York Times* Jan. 17, 1978: 14.

Maggin, Elliott S. (w), Jose Delbo (p), and Vince Colletta (i). "Maximum, Emperor of Hollow Mountain!" *Wonder Woman* Vol. 1 #225 (Aug.-Sep. 1976). New York: DC Comics.

Messner-Loebs, William (w), Lee Moder (p), and Andé Parks (i). "Loses." *Wonder Woman* Vol. 2 #73 (Apr. 1993). New York: DC Comics.

Morrison, Grant (w), Cameron Stewart (a), Chris Burnham (a), and Frazer Irving (a). "Black Mass." *Batman and Robin* Vol. 1 #16 (Jan. 2011). New York: DC Comics.

Moulton, Charles. "Wonder Woman Comes to America." *Sensation Comics* #1 (Jan. 1942). New York: DC Comics.

Moulton, Charles. "A Spy in the Office." *Sensation Comics* #3 (Mar. 1942). New York: DC Comics.

O'Neil, Dennis (w), Curt Swan (p), and Murphy Anderson (i). "Superman Breaks Loose." *Superman* Vol. 1 #233 (Jan. 1971). New York: DC Comics.

O'Neil, Dennis (w), Mike Sekowsky (p), and Dick Giordano (i). "A Death for Diana." *Wonder Woman* Vol. 1 #180 (Jan.-Feb. 1969). New York: DC Comics.

_____. "Wonder Woman's Last Battle." *Wonder Woman* Vol. 1 #179 (Nov.-Dec. 1968). New York: DC Comics.

O'Neil, Dennis (w), Mike Sekowsky (p), and Dick Giordano (i). "Wonder Woman's Rival." *Wonder Woman* Vol. 1 #178 (Sep.-Oct. 1968). New York: DC Comics.

Simone, Gail (w), Aaron Lopresti (p), and Matt Ryan (i). "Rise of the Olympian, Part One: Plague and Pestilence." *Wonder Woman* Vol. 3 # 26 (Jan. 2009). New York: DC Comics.

Simone, Gail (w), Nicola Scott (p), and Fernando Dagnino (p). "Wrath of the Silver Serpent: Part 1 of 3, Contagion." *Wonder Woman* Vol. 3 # 42 (May 2010). New York: DC Comics.

Smith, Matthew J. "The Tyranny of the Melting Pot Metaphor: Wonder Woman as the Americanized Immigrant." *Comics and Ideology,* edited by Matthew J. McAllister, Edward H. Sewell, Jr., and Ian Gordon, 129–150. New York: Peter Lang, 2001.

Wein, Len (w), Curt Swan (p), and Tex Blaisdel (i). "The Man Who Mastered Woman." *Wonder Woman* Vol. 1 #212 (Jun.-Jul. 1974). New York: DC Comics.

Backlash and Bracelets

The Patriarch's World, 1986–1992

D. R. HAMMONTREE

The dominant cultural rhetoric of the United States in the late 1980s can be described as a backlash to the socio-political movements of the 1960s and 1970s. The state of affairs in the Patriarchally dominated environment of 1987 sees a backlash culture where the feminist movement is commodified into the larger cultural pathos of the time. The 1980s sees a domestic economic and political climate that values economic neoliberal notions. Social and counterculture gains of the late 1960s are undermined. The spirit of détente in Cold War politics would also give way toward more aggressive stances. In all, the 1980s is a time Adrienne Rich describes as "a growing middle-class self-absorption and indifference both to ideas and to the larger social order" (37).

This cultural backlash takes the form of "a knee-jerk reaction on the part of the mainstream in defense of the status quo" (Gamble 46). This is a post-feminist time when the political aims of movement-oriented politics are challenged by a neoliberal framework promoting "free market" economics along with inclusion rather than resistance to the political and social structures that perpetrate anti-feminist attitudes. It is a push back against progressive-leaning outlooks of the 1960s. The cultural products of the era also lead to more insular behavior: this is the era of Music Television (MTV), home video, the portable cassette player, and personal video game systems. A materialistic mind-set is at the forefront of this era as the gains from the social movements of the 1960s were promoted as out of fashion.

Through popular media, social attitudes about the domestic protest over the Vietnam War began to shift away from sympathy for the anti–War movement and various social movements attached to the aims and scope of the movement. In turn advances in Civil Rights slow and the Women's liberation advocates looked for higher ground after the defeat of the Equal Rights Amendment. This era also sees the beginning of the postfeminist and anti-feminist[1] effort, as a reaction to the liberating messages of second wave feminists. This postfeminist attitude would counter previous feminist notions that saw "the principal objective of feminist criticism [as] political: [seeking] to expose, not to perpetuate, patriarchal practices" (Moi xiv). It would seem that in the 1980s the personal was more narcissistic rather than political. It is in this environment that a culture icon embraced by the feminist liberation movement a decade before would be revised. This article will focus on how the revised *Wonder Woman* (published from 1986 to 1992) was an ambitious attempt to explore complex cultural (political, social, religious) issues through a feminist lens within the backlash environment of the late 1980s.

Background

The Post-*Crisis* DC[2] from 1986 to 1992 is a study in experimentation, a time when mainstream superhero comics emphasized realism by creating believable characters to attract a new generation of readers. This "Era of Ambition" (See Duncan and Smith, 71) produced *Watchmen* and *Batman: the Dark Knight Returns* (two canonical readings in Comics studies) and brought more complexity to the standard superhero narrative. It was also a time of revamping and reimagining for the DC monthly titles. While most of the mainstream attention went to John Byrne's *Superman*, all the DC books were going through a mild renaissance in character development and writing styles. Experiments and innovations of the time included the light-hearted *Justice League International*, a new Flash, and Keith Giffen's complex *Legion of Superheroes*. The editorial direction at DC Comics uses this Post-*Crisis* period to attract readers beyond the typical superhero demographics (teenage males) in a time that comics competed with VHS, video gaming innovation, and the compact disc. Post-*Crisis* DC comics exhibit writing breaking away from the mainstream conception of comic books, directed toward mature fans with disposable income (see Brown).

Given this backdrop, DC Comics could draw from a storehouse of well-known but traditionally underdeveloped characters. Wonder Woman was one such overlooked character with potential to reach female readers. The character maintains its status in popular culture as the book is "one of only seven American comic books that has been consistently published" since the 1940s (Emad 956). What accounts for such a sustained run is that the character manages to resonate in a popular medium despite her World War II origins and because she remains the predominant female superhero. However, as addressed in other entries found in this volume, the characters' potential was seldom realized. While the general public (and comic book readers) knew of Wonder Woman, the development within the books itself was quite lackluster.

Although the editorial environment was open to developing a complex narrative for the character, they had few ideas as to the overall direction this would take (Pérez, *Gods*). Editor Karen Burger, artist George Pérez and writers Greg Potter and Len Wein worked on the redevelopment (although the overall run would be identified mainly with Pérez, who worked on the series in the capacity of artist, plotter, or writer for five years). The result was a reimagined Wonder Woman that retained many of the essential elements of the character (costume, magic lasso, tiara). Other elements put aside included the "Diana Prince" secret identity and Steve Trevor as a love interest. Indeed, Princess Diana of Themyscira would have no secret identity. Emphasis is also placed on the mythological background rather than a military driven backdrop. Potter developed the origin of the Amazons as "reincarnations of women murdered through pre-history" (Pérez). As well, much more emphasis was placed on the Greek Pantheon as supporting characters (specifically Ares and Hermes).

The reboot was very much grounded in realism with an addition of a new supporting cast (as well as traditional characters like Steve Trevor and Etta Candy). A female audience was the specific goal for Karen Berger, who would stay with the title throughout Pérez's time with the series. Indeed, this was "the only time Wonder Woman continuously broke sales records [as] Pérez shifted the books focus to include women readers" (Goetz qtd in Emad 970). Pérez's artistic run on the book would last the first twenty-four issues and he would plot or co-write issues until issue #62 (Feb. 1992). Although Pérez is most associated with this series, the book would also feature pencils by Jill Thompson and Cynthia Martin.

Themyscira and the Amazons

The revamp of Themyscira from its previous incarnation of "Paradise Island" is most significant in viewing this new version of Wonder Woman as a counter to the cultural anti-feminist backlash of the late 1980s. Before the island was simply Wonder Woman's home and not much was done with Queen Hippolyta and the Amazons in terms of origin, sociology, and political structures. The Amazons are now given a fuller origin as the realization of all the lost souls of battered and murdered women from the dawn of time with Hippolyta as their Queen. In turn for their protection and loyalty to the Gods (specifically Aphrodite, Artemis, Athena, Demeter, and Hestia who are the island's protectors), they are given immortality. The Amazons are charged by Artemis to "establish new ways of justice and equality" (Pérez, *Wonder Woman: Gods* 187). The Amazons are also selected to protect "Doom's Doorway" which holds various evils the likes of demons or other mystical creatures. The Amazon bracelets are a reminder of their previous bondage (thanks to Hercules) and serve as recalled in issue #50 (Jan. 1991) "a reminder never to err again" (Pérez, "Embracing" 50). It is in trusting men that led to the initial fall of the Amazons and, thanks to the Goddesses, they remain for centuries, sentries protecting an unknowing world from various evils until that time where men would have matured beyond his aggressive lust for power and domination over others. With these revised Amazons, readers are confronted with a cultural critique of the patriarchal world as a flawed and conflicted.

For centuries the Amazons seem to function in harmony, hidden from the world, without outside contact (specifically without any male contact). With these protections in place, the Amazons of Themyscira become a self-sufficient warrior and artisan culture, advancing scientifically, artistically, and mystically as a communal matriarchy. The very nature of this sociological arrangement (immortality aside) seems to run counter to the capitalist, and defensive ideology of the United States in the 1980s on various levels. Indeed, the Amazons are both "theoretically and politically astute and aware of their cultural positions" (Moi 175) in relationship to the outside world. Their system is an alternative to the inclusionary tendencies in a backlash culture.

A deeper look into the culture of Themyscira sees a utopian community runs on a democratic-matriarchal model with Queen Hippolyta as the central leader. Specifically Themyscira is a "benevolent monarchy" as Hippolyta explains in issue #38 (Jan. 1990), " I do not rule with terror, and I bend to the will of the majority" (Pérez, "Forbidden" 9). Yet, the community is not overly utopic as readers are shown various disagreements among the island's inhabitants. Various governments view the island as a danger and make efforts to suppress public knowledge of its existence. In issue #27 (Feb. 1989) the conservative faction on the island represented by Hellene, Iphtime, and Oenone denounce interaction with patriarch's world and, specifically oppose diplomatic attempts to bring outsider to the island. Indeed, it seems that the most divisive issues among the Amazons concerns the influence that the outside world will have on the island (Pérez, "The Immortal"). As well, many Amazons are concerned that outsider may attempt to take advantage of the island's hospitality. The inhabitants of Patriarch's world are seen as savages overall and not ready for the island's technological or spiritual advances. Indeed, the outside is word is described by a reporter in issue #49 (Dec. 1990) as "a world grown hardened and weary by prejudice, intolerance, and economic and political manipulations" (Pérez, "Wonder" 9). This debate among the Amazons parallels the debates within feminist critical theory.

The internal debates on the island are featured in a subplot running as early as issue #27 (Feb. 1989) with Steve Trevor's visit to the island and culminating in issues #36–40 as United Nation representatives visit Themyscira. Hellene objects to any unstable elements on the island and Hippolyta quickly silences her stating the "the vote was taken, the majority willed for this day" (Pérez, "Strangers" 13). The UN cultural exchange storyline is the most reflective of the series in terms of exploring the religious, political, and social issues. The arch is narrated as a Lois Lane *Daily Planet* story. This plotline touches on the various reactions that second-wave feminist have toward the 1980s backlash and the inclusionary approach of post-feminist thinking. The Amazons stand in for the second-wave, politically oriented feminist movement as they, from a position of power on Themyscira, view the cultural attitudes and values of the era.

However, the conventions of comic book writing make it a bit impossible for so many issues to be devoted to exploring the cultural and political issues alone as Eris, the Greek Goddess of discord, begins to manipulate tensions between the delegates. Yet a closer examination of this story arc demonstrates an innovative approach to understanding the influences behind critical sociopolitical debates. Discord and influence, indeed play an obvious role in backlash politics. Although all is tied up nicely at the end, the story arc does remind readers that Eris (standing in for the dominant cultural forces of discord) may only manipulate what already exists, asserting that we all play a role in advancing the predominate ideologies of the time. All and all this subplot is unique in that it brings a sociological debate in to the realm of comics. A discussion, indeed, that does not appear to be happening in much of the larger culture.

The Amazons begin to question their faith in *Wonder Woman* #50 (Jan. 1991). In a similar vein the series asks readers to question their own faith in a decades-long build-up of political tension and conflicted patriotism. A broader analogy relates to the cultural shift in the feminist movement overall all as the internal conflicts of the Amazons of Themyscira parallel and at times counter a similar cultural narrative of the post-feminist mind-set of women conforming to dominating cultural values rather than attempting to change or resist those values. With the Amazons, readers have the opportunity to view the dominant culture through another lens but that lens is also used to express the frustrations of the times as the Amazons, long isolated, face similar challenges to their own faith, security, and mind-set. As the Amazons also function as a communal religious order, themes in play can question issues of faith in the onset of the Culture Wars. However, the key difference here is that Olympian gods are omnipotent but not omniscient, so that they may be portrayed in a way that won't offend all readers. It is a portrayal that parallels other books in the DC Universe, including *Sandman*, also edited by Karen Berger.

Supporting Cast

Religious overtones are difficult to ignore in a book featuring the Greek Pantheon as a supporting cast. However, the Gods spend most of the run away from Earth on a spiritual quest. Left behind is Hermes on a quest of his own throughout this run, first mourning the loss of his offspring, Pan, then gradually going insane. The insanity of Hermes comments on the generational cultural shift of 1980s as the individual becomes fragmented from a larger social identify (giving way to self-absorption). At the same time, the cultural abandonment of social, progressive communal notions leave the culture apathetic and disillusioned. Hermes exhibits all these qualities as he attempts to make sense of his role in this culture.

The supporting cast also features very strong women. Julie Kapatelis, a Harvard Anthropology professor, is chosen by Hermes to serve as Diana's guide in "Man's world." Her portrayal goes against the cultural attitudes of the backlash culture in that she is a successful academic and single mother (widow) in a time of "welfare queens" and the stagnation of the Women's equality movement that looked to blame the degradation of the "traditional families" as the cause (rather than the result) of various social ills. The running narrative during these years sees Julie as on various archeological digs to the frustration of her daughter Vanessa, who exhibits typical teenage angsts combined with the psychological trauma of losing her father at age five and the suicide of her best friend, Lucy. Vanessa is an emotionally unstable but an overall sympathetic character that would appeal to a would-be new demographic of teenage, female readers.

Diana's "publicist" Myndi Mayer embodies of the business ethos of the 1980s and serves as an important example of how the Pérez's *Wonder Woman* message runs counter to the prevailing materialistic views lauded at the time. Myndi embodies most of the 1980s corporate materialism: she wears furs, smokes, seems fashionable, flashy, and brazen. Employed to shape the public persona of this new "Wonder Woman," Mayer is portrayed as a no nonsense business woman and social climber. Readers are first introduced to her in a panel of only her purple heals as they "tak, tak, tak, tak, tak," to the office of Julie Kapatelis. The next panel is a reaction shot of three students looking a bit aghast (it is also in this shot we see cigarette smoke). Two panels later is the wider reveal of Myndi (note the non-traditional spelling to enhance the marketability of the characters personality) in a white fur coat. She attempts to persuade Julie Kapatelis to introduce her to Wonder Woman promising to "make it profitable" (Pérez, *Wonder Woman: Gods* 177). Julie rejects Myndi and her offer, further labeling her as a "loudmouth" and a "cheap shark." Indeed, it seems that in Julie readers have an idea of traditional feminist image, while Myndi offers readers a static characterization of an anti-feminist 1980s archetype. Julie's reaction is one of disgust and a bit of outrage as Myndi stands in for the very "loudmouth" and "cheap shark" cultural values that are promoted during this time. After having the door slammed, Myndi motivates herself by articulating her desire to "ink this Diana dame" and with a bit of emotional reinforcement states to herself (while speaking to her compact) "Whatever else Myndi Mayer may be ... she certainly ain't cheap!" Here readers are confronted with an embodiment of the 1980s anti-feminist ideal. Nonetheless, Diana, in the spirit of eternal sisterhood, accepts Myndi.

The work as Diana's promoter begins to take a toll of Myndi as it seems clear that Diana finds little of interest in her promotional goals. While she is first seen as very two-dimensional in her cutthroat approach to marketing, by her second appearance she is seen at work on a campaign arguing for the role individuals play in shaping and creating cultural values. Myndi's efforts with Diana can be seen in a larger a meta-textual scope paralleling Pérez et al.'s intentions at revamping Wonder Woman's public persona.

As Myer's character develops, the mind-set behind the "greed is good attitudes" of the 1980s is addressed on its own merits. However, the final argument as to the virtues of such selfishness is revealed to readers with the downfall of the character. Myndi becomes entangled with a male lover working for the mafia. An extortion attempt is made and although she is appears to have been murdered, her death resulted from a drug overdose. The story then becomes a lesson as to the effects of drugs but in a broader sense Myndi stands in for the wasteful and ultimately self-destructing mentalities exhibited by the materialism of the 1980s (which feminist theory would attribute to male-driven dominant attitudes and behaviors). Although the suicide and murder plot do address the surface issues of drug overdose, a deeper analysis of the Myndi Mayer character finds a subversive critique of market driven cultural attitudes.

The overall message, as seen with the resistance attitudes of the Amazons, calls into question the pervading cultural ethos of the 1980s expected of professional women after the fallout from the defeat of the Equal Right Amendment. So, at first Myer seems to represent the idea of anti-feminist backlash where "the career woman" is depicted as "coping with stress-induced illness" brought out about by "a deep sense of unfulfilled needs and desires" (Gambel 193). It seems obvious that with Myndi is an attempt to illustrate what happens when a subjugated class endeavors to fit into the culturally dominant idea of privilege.

Military (Critique of War and Patriarchy)

Before the reboot, the U.S. Army Intelligence agency headquartered in Washington D.C. was the base of operations for Wonder Woman in her secret identity of Diana Prince. Indeed, the U.S. Military played a central role in Wonder Woman stories since the character's World War II era development (with the exception of a brief period in the late 1960). The 1940s Queen Hippolyta's reasoning for sending a champion to "Man's World" was to aid the U.S. Army in fighting the Axis powers. Nevertheless, the 1987 Wonder Woman is "no longer an ally to an explicit war effort" (Emad 973) and becomes a peace ambassador.

The 1986 Steve Trevor is a notable example of how this new take on Wonder Woman seems to go against the tide of the military portrayals in the 1980s. Now a veteran (and much older) U.S. Air Force Colonel, Trevor finds himself torn over his participation in the Vietnam War and comes into conflict with his "top brass" over his pacifist views. Trevor bridges the culture attitudes of the 1960s while addressing the cultural narrative of Vietnam (and in turn attitudes toward the military) that develop in the 1980s due to an onslaught of Vietnam-era related motion pictures (*Platoon, Full Metal Jacket*), television programs (*Tour of Duty, China Beach*), and comics (*The 'Nam*). A reflective Steve Trevor exhibits many of the qualities of the conflicted American cultural clash over Vietnam; social values deeply tied to the various social movement of the 1960s. With Trevor, the feminist social movement gains a sympathetic representative from "Man's world" no longer directly associated with the any militaristic effort. Trevor's position and experience give him some protective privilege as he resists the elements of the military more susceptible to Ares' influence. Further, there would be no love interest between Steve Trevor and Diana. Now, Trevor has an on and off relationship to Etta Candy.

The Cold War backdrop may also be viewed as a critique of Patriarchy in an era that sees the end of détente in U.S. Cold War relations with the Soviet Union for a more aggressive rhetorical stance. Yet, while the depiction of Cold War relations may be taken at its face value, a deeper reading sees a critique of the prevailing foolishness of international relations in Patriarch's world. To begin, Diana is sent to "man's world" to combat the influence of Ares, the God of War. The initial story arc sees Ares attempting to influence both U.S. and Soviet generals as to precipitate a nuclear conflict. In the attempt to create a final war, Aries pits the two superpowers against another. The underlining tone of the Ares storyline reflects the Cold War anxieties of the late 1980s and the cost of nuclear destruction. These themes, of course, were not unique in the popular fiction of the time.

In an early story arc, Ares influences both American and Soviet generals to take over nuclear facilities and begin an attack. The story seems typical of Cold War fears but also reaches beyond the ideological political conflict which is now portrayed as small compared to the influence of the War God Ares (whose strength and power derive from strife). Ares' goal of world domination is ultimately misguided and self-destructive. However, Ares' plan only fails when confronted with the repercussions of his actions. Indeed, whilst bound in the "lasso of truth" Areas sees himself as the master of a world laid waste by nuclear fire and devoid of life. Realizing that his very being relies on the worship of others Ares discovers that by destroying the world he destroys himself. However, the plot doesn't go much deeper than this. What is curious here is that Ares, as the God of War, would more than likely see the benefits of permanent war over nuclear annihilation and do his best to maintain strife among the geopolitical landscape as it continues to exist to this day. Here Ares is a stand-in for the short slightness of a self-absorbed cultural ethos.

Nevertheless, it seems that, again like much of the popular fiction, the Cold War is only nuclear in nature and the narrative doesn't take the opportunity to comment on the effect of the Cold War regionally (Southeast Asia, the Middle East, Central America, etc.). With Ares a message of the waste and ultimate consequences of total war are realized in a time that mutually assured destruction was seen as a reasonable deterrent. These anti-war notions stand against the political backlash toward the social and cultural movements of the time.

Conclusion

What seems to be absent in this overview is any specific discussion of the central character herself. It is intentional since the potential of the character is limited by its various interpretations. In other words, the character herself is limited by "cultural power and textual interpretation" (Brooker 3). As a cultural icon the character is too much a part of the prevailing cultural ideology to make any individualized statement. In turn, her development seems to be open to interpretation. Wonder Woman is a cultural product, a character that is best understood in how others react to her. Pérez draws her as she was designed to be, beyond the reach of mortals. This is not to say that Diana does not make any specific statement, as her role as a peace ambassador seems to already embody her message. Overall it is difficult not to see Diana as anything but a fetishized object as her personality is vague and left up to "audience-identification" (Carson 121).

Only when the various social justice movements of the 1960s and 1970s give way to more materialistic endeavors in the 1980s does Wonder Woman become a voice of resistance (perhaps dissonance) to the prevailing cultural ethos. Indeed, in the 1970s Wonder Woman was used by DC Comics to portray the Women's Rights movement as a "threat [of] female power unleashed [and] uncontrollable" (Emad 968), while the Pérez Wonder Woman embraces peace, justice, and diplomacy. It not without irony that at the moment when the Equal Rights Amendment is defeated and the Women's Liberation movement is seen by many as a radical or fringe movement that this comic, perhaps in hopes of gaining a new readership beyond adolescent males, takes another direction to attract new readers. This "era of ambition" is not without its various comic works that critique the neo-conservatism of the 1980s (indeed these are touchstones of both *Watchmen* and *The Dark Knight Returns*), but now a feminist narrative is embedded into this monthly series.

It is indeed this very narrative that "becomes part of the information we use to process our other experience and live in it" (Robinson 134). On the surface these stories may seem empowering, but they do not overtly challenge any particular cultural status quo. A feminism with emphasis on social criticism gets closer to Simone de Beauvoir's assertion of taking "words and the truth to be of value" (Moi 183) rather than having truth misinterpreted in cultural texts which may serve to pervert political goals of meaning and empowerment into fetishized categories (which a narcissistic culture would be prone to do). The *Wonder Woman* stories during this time address the conflicts within the limitations of a popular entertainment form. *Wonder Woman* from 1987 to 1992 works as a form of cultural pedagogical praxis by framing the *essence* of complex topics of patriarchal power within its pages. And although the intention was to frame a narrative for female readers, it should not be discounted that series also carried the potential to engage male adolescences readers as well.

The broader argument here is the issue of the text as part of the prevailing patriarchal ideology in the first place (see Moi 8) which runs the risk of delving into post-feminist notions that confuse feminist empowerment in the guise of masculine fetishized oppression. The years 1987 to 1992 seem to be an island during which time the *Wonder Woman* comic books moved beyond a too-frequently encountered tradition of base consumerism and sexual essentialism.

How lasting or influential the attempt was is questionable. Much of what was attempted under the guidance of Karen Burger was undone after 1992. Yet overall, in the attempt to use feminist language to engage the dominant values of patriarchy and offer engagement with such norms via an unsuspecting and unserious medium, the Pérez-era Wonder Woman succeeds but, of course is limited. There is always the worry of alienating readers. Yet it is of historical note that these stories criticize and provoke readers to reflection. The run succeeds in addressing conflicts and, perhaps through its own progressive praxis may entice its audience to see beyond their own frames of reference.

NOTES

1. Anti-feminist backlash (as part of the "Culture Wars") comes to the forefront in the 1980s demonstrated predominately in the Anita Hill sexual harassment controversy over the appointment of Clarence Thomas to the U.S. Supreme Court in 1991.

2. This is the name for DC continuity following *Crisis on Infinite Earths*, a series that rebooted the DC narrative continuity.

WORKS CITED

Baker, Martin. *Comics: Ideology, Power and the Critics*. Manchester: Manchester University Press, 1989.

Brooker, Will. *Batman Unmasked: Analyzing a Cultural Icon*. New York: Continuum, 2000.

Brown, Jeffrey A. "Comic Book Fandom and Cultural Capital." *Journal of Popular Culture* 30.4 (1997): 13–31.

Carson, Fiona. "Feminism and the Body." In *The Routledge Companion to Feminism and Postfeminism*, edited by Sarah Gamble, 117–128. London: Routledge, 2001.

Duncan, Randy, and Matthew J. Smith. *The Power of Comics: History, Form and Culture*. New York: Continuum, 2009.

Gamble, Sarah, ed. *The Routledge Companion to Feminism and Postfeminism*. London: Routledge, 2001.

Emad. Mitra C. "Reading Wonder Woman's Body: Mythologies of Gender and Nation." *Journal of Popular Culture* 39.6 (2006): 954–84.

The Grand Comics Database. The Grand Comicbook Database Foundation, www.comics. org. Accessed Jan. 2013.

Moi, Toril. *Sexual/Textual Politics: Feminist Literary Theory*, 2d ed. 1985. New York: Routledge, 2002.

Overstreet, Robert. *The Official Overstreet Comic Book Price Guide*, 37th ed. New York: Gemstone, 2007.

Pérez, George (w), and Chris Marrinan (a). "The Immortal Storm." *Wonder Woman* Vol. 2 #27 (Feb. 1989). New York: DC Comics.

Pérez, George (w), Colleen Doran (a). "Wonder Woman." *Wonder Woman* Vol. 2 #49 (Dec. 1990). New York: DC Comics.

Pérez, George (w), and Jill Thompson (a). "Embrace the Coming Dawn." *Wonder Woman* Vol. 2 #50 (Jan. 1991). New York: DC Comics.

Pérez, George (w, a), Len Wien (w), Greg Potter (w), and Bruce Patterson (a). *Wonder Woman: Gods and Mortals*. New York: DC Comics, 2004.

Pérez, George (w), Mindy Newell (w), Chris Marrinan (a). "Forbidden Fruit." *Wonder Woman* Vol. 2 #38 (Jan. 1990). New York: DC Comics.

_____. "Strangers in Paradise." *Wonder Woman* Vol. 2 #37 (Dec. 1989). New York: DC Comics.

Rich, Adrienne. "Credo of a Passionate Skeptic." *Monthly Review* 64.2 (2012): 36–41.

Robinson, Lillian S. *Wonder Women: Feminisms and Superheroes*. New York: Routledge, 2004.

The Dark Amazon Saga

Diana Meets the Iron Age

NICOLE FREIM

Wonder Woman has a fairly unique distinction among comic book women: she is widely recognized. Thanks largely to television, Diana the Amazon Princess and her colorful uniform carry iconic power similar to Superman and his "S." With versions of the character appearing in television shows like *Wonder Woman*, *The Superfriends*, and several recent DC animated superhero shows, Diana is indeed a permanent part of our culture. A good overview of some of the character's high and low moments can be found in Les Daniels' *Wonder Woman: The Complete History*. For example, Diana served as a feminist symbol in the 1970s and was celebrated in 1981 by the creation of the Wonder Woman Foundation to "honor women whose lives have inspired countless other people" (Daniels 151). And for a woman who's been around since 1941, she looks pretty good.

That is not to say that Diana has been a static character. Like most members of the comic book universe, she has been transformed many times as the years have gone by. These transformations have two main motivating factors: new creative teams on the book and the passage of time. The first change usually heralds what has come to be known as the "Bold New Direction"; like many unfortunate phrases, it was simply used too often and has now entered the realm of cliché. The second change is in some ways obvious. A character like Wonder Tot may work in the 1950s under the Comics Code, and crime-fighting jumpsuits may work in the 1960s and 1970s, but the realities of current society need to be reflected in the text in order for the character to stay relevant and interesting to a continually developing audience.

The passage of time, however, cannot fundamentally alter the sensibilities of the superhero. While a character may have doubts about her mission, moments of selfishness, or rampages while mind controlled, the innate goodness of the hero must re-emerge. Richard Reynolds discusses this in the context of superheroes as modern myths for our age. He believes that "a key ideological myth of the superhero comic is that the normal and everyday enshrines positive values that must be defended through heroic action ... the superhero has a mission to preserve society, not re-invent it" (77). The heroes are there to affirm the rightness of our world and so cannot be permanently shifted from being a positive force. This "rightness," however, comes from the current state of affairs of whoever is writing the book at the time.

The genre's need for changeable yet unchangeable characters has resulted in bizarre storylines in the comics industry over the years. Many characters have had their powers expand and their origin stories revised as writers became even more fanciful in their imaginings. Whole storylines have been presented as "What if?" events (possible, but not part of accepted continuity) or simply later erased as dreams (long before *Dallas* ever used it on Bobby). Even a death seen as "canon" is sometimes simply revised in a deus ex machina style, or ret-con in comics parlance (Jean Grey/Phoenix, for instance). So some aspects of the characters do change over time: costumes, back stories, supporting cast, love interests, etc. But the underlying heroic aspect does not vary much.

While individual characters can transform on a yearly or monthly basis, the comics industry as a whole has also undergone several major transformations. These changes to the overall tone and style of mainstream comics are generally referred to as "ages." The Golden Age kicked everything off, with a wide variety of stories and genre comics alongside the superheroes. The Silver Age suffered through the restrictions of the comics code, producing family friendly and often silly stories. The Bronze Age struggled with real issues like drug abuse and discrimination but also embraced franchising with comics based on films and television shows. The Iron Age (also called the Dark Age or Modern Age, although I prefer "Iron" for the symmetry) seemed to introduce a more pronounced shift in storylines, attitudes, and motivations.

This period of comics is generally acknowledged to start in 1986 with the publications of *The Dark Knight Returns* and *Watchmen*. These books were limited series and darker in tone than was usual for mainstream comics. The deconstructionist view of heroes and the characters' intense questioning of themselves seemed to strike a chord with the audience. The heroes became less heroic, more like anti-heroes working against the corrupt establishment or outside accepted channels. Characters like Venom, Spawn, Deadpool, and Cable were selling like crazy. The Punisher had three titles and a film (with Dolph Lundgren) by 1989. Lobo, introduced in 1983 as a villain, was revamped as a bad boy anti-hero with a motorcycle in the early 1990s. Paralleling this, movies such as *Die Hard, Lethal Weapon,* and the *Rambo* series were raking in money with violent takes on human nature and antisocial yet somehow nobly driven heroes. The music scene was being swept by "grunge" bands whose lyrics were filled with angst and apathy. A general sense of disenchantment with society seemed to be seeping in to many aspects of popular culture.

So where did this wave of pathos and alienation leave a character like Wonder Woman? The *Wonder Woman* title had been cancelled and restarted with a new #1 (volume 2) after DC's *Crisis on Infinite Earths* in 1985. The new series attempted to bring Diana back to her roots in Greek myth and featured more connections to characters and ideas from mythology. Diana's position was now that of an ambassador, bringing Amazonian ideals of peace and equality to the outside world. During the beginning of the series, artist and writer George Pérez consciously tried to "make [Diana] a nice person ... a peace character" (Daniels 169). As a result, Diana did perhaps more talking than some other heroes of the punch-first-ask-questions-later persuasion popular at the time.

When Pérez stopped writing the book at issue 62, William Messner-Loebs took over as writer. A new editor, Paul Kupperberg, wanted to give Diana a new look, drawing "attention to a familiar character that readers might be inclined to take for granted" (Daniels 184). Part of this was motivated by flagging sales; Diana was having trouble keeping up with the grim and gritty gun-toting anti-heroes. By this point, many characters had already undergone a metamorphosis and emerged not as a butterfly but as a beat-up caterpillar with attitude. Mark Voger runs through a list of some of the changes in his retrospective *The Dark Age.* In fact, he considers the "makeover" to be the number one cliché of this time in comics. Voger cites such changes as Aquaman's loss of a hand while gaining a hook and beard, Azrael's assumption of and modifications to the Batman uniform, and Superboy's black leather jacket, spiked gauntlets, and shredded pants as attempts to revive characters through edginess (124). But what was DC Comics to do with Wonder Woman? How could they take their foremost female character, one whose very reputation was based on goodness and purity, and make her "dark and gritty" without losing sales from confused or resentful fans?

Enter a new Wonder Woman, one whom the readers could accept as more forceful and violent because she had no history to contradict that. Kupperberg hired Brazilian artist Mike Deodato Jr. to work with Loebs on this storyline (Daniels 184). Deodato's art was exaggerated, with the kind of physical proportions of women that earn comics a bad reputation as male fantasy. His style earned a lot of attention and a fair amount of criticism; for example, the bottom of Wonder Woman's costume shrank until it was a thong. Deodato worked with Loebs for issues #90–100 (and #0 — an extra issue from a crossover event) in a story arc that was able to use elements of the Iron Age while still preserving Diana's character. The team created the red-headed (i.e., hot-tempered) Amazon Artemis, who would replace Diana in the star-spangled bathing suit. The story arc ran from September 1994 through July 1995, at which point Artemis' story came to an unfortunate end. (Naturally, she felt better soon — almost no one ever really dies in comics.) Because Artemis had used the Wonder Woman identity during this time, rather than using "Wonder Woman" I will refer to Diana and Artemis by name.

Issue #90 begins with Diana returning to Themyscira after a long absence; the Amazons were gone and Diana thought them all dead. She learns that the island was caught in a spell by Circe (yes, that one from Greek myth) and cast into another dimension, where the Amazons were trapped for nearly ten years (only months to Diana). Diana's mother Hippolyta expects that Diana has "reformed" patriarch's world by this time, freeing women from oppression, protecting children from poverty, and stopping violence between men and women. Diana tries to explain that she has made a beginning, but Hippolyta believes Diana has not done enough — in fact she destroyed half of Boston "in a selfish rage" (Hippolyta's words) because one person was in danger (Messner-Loebs, "Homeward Gazings" 13). Her mother proclaims that Diana has not properly promoted the Amazon ideals of peace and harmony (interesting to remember when we get to discussing Artemis) and she calls Diana's behavior "extreme" and "violent." Since Diana isn't getting the job done, Hippolyta calls for a contest to choose a new Wonder Woman.

Artemis is part of a splinter group of Amazons who left the island centuries ago to live in man's world. They consider themselves the "true" Amazons, toughened by the harshness of the outside world. These Amazons are regarded by the Amazons of Themyscira as little more than barbarians, corrupted by the violence of patriarch's world. (They were recently used as pawns in an attack on the island.) They are almost exclusively depicted as angry at the other Amazons:

> DIANA: You might at least wait for me to attack you before striking back.
>
> ARTEMIS: I've no intention of waiting for anyone ... least of all you! [Messner-Loebs, "The Contest: Part 2" 12].

Artemis, however, does show intelligence in her grasp of the situation between the two groups of Amazons. She was the only one in her tribe who spoke against attacking the Themysciran Amazons, saying "Whatever their crimes against us, Amazons shouldn't war against one another" (Messner-Loebs, "The Contest" 16). She believes that Hippolyta is merely punishing her daughter with the new contest and that Diana will win in the end, but if her tribe can make a good showing, they can begin to earn respect. Artemis helps other contestants in trouble (even if she is grouchy about it) and shows a savvy understanding of the contest's maneuverings. She is a skilled archer and warrior and has the most impressive ponytail known to the world. Her hair is always long, wild, and curling around her legs and framing her body.

Surprisingly, Artemis does in fact win the contest (Diana trips at the last moment) and is awarded the Wonder Woman costume and extra weapons to make up for her lack of Diana's natural talents. (The Sandals of Hermes let her fly and the Gauntlets of Atlas increase her strength by ten.) Hippolyta proclaims Artemis "worthy to carry our message of peace and love into patriarch's world" (Messner-Loebs, "Violent" 1). Although no longer Wonder Woman, Diana returns to America as well and begins a career as a private investigator. She gets a new costume (black biker shorts, bra top, and boots with a blue cropped jacket) and hair style — suddenly her waist-length curls are gone in favor of shoulder-length straight hair.

Upon arriving in New York City, Artemis somehow joins up with a meta-promotions team who promise to help her get her message out. She does question what they get out of it and is told "Hey, babe, all you have to worry about is being good enough! We don't want to waste our time bailing you out if you can't cut it!" To which she replies: "Do not worry. I am good enough" as she pins the man to the wall with seven arrows (Messner-Loebs, "Violent" 14–15). The male promoters set up a press conference for her where Artemis announces that she will fight to end oppression of women and children and that her first priority will be "to end the violence that mars world society" (Messner-Loebs, "Violent" 17). Talk about biting off more than she can chew!

The first villains she fights are caricatures of men. She clashes with The Chauvinist, The Exploiter, and Involute the Conqueror, all of whom are absurdly large, muscled beyond belief, and wielding chains, whips, and big guns. These confrontations take place at locations where she has gone on the advice of her promoters (such as a shelter for battered women or a sweat shop) and all the conflicts end badly. For example, when at the women's shelter, she asks a woman why, when her husband hit her, she did not hit him in return. When the woman says her husband would have killed her and her children would have starved, Artemis replies "Good! Better they starve than have a mother who is a parasite and a coward!" (Messner-Loebs, "Poison ... Part 2" 4). This earns a comment from the press calling Artemis "the she-wolf of the S.S." During her fight with the Chauvinist, when Artemis is on the ground, the same woman jumps in front of a man's gun and sacrifices herself so Artemis won't think she is a coward. When fighting the Exploiter, Artemis shoots an arrow into the barrel of the gun which then explodes when he fires it. As he is screaming about his injured hands, her response is: "What kind of idiot fires after he sees the barrel is blocked?" (Messner-Loebs, "Joker's" 15). Facing the Conqueror, she uses the magic lasso against him, and when he realizes what horrors he has committed, he shoots himself and Artemis is unable to stop him.

After these "successes," Artemis comes to Boston to clean up Diana's city for her. She berates Diana for letting the Joker get away in a recent fight, even though she doesn't know who the Joker is. Diana starts to explain:

> DIANA: Patriarch's world is a complex place, Artemis. I've been trying to *learn* its ways before ...
>
> ARTEMIS: Whine and temporize all you want, sister, it proves my point. You are *incapable* of real action. Your weakness has cost you your home, your name, and your legend. It has cost you the love of your mother. I have replaced you in everything [Messner-Loebs, "Sisters" 3].

Artemis proclaims that she will start cleaning up the city beginning with the mob boss, Juliana Sazia (the only woman Artemis faces). She arrives at Sazia's house and simply starts ripping into the guards. When she reaches the front door, she is greeted by a hologram of Sazia who says "By this time you've probably already tried to kill me ... assuming you're the new Wonder Woman and I think you are. Artemis, isn't it? You're much more impulsive than Diana, and therefore more likely to try a direct attack" (Messner-Loebs, "Sisters" 10). Sazia pronounces her "too unstable" to leave alive and likens her to "someone else who thought force wins over brains" (11). This is in reference to Sazia's male rival.

Artemis escapes with her life, but just heads right into an argument with Diana. She believes that Diana is working against her (that's what her promoters told her). Diana, meanwhile, has been doing a little research on the company promoting Artemis and the villains she fought. She even tracks down the Chauvinist from the business card he left at the shelter. After fighting with Artemis, Diana reveals what she has found out about all the villains Artemis has been facing:

> DIANA: These files are locked. My guess is they hold records that show your friends *hired* the villains you've been fighting ... and beating. They've been paid to lose.
>
> ARTEMIS: But ... *why?*
>
> DIANA: Because the media are lazy. Once you "defeated" an evil man, the pressure went away. No one bothered to check to see if the underlying problems were still there. Nothing has changed. You were just entertainment [Messner-Loebs, "Sisters" p. 22].

Artemis realizes some of what has been going on and tries to find out who is behind this arrangement. She tries to force the information out of people by having a little target practice: "I cannot hear you. Perhaps there is room for one more arrow between the last one and your head. Shall we see?" (Messner-Loebs, "The Rest of the Story" 17). After watching Artemis beat up a monster, the man confesses the White Magician was behind it and he has a private airfield where he goes to be alone. Artemis thanks him and advises him to run away in case she cannot beat the Magician. As she flies off we see the man smiling to himself. This too was part of the set-up. It's hard to explain why she didn't just use the magic lasso and get the truth. Maybe because she hasn't been Wonder Woman long enough to think of it or she thinks she's just that intimidating. But it's probably because then she wouldn't have fallen into the trap set for her and the whole death scene would have to be scrapped.

And it is a stunning death scene. Twelve pages (out of thirty-eight) of Artemis getting beaten, thrown into walls, and shot. (Plus a few pages of Diana getting some of the same when she shows up.) In the end, Diana must come to the rescue and slay the foe Artemis was unable to defeat. Diana has discovered that her mother orchestrated the contest because of signs from the gods (still taken very seriously on Themyscira) that Wonder Woman was going to die. Not wanting to lose her daughter, Hippolyta arranged for Diana to lose the contest, knowing that whoever replaced her would die in her stead. Diana rushes to help Artemis but she is too late. Artemis gives her the Gauntlet of Atlas, and with her natural strength increased by ten, Diana is strong enough to defeat the White Magician. Artemis dies in her arms with the words "Take back your uniform, Diana. I have ... dishonored it. My ambition and ... arrogance nearly got ... us both killed ... *You* are Wonder Woman" (Messner-Loebs, "Blank Madness" 37). Diana buries her head in her hands.

The death of the character is perhaps another cliché of the Iron Age. Starting with the death of the Flash (Barry Allen) and Supergirl in *Crisis on Infinite Earths* and following through to such "events" as the death of Superman (the issue was sold bagged with a black armband), these tragedies seemed to capitalize on the times' sense of pessimism while simultaneously providing reasons for the remaining characters to be angry and violent. Aside from the death (issue 100 proclaims "The Fall of an Amazon" on the cover with a silhouette of Diana), this particular story manages to dovetail into the dark and gritty philosophy of the Iron Age in several other important ways.

Artemis provides the first and most clear embodiment of the dark times in her personality and actions. Artemis knows that she is representing the outcast tribe of Amazons and that if she fails, it will have ramifications for all of them. This pressure combined with years of resentment from being forced off the island and ten years of war in an alternate dimension have produced a lot of bottled anger and hostility at a world she does not believe will help her. Her version of Amazonian ideals do not seem to include peace and harmony because she has not lived that way. Her life has been hard and brutal, so that is how she lives, just like the Punisher or Deadpool.

The brutality and hostility of the male characters in the Iron Age is often discussed, but the female characters were just as tough. Artemis was simply building on the action heroine type that had been recently established. Rather than being cast as femme fatales, women were creeping into the action genre, thanks to characters such as Ellen Ripley in *Aliens* (1986) and Sarah Connor in *Terminator 2: Judgment Day* (1991) — interestingly, both characters are much tougher in these sequel films. Women in comics were getting tougher and sexier, in what came to be known as Bad Girl comics. Theorist Scott Bukatman acknowledges the ridiculous proportions these female characters had, but he points out that "it's worth observing that they're now as powerful as their male counterparts. They no longer need protection; they are no longer victims or hostages or prizes" (qtd. in Brown). These women carry weapons and can act as men do; this may help explain both Artemis' lack of sympathy for women at the shelter and her callous treatment of her injured foe.

The attitudes of the times are also seen in the villains featured in this storyline. Artemis was not facing gods or creatures from another planet. She was fighting men who represented practices that are despised by the majority of society. A character like The Chauvinist, leading a group of men to reclaim their "property," i.e. wives, echoes the slum lords that Superman fought in his early years. The readers were feeling pessimistic about society; addressing a problem that was real both validated the problem and underscored the immensity of it. Beating up bank robbers may be entertaining, but Artemis was facing actual problems that might concern the reader. Her naiveté in thinking that by shutting down The Exploiter's sweatshop she has made real progress is simultaneously endearing and stupid. But letting the character attempt to do something about battered women or the ruin of the rain forest does in some ways acknowledge that the reader is right to be concerned about the issue.

Even Diana's first case as a private investigator when she returns from Themyscira is to take care of a woman's ex-boyfriend who is stalking her. While Diana does use some physical force against him, her ultimate solution is more practical than a beating. She takes him to Wyoming (far away from the lady he's stalking) where she has arranged a therapist for him and a job opportunity. The issues of stalking and mental abuse were becoming more well known in the 1990s (see 1991's *Sleeping with the Enemy*).

While the overall villain of the story was the White Magician who'd made a pact with a demon, this was behind the scenes for most of the run. The problems at the forefront of the story were real problems that any reader had heard of and could understand. This reflects Generation X's general disenchantment with society, especially in the sense that none of the problems could be fixed in a single issue. Social problems are complicated and wide reaching; action at one battered women's shelter will not go far in addressing the problem. Artemis could be excused for not understanding that the problems remain; she has no real conception of the way the outside world functions. It does not occur to her to follow up because she believes she has solved the problem. Diana has been in "man's world" for much longer. She, like the reader, realizes that the nature of these problems precludes an easy fix.

This becomes the key to the third element of the Iron Age that this story embodies: angst. Diana feels betrayed by her mother's decision to hold a new contest. The feeling is worse after she discovers that it was all because Hippolyta knew Wonder Woman was going to die and was willing to let another die in her daughter's place. When Diana returns to Boston, she must take on a new costume and identity. She also gets a new hairstyle, severe and restrained compared to her earlier riot of curls. What she was has been stripped away and she is unsure of where she fits into the world now. Although scared of what might happen, Diana meets with the Justice League, asking "Wonder Woman was the leader of the Justice League. As Diana ... do I belong here? You have to tell me." When the others assure her that she is welcome, she says "Thank you! I was hoping you would say that, but this has all left me so —" (Jones, JLA 5–6). She is interrupted by a fight scene, but it is safe to assume that the way it has left her has not been cheery.

Diana is deep in the throes of self-doubt. Her title was removed because her mother claims Diana had failed at her mission. As much as we all try, we often cannot ignore criticism from those closest to us. Diana is having to create a new identity for herself while feeling that her last one was a failure. Artemis complicates the situation when she comes to Boston and lectures Diana on how ineffective she was as Wonder Woman. Diana is upset when Artemis leaves. Her companion, Inspector Delicato, asks her if she is all right. Diana says "everyone should be able to take a little constructive criticism." He insists that Artemis treated her like "garbage" and says she's been through so much lately that "nobody'd blame you if you let out a little-" (Messner-Loebs, "Sisters" 4) at which point Diana flattens a filing cabinet with one punch. She then straightens it back out. She considers it "inappropriate" to rant at Artemis and tries to find a better way to handle the problem.

The ultimate expression of angst comes when she realizes that Artemis is about to die alone in Diana's place. Even the White Magician calls it "melodrama" as a dying Artemis insists Diana take the gauntlet of Atlas in order to win the fight. The last image of Diana hunched over Artemis' body tells quite clearly how tormented Diana is by the outcome. The anguish Diana feels mirrors the extreme sensibilities of Generation X. Although not the "lost" generation by name, Gen X is marked by a sense of purposelessness and social alienation often due to hopelessness about the state of society. What would have happened to Diana after the death of Artemis? How would Loebs and Deodato have had her grapple with the sacrifice of another in her place, even it was not by Diana's choice? It would have been interesting to see how losing her title and searching for a new purpose affected Diana and her dedication to her path. Issue 100, however, featured a spoiler for *Wonder Woman* #101 announcing "an exciting new era for the Amazing Amazon" as John Byrne took over and relocated her, taking the character in a new direction. He did recognize that Artemis was popular, so he brought her back from Hell as a supporting character. The heyday of the Iron Age was over, however, so a new black and green costume covered Artemis completely, she became a mentor to the new Wonder Girl, and overall she behaved quite decorously — at least for a little while. Bad girls can't ever be completely reformed; where's the fun in that?

Works Cited

Brown, Jeffrey A. "Gender, Sexuality, and Toughness: The Bad Girls of Action Film and Comic Books." In *Action Chicks*, edited by Sherrie A. Inness, 47–74. New York: Palgrave Macmillan, 2004.

Daniels, Les. *Wonder Woman: The Complete History*. San Francisco: Chronicle, 2000.

Jones, Gerard (w), and Chuck Wojtkiewicz (a). *Justice League America* 95. New York: D. C. Comics, 1995.

Messner-Loebs, William (w), and Mike Deodato, Jr. (a). "Blank Madness." *Wonder Woman* Vol. 2, #100 (Aug. 1995). New York: DC Comics.

_____. "The Contest." *Wonder Woman* Vol. 2, #92 (Dec. 1994). New York: DC Comics.

_____."The Contest: Part 2, The Blind Eyes of Time." *Wonder Woman* Vol. 2, #0 (Oct. 1994). New York: DC Comics.

_____. "Homeward Gazings." *Wonder Woman* Vol. 2, #90 (Sep. 1994). New York: DC Comics.

_____. "Immortal Combat." *Wonder Woman* Vol. 2, #91 (Nov. 1994). New York: DC Comics.

_____. "Joker's Holiday." *Wonder Woman* Vol. 2, #96 (Apr. 1995). New York: DC Comics.

_____. "Joker's Holiday Part 2." *Wonder Woman* Vol. 2, #97 (May 1995). New York: DC Comics.

_____. "Poisons, Claws, and Death Part 1." *Wonder Woman* Vol. 2, #94 (Feb. 1995). New York: DC Comics.

_____. "Poisons, Claws, and Death Part 2." *Wonder Woman* Vol. 2, #95 (Mar. 1995). New York: DC Comics.

_____. "The Rest of the Story." *Wonder Woman* Vol. 2, #100 (Aug. 1995). New York: DC Comics.

_____. "Sisters." *Wonder Woman* Vol. 2, #98 (Jun. 1995). New York: DC Comics.

_____. "Violent Beginnings." *Wonder Woman* Vol. 2, #93 (Jan. 1995). New York: DC Comics.

Reynolds, Richard. *Superheroes: A Modern Mythology*. Jackson: University Press of Mississippi, 1992.

Super-Wonder

The Man of Steel and the Amazonian
Princess as the Ultimate 1990s Power Couple

Jeffrey K. Johnson

In August 2012, American media members frenziedly reported that Wonder Woman and Superman would soon become the nation's newest power couple. The Amazing Amazon and the Man of Steel would kiss in *Justice League* #12 and begin to pursue a romantic relationship shortly thereafter. Writer Geoff Johns noted that this was no attention-grabbing stunt but instead was the "new status quo" (Jensen). While few news sources acknowledged the characters' past dalliances, many comic book fans knew that Superman and Wonder Woman had flirted with a relationship previously. The two heroes that often fought alongside each other sometimes also battled a mutual attraction that appeared to them to be unacceptable. Two non-continuity tales from 1996 and 2002 respectively, do display unique views of a possible Man of Steel and Amazonian princess coupling though. These storylines in *Kingdom Come* and *Batman: The Dark Knight Strikes Again* provide two very different understandings of what it would mean for Superman and Wonder Woman to become lovers. Both tales introduce near apocalyptic possible futures and place the romantic duo as leaders in the effort to reform/rebuild society. Both members of this super-pair channel their romantic desires and remake the world using their union as an example of what can be.

While other in-continuity stories portray the couple's love as an unacceptable weakness, these two tales depict their passion as the basis to transform the world. Interestingly, while both tales differ in tone and presentation, they both ultimately reveal unequal relationships that propagate the notion of a male-centered hierarchy. While Superman does appear to personally benefit most from the super-coupling, ultimately the superhero relationship helps to save the world. *Kingdom Come* and *Batman: The Dark Knight Strikes Back* showcase realities in which super-love conquerors all and feature unique, albeit one-sided, understandings of what could happen if two nearly godlike beings merged into one couple.

The idea of a Superman and Wonder Woman relationship is at once both reasonable and irrational. The notion that two of the most iconic, popular, and physically powerful superheroes in the DC universe would romantically bond seems to be a sound and rational proposition. The two ultra-powerful heroes share many of the same problems and experiences that come with fighting crime, being a super-powered celebrity, and experiencing the world as societal outsiders. The pair is also on a short list of individuals who understand the challenges and gratification that comes with being super-powerful. These commonalities, combined with several others, would seem to indicate that it could be wise for the two to consider a romantic relationship and thus engage with someone that understands a superhero's unique lifestyle.

Another point of view suggests that the Man of Steel and the Amazonian Princess are ill-matched though, and, in fact, share little in common except trivial surface elements. The two heroes had dissimilar upbringings and because of this they view the world in divergent ways. Superman is the orphaned son of a dead planet, leaving him one of the few remaining members of his race. A kindly Midwestern couple adopted the young alien and raised him to have middle American values and morals. Because of this, much of his thinking is based on Bible Belt beliefs and conservatives understandings. In the past he has primarily dated non-powered human women like Lana Lang and Lois Lane (although the pre–Crisis Man of Steel was in a relationship with the mermaid Lori Lemaris during college).

By contrast, a group of women raised Wonder Woman on a secluded island and trained her to be independent, to fight, and to hunt. The Amazon is a warrior by nature and inclination and often feels uncomfortable in a society half-populated by men. Amazonian civilization follows ancient Greek culture and traditions and is very different from middle–American society. Additionally, the superheroine is also a princess and sees the world though royalty's lens. While Wonder Women has dated human men like Steve Trevor in the past, she appears to value the company of women more than men and seemingly is more interested in superheroics than dating. On a practical level the pairing of a Midwestern farm boy and Amazonian royalty would seem to be mismatched at best and one can imagine numerous difficulties for a couple in which the two members are literally from different worlds. These are some of the many reasons that the two did not become an in continuity couple during most of their fictional existences, although fans have often suggested the pairing. Several writers did explore a Superman and Wonder Woman relationship in non-continuity stories though, and these tales showcase the consequences and benefits of a super couple romantic bond.

Like most couplings, a Superman and Wonder Woman relationship would have both personal and professional problems and benefits. Unlike the majority of romantic pairs, the two iconic superheroes coupledom would undoubtedly dramatically change the world around them. In times of peace and prosperity, the duo would most likely keep the social order intact in the classic post-war superheroic manner. The pair would continue to work as guardians of the state and commit to tasks like apprehending criminals, stopping natural disasters, and battling super-villains that attempted to create change.

Traditionally (except for a brief period before World War II), Superman and Wonder Woman have been reactive in nature and rarely have pushed a proactive agenda. Without the specter of conflict or societal breakdown this outlook would probably continue even as the two more completely bonded. If society did suffer a natural or manmade disaster then it is less clear how the Man of Steel and Amazing Amazon would react. Superman's background and training have traditionally made him unwilling to lead a political or social revolution. Traditionally, Wonder Woman also has shied away from aggressive political and social postures but her warrior background would seem to indicate that she would likely spearhead a movement if she deemed one necessary. If a Superman and Wonder Woman union were faced with social upheaval, how would the pair react? What sway would each of the heroes have on the other? What kind of world would such a power couple ultimately create? These are questions that Mark Waid and Alex Ross address in *Kingdom Come* and Frank Miller and Lynn Varley also consider in *Batman: The Dark Knight Strikes Again*.

Mark Waid and Alex Ross's *Kingdom Come* provides a non-continuity look at a bleak future in which older superheroes battle young upstarts that no longer respect the morals and values of their super-human predecessors. DC Comics originally published the graphic novel in 1996 as a four part miniseries that addresses the dark and violent tone of many 1990s' comic books. As numerous heroes metamorphosized into hyper-violent vigilantes Waid and Ross envisioned a showdown between the older and younger heroic generations in order to define a hero's role at the end of the twentieth and beginning of the twenty-first centuries. Unsurprisingly, Superman and Wonder Woman lead the traditional heroes' camp and work together to save the world and refashion American society.

The story begins with the Man of Steel in self-exile after the Joker murders ninety-three people including the love of his life, Lois Lane. Another hero, named Magog, kills the Joker and eventually the court acquits this ultraviolent vigilante and the public rewards his efforts. Society has seemingly changed and now appears to want a more violent and proactive type of hero. Superman, unable to save his wife and having lost community favor, retires from public life and locks himself away at a make believe farm. Emotionally despondent and broken, the once great hero no longer believes in himself or the world around him and has turned his back on his former values and ideals. Superman was unable to protect his fragile human mate and also could not prevent super-villains from harming those around him. As the world begins to fall apart around him and a nuclear accident threatens the environment the Man of Steel is listless and lost. Whether her knows it or not, Superman needs Wonder Woman in his life.

Wonder Woman first appears in *Kingdom Come* as she visits a hermit-like Superman who seems to be building a barn near a golden wheat field. At first glance the reader assumes that the Man of Steel has returned to his Kansas boyhood home but this is soon revealed to be an illusion. Instead, we come to understand that Superman is farming insider a holodeck-like area within his arctic Fortress of Solitude. The Metropolis Marvel has lost his psychological and emotional center and now engages in pointless tasks to fill his time. Wonder Woman goes to see Superman in order to remind him of his humanity and to show him how much the world needs him. The Amazonian princess tries to induce the Man of Tomorrow to return to his role as a hero by sympathizing with him, provoking him, cajoling him, and reasoning with him. Wonder Woman sermonizes, "Do you live in nothing but lies? Here are two words. See if they sound familiar. Truth and justice. You can't have completely forgotten them" (34–35). Superman has lost Lois Lane, his wife and companion, and now has no one to tether him to the world and humanity. Diana attempts to serve as the Man of Steel's confidant, friend, and support system in this early part of the story. While there is no hint of romance at this juncture, Diana wishes to provide the type of guidance that a spouse would often supply. Superman at first refuses the Amazing Amazon, but he later rethinks his stance and returns to the world in an attempt to restore order and remake society. The Amazonian princess convinces the Man of Steel to resume his heroic duties and begin a war against many of the new younger meta-humans.

The super-pair are not exactly dating at the beginning of *Kingdom Come* but they do form a partnership and begin to grow closer. The two engage in a pseudo-courtship that builds slowly over time and follows the traditional methods of courting except Superman and Wonder Woman are also fighting a war and remaking the world. The two are pre-dating and already changing the course of history even though they have yet to even kiss.

As Superman and Wonder Woman grow closer in *Kingdom Come* their friendship turns into a solid working relationship in which the Amazonian princess serves as the Man of Steel's top advisor. Diana's loyalty to Superman makes her an excellent lieutenant as she and the Man of Tomorrow attempt to return the world to its previous state. Unsurprisingly, her warrior inclination and nature soon clash with Superman's Midwestern morality and the two quarrel over the proper manner in which to deal with the renegade super-heroes. While it would at first glance appear that the Amazon is subservient to the Metropolis Marvel, a closer inspection reveals that Diana is slowly molding the Man of Steel's social, political, and tactical views to become more in line with her own. At the beginning of *Kingdom Come* Superman holds the naïve belief that he can quickly and painless convince the world's heroes to align with him. As the campaign progresses Wonder Woman gradually persuades him that the older heroes must be more punitive and warlike and eventually the pair decides to incarcerate the rebel meta-humans (Diana's idea that Clark originally rejected.)

Interestingly, Diana's increasing sway over Clark has an underlying sexual component that suggests the Amazon is much more in touch with her emotions than the Kryptonian. In chapter two, as the pair fight over the idea of building a prison, Diana voices her sexual desire for Clark and the Man of Steel seems unable to resist the Amazon (93). It would be a stretch to suggest that Wonder Woman used sexual attraction to manipulate Superman in order to gain her wishes but the princess does stir the Man of Steel's passion and eventually changes his mind. Tellingly, Wonder Woman does not attempt to proactively make change but rather invests her efforts in reestablishing Superman and convincing him of her idea's correctness. Even though the pair are not in a relationship, her actions already resemble those of a traditional wife.

The underlying dynamic in *Kingdom Come* is one of Wonder Woman helping Superman to regain his humanity and to return to a society that he had abandoned. As the Man of Steel and the Amazon warrior's relationship progresses, Superman re-embraces his Kansas farm boy identity, working to rekindle traditional social superhero values and punishing those that resist. At Superman's core is the notion of the duality between his alien and Midwestern American identities. During the best of times the Man of Steel is able to maintain a delicate balance within his dual nature. In attempting to restore society, the Man of Tomorrow is also working to reestablish his desired mental and emotional equilibrium. Interestingly, Wonder Woman is also facing losses of her own. Having failed in her mission as the Amazonian ambassador, her sisters stripped her of her ambassadorial title and her royalty. The former princess no longer serves as a leader of her people and now carries the shame of having lost her royal birthright. Surprisingly, the story rarely addresses Diana's internal conflicts and instead focuses on Superman's struggles and his efforts to overcome social and psychological disasters. Although, she is trained as a warrior and an ambassador, Diana seemingly takes on the position of friend, confidant, and caregiver. Wonder Woman's role is in *Kingdom Come* is to help Superman and to make him a better hero and person. This traditional understanding of femininity leaves little room for Wonder Woman to worry about her own problems and instead she seemingly happily takes a backseat to Superman's needs and desires. Eventually in the story, Superman and Wonder Woman's plan goes terribly wrong and numerous superheroes die as a result.

By this point, the Man of Steel and the Amazing Amazon have embraced their new romantic roles and the pair has become a traditional couple. Now the two decide that superheroes must take a new role in society and no longer act as protectors but rather will integrate into the social fabric. The heroes will take a "third path" that differs from the traditional heroic defender role and Superman's earlier option of abandonment (194–195). The pair's new relationship status showcases a traditional romantic pairing that leads to a new superheroic understanding. Wonder Woman pairs with Superman to change society by utilizing the traditional couple model. Wonder Woman has become a good and supportive girlfriend and the world is better for it. Unfortunately, she seems to have gained far less personally than Superman did from the relationship.

As Superman and Wonder Woman's relationship progresses during *Kingdom Come*, the Amazon transforms from a helpful friend to a trusted romantic partner as she and the Man of Steel reconstruct society. At the end of the story, the super-pair reveal that they are married and that the Amazonian princess is pregnant. The two ask Bruce Wayne (Batman) to be the child's godfather and talk about superheroes' new integration into society. Superman and Wonder Woman have become a couple that works within social conventions and dictates instead of pursuing their previous course of creating extralegal displays of superheroics. Society has benefited from Diana's efforts to humanize Superman and normalize superheroes but she in turn has paid a steep price. While the Amazons reinstate Diana's royal titles, she simultaneously chooses to be less super and to become subservient to Superman's and society's needs. While Superman focuses on agricultural problems and blends into society at story's end, he continues to retain his leadership position and loses little of his status and authority. Wonder Woman, on the other hand, takes a traditional spousal role in which she supports her husband's needs and career goals. While she remains intelligent and strong, she now compromises many of her needs and desires and becomes a superpowered version of a stereotypical wife and mother. While Superman and society gained much for the Man of Steel/Amazing Amazon romantic pairing in *Kingdom Come*, Wonder Woman was forced to relinquish much. In the end, traditional couplehood saved the world, although it might not have been very good for Wonder Woman.

If the underlying theme of Superman and Wonder Woman's relationship in *Kingdom Come* is that their traditional romantic partnership can save the world, then *Batman: The Dark Knight Strikes Again* presents a much different thesis. Mark Waid and Alex Ross stress compromise and neo-traditional values in *Kingdom Come*. Conversely, Frank Miller and Lynn Varley press for revolution and a break from the past in *The Dark Knight Strikes Again*. This sequel to 1986's *Batman: The Dark Knight Returns*, restores the Caped Crusader to a frightening dystopia replete with sex, violence, and moral deprivation. Batman and his social modifying team are society's sole agents of justice, while Superman and Wonder Woman long ago became frightened servants of a corrupt establishment. Villains like Lex Luthor and Braniac control society and Superman and Wonder Woman kowtow to the criminals' demands in order to seemingly keep the world peaceful and safe. Although the Man of Steel remains in the public eye, he has withdrawn from his traditional duties and is no longer actively serving the public good. In much the same way as in *Kingdom Come*, Superman has lost his way and Wonder Woman is the only person who can help him remember his true social role. As in Mark Waid and Alex Ross's story, the Amazon warrior's main function in *The Dark Knight Strikes Again* is to rehabilitate Superman and thus allow him to return to being his authentic self. While this role is very similar to the Amazing Amazon's position in *Kingdom Come*, it differs in nature and degree. If *Kingdom Come* is a treatise on how neo-traditional values can save the world, then *The Dark Knight Strikes Again* is a rallying cry against conventionalism and the conservative orthodoxy that abounds within American society. Waid and Ross's Wonder Woman is a populist who embraces her domestic and maternal nature in order to support her love and help him to rehabilitate. Miller and Varley's Amazonian princess becomes a radicalized weapon against the traditional social structure and uses her passion and sexuality to convince Superman to abandon his former understanding of both himself and the world around him. While both forms of Wonder Woman serve as Superman's lover, confidant, and rehabilitator, in Miller's version the Amazon wants more than to save the world, she wants Superman to reinvent and rule it.

Unlike *Kingdom Come*, Miller and Varley's tale features no slow romantic build up or long courtship. Miller rejects the traditional dating process and instead focuses on a quick but intense sexual experience. Because of this, Wonder Woman appears relatively very little in *The Dark Knight Strikes Again*. The Amazon's first major scene occurs about halfway through the storyline when she encounters a beaten and battered Man of Steel, who has lost his physical prowess and seemingly also his will to live. The mighty Amazon flies to Superman's arctic Fortress of Solitude and confronts the Kryptonian that she describes as, "My love" (112).

It is soon revealed that the pair has a daughter (named Lara, presumably after Superman's birth mother) and stay apart in order to avoid the notice of the numerous villains that seemingly control society who would almost certainly harm their child. The two lovers fight over how to proceed, with Wonder Woman stating that they should fight and die if necessary and Superman claiming that his time is over and Diana should protect Lara from harm at all costs. The Man of Steel emphatically contends, "Forget it, Diana. It's too late. Look at me. I'm as good as dead. Bruce broke me down into pieces like I was a high school geometry project. I've lost it. I'm finished. I had a good run..." Diana counters, "Damn you! I could kill you myself! Where is the man who stole my Amazon heart? Where is the hero who threw me to the ground and took me as his rightful prize? Where is the god whose passion shattered a mountaintop? Where is that man? Where is that Superman?" While making this impassioned plea, the Amazon kisses the battered Metropolis Marvel and the Man of Steel answers, "Right here" (113–116). The two then proceed to crash through the Arctic ice and then ascend to the heavens as they embrace. Superman, who has been shown in dark and muted tones until this point, suddenly is engulfed in bright colors as both his body and uniform appear to be rejuvenated. The Man of Steel's "S" insignia now closely mirrors the Joe Shuster drawn symbol of Superman's early Great Depression appearances, seemingly signaling that the Man of Tomorrow has become revitalized and renewed. Superman and Wonder Woman's coupling turns more intimate as they rise into outer space and then descend into the ocean, all the while fulfilling their sexual needs. The force of the couple's impact causes havoc around the world setting off earthquakes, tsunamis, and a hurricane. The two seem unworried about the destruction as they rush off to dinner and Diana jokes that the earth moved for her (116–124).

The pair's sexual coupling seems to be the cure that returns Superman to his naturally omni-powerful state. The Man of Steel becomes the embodiment of a mythological Greek-like god, who basks in his own power and cares little about the minions that surround him. Wonder Woman's statement almost immediately after sexual intercourse that she is pregnant lends credence to the notion of the Man of Steel's godlike prowess and brings to mind Zeus's dalliances that always produce offspring. It is unclear if this transformation is the result of the sex act itself, Superman's love for Wonder Woman, the opportunity to release his pent up desires, or something unique about engaging in intercourse with Diana. If Superman now resembles a Greek god then it is also possible that sex with Wonder Woman imbided him with the traits of her mythological pantheon. This is the inverse of Larry Niven's famous 1971 essay "Man of Steel, Woman of Kleenex," which discusses the dangers of Superman having sex with his long-time girlfriend Lois Lane. Niven states, "Superman would literally crush [Lois Lane's] body in his arms, while simultaneously ripping her open from crotch to sternum, gutting her like a trout. Lastly, he'd blow off the top of her head [when he ejaculates]. ...In view of the forgoing, normal sex is impossible between [Lois Lane] and Superman" (Niven). None of these problems hamper sex with Wonder Woman though; rather the act seemingly provides the Man of Steel with almost mystically attributes and powers. Sex with the Amazon is a nearly mythical experience that physically, emotionally, and mentally rebuilds the Man of Tomorrow. While Wonder Woman seems to have enjoyed herself, it appears that she did not receive most of the same benefits as Superman.

Much like *Kingdom Come* Superman and Wonder Woman's relationship in *The Dark Knight Strikes Again* primarily focuses on the Man of Steel's needs and well-being. In this story, Wonder Woman's key character trait is her aggressive sexuality. Her purpose is to reinvigorate Superman with sexual healing that Marvin Gaye could only dream about. Besides her joke about her "earth moving" orgasm and a submissive sexual encounter, Wonder Woman's needs are not considered. Her body serves as a catalyst that revives the Man of Steel and gives him the strength, stamina, and new outlook to save the world. The Amazon's greatest contribution to saving the world is to sexually submit to her Kryptonian lover. After the Man of Steel and Amazonian princess have sex, Diana barely appears again and her appearances provide little lasting contribution to the plot. Her role as revitalizing sexual partner has been fulfilled and now she is of little use. There is no happy ending in which the super-pair grow old together, because Wonder Woman is symbolic of sexual longing and fulfillment and can be easily cast away after Superman's needs are satisfied.

In *The Dark Knight Strikes Again*, Diana is not a partner but rather a sex object to be used and then discarded. Wonder Woman's other plot purpose is to give the Man of Steel a superpowered heir to help him defeat the story's villains. Lara is the perfect mixture of her mother and father and is able to accomplish things that never of them could. The young superhero encourages her father to revel in his godlike status and to become an aggressive and proactive champion. Wonder Woman uses sexual contact to begin Superman's metamorphosis and Lara finishes the task by appealing to his paternal instincts. At the story's end, Superman and his daughter look out at the new world and the Man of Steel asks, "What exactly should we do with our planet, Lara?" (247). Wonder Woman was instrumental in producing this triumph but was not important enough to physically experience it with her lover and her daughter. She fulfilled her purpose as sex object and mother and then was unneeded and subsequently cast out.

Comic book fans have long debated the merits of a Superman and Wonder Woman relationship, though the two iconic superheroes have rarely acknowledged any romantic or physical attraction during in continuity stories. What would a Wonder Woman/ Superman pairing look like and how would the two heroes react to this new development? Mark Waid and Alex Ross's *Kingdom Come* and Frank Miller and Lynn Varley's *The Dark Knight Strikes Again* features tales in which the two heroes engage in both a romantic and business partnership. The super-duo works together to save the world while also engaging in a romantic/ sexual relationship. Though the nature of this relationship differs greatly, both sets of creators primarily see the intimate pairing as a way for Wonder Woman to heal and rehabilitate a beaten and battered Superman. Seemingly little thought went into determining the Amazon's needs and desires but rather all parties chose to focus on the Man of Steel. In *Kingdom Come*, Diana becomes a conservative spouse-like figure who must reinvigorate the Man of Tomorrow while nudging him to follow her tactical and political ideas. In *The Dark Knight Strikes Again* the Amazon warrior is little more than a sexual object that reinvigorates Superman through carnal contact and then disappears after leaving him a daughter to fight alongside. Strangely, the two very different versions of a Clark and Diana romance feature an unequal relationship that focuses almost exclusively on the Man of Steel's needs. The Amazonian warrior is transformed into either a maternal/ domestic or a sexual figure and the Man of Tomorrow is restored to his proper heroic self. Although Wonder Woman has made enormous progress since her early often submissive appearances, in this late twentieth and early twenty-first century stories the Amazon is once again culturally and socially bound and tied.

WORKS CITED

Jensen, Jeff. "'Justice League' #12: DC Reveals Superman's New Leading Lady ... and It's a Doozy — EXCLUSIVE." EW.com. Aug. 22, 2012. Web. Dec. 12, 2012.

Miller, Frank (w), and Lynn Varley (a). *Batman: The Dark Knight Strikes Back*. New York: DC Comics, 2002.

Niven, Larry. "Man of Steel, Woman of Kleenex." *Man of Steel, Woman of Kleenex*. Dec. 1, 1994. Web. Dec. 16, 2012.

Waid, Mark (w), and Alex Ross (a). *Kingdom Come*. New York, NY: DC Comics, 1997.

War, Foreign Policy
and the Media

The Rucka Years

FERNANDO GABRIEL PAGNONI BERNS

Following *Crisis on Infinite Earths* (1985), George Pérez took over the job of revitalizing Wonder Woman, recounting her origin and her adventures. The secret identity of Diana Prince was left aside and Wonder Woman assumed the identity of Diana, princess of Themyscira in the world of men and ambassador of peace. In this time Diana's adventures begin to suffer from complexities that give the character depth, but contradictions too.

Diana is princess of the Amazons, mythological creatures whose very essence is war. However, Diana is sent to the patriarchal world to ensure peace. In other words, Wonder Woman is asked to deny her essence. On the other hand, Diana is continually depicted like a superhero who tries dialogue before engaging in a fight with the enemy. Her ways are those of peace, empathy, and forgiveness. Her ways are diplomatic. This contradicts the popular view held about the Amazons as bloodthirsty warriors who are always eager to fight to death. But the amazons of Themyscira are presented on many occasions, in different years and under the hands of different authors, as daily practitioners of the art of war.

It did not help to resolve these contradictions that virtually every author who followed Pérez treats Wonder Woman like a *tabula rasa*. Supporting cast, spatial location, and personality were ignored for the most part to create a new universe that better suit the situations that the new author wants to create.

The character's constant "reboots"[1] have resulted in Wonder Woman not having a very defined personality, which, in a cycle that continues the problem, allows each author to recreate the character. It is this freedom in creating new story arcs which causes the most important female character in DC Comics lacks definitive and defining outlines.

At the heart of these contradictions, in addition to the aforementioned tendency for the authors to take the character and make an unofficial "reboot" for their own stories, lies the problem of the relationship that Diana has with war in the patriarch's world. She is a creature bred for war that works as a figure of peace. These disjunctive lines are those that help to make it difficult to create coherent story arcs for her.

Diana's relationship with war and with the outside world that makes these wars takes center stage in the years when Greg Rucka wrote *Wonder Woman* from 2003 to 2006. At times Rucka falls into the same patterns his colleagues followed: taking one of Diana's particular traits and using it as the basis for the stories, ignoring the character's other facets. So, Rucka focuses almost exclusively on Diana as a Themyscirian ambassador in the patriarchal world and the problems that this role brings to her. But Rucka also created memorable stories in which Wonder Woman found herself in the midst of a war for the throne of Olympus, stories in which she must battle with a resurrected Medusa, or engage in an epic battle with Maxwell Lord, without forgetting the constant friction with the successful businesswoman Veronica Cale.

What makes this Wonder Woman run exciting? Not only the great creativity in the construction of plots and sub-plots, the pace, or the creation of very well developed characters such as the Minotaur and chef Ferdinand. What makes these stories stand out is the fact that they are framed in the echoes of a real event that shocked and changed the history of not only America but the whole world: the attack of 9/11 on the United States.

The first issue of *Wonder Woman* created by Rucka is #195 (Oct. 2003), just slightly over two years after the attack on the World Trade Center. Not only were these two years not enough for the trauma to heal (which probably will remain forever open), but the pain and the impact caused by the terrorist attack had not even settled yet. Diana mirrors in her actions and contradictions,[2] especially in her role as ambassador, the doubts and determinations of a nation which faces the dilemma of answering terror with terror or attempting a diplomatic response.

The leading idea of this chapter will be to find the similarities that allow reading *Wonder Woman* Vol. 2 #195–226 as a cultural artifact that channels and reconstructs themes that permeated the "new normality" after the 9/11 (Daniel). In this sense it is interesting to observe how *Wonder Woman* Vol. 2 #195, Rucka's first issue, includes several of the topics that will be developed throughout the following years.

First, Wonder Woman's life in the embassy. Rucka highlights this by choosing to narrate the arrival of a new personal secretary to Diana, Jonah McCarthy. The embassy will also function as the epicenter of Themyscira's difficult relationships with the outside world in the defense of its borders and sovereignty. Second, Diana Prince's absence from the embassy, in this case because she is on a mission outside U.S. frontiers, in a territory that appears as "invaded." Third, a deliberate multicultural approach that permeates Rucka's run. The employees of the embassy come from ethnic groups and nations, from an Italian, Peter Garibaldi, in charge of the media affairs to a Latina secretary, Alana Dominguez, to the individual in charge of the affairs for international law, Rachel Keast, a black woman. And, significantly, the chef of the embassy is a minotaur extracted from distant lands and times. Fourth, the topic of the clash of religions is announced in the title of a book that Diana wrote: "Reflections. A Collection of Essays and Speeches." Fifth, the significance of topics such as the handling of international law and the mass media, embodied in Keast and Garibaldi respectively, since they are responsible for such matters.

This first issue allows Rucka to show what will be Diana's habitual environment during several years: the daily life in the embassy, and the daily fights that Wonder Woman should face not in her super-heroic figure, but as an ambassador. Supposedly Diana has already been the ambassador of Themyscira in the United States since George Pérez's years, but Rucka is the first author that takes this aspect of her life and places it in center stage.

It is in the embassy's everyday life where the author put his focus while Wonder Woman has a mission that cleverly mixes two of her roles: super-hero and ambassador. Diana is in an unnamed foreign country, which has features that mirror the common imagery that accompanies Islamic culture, such as the soldier's physical features and their leader's name: General Abaku.

This issue leaves the true nature of what is happening unclear to the reader. Is Wonder Woman invading an Eastern country on behalf of the United States? Is she stopping an alleged invasion of a sovereign nation over another one? If so, is it in behalf of the United States? Is Abaku really a dictator or a democratically elected president? Does she arrest him by the authority conferred to her for being a messenger of peace? From where/whom she obtains the authority?

These arguments were very important when responding to the attacks of 9/11. It is possible that for many citizens, the United States had sufficient reason to invade the countries that gave shelter to Al Qaeda and its leader, Osama bin Laden. Thus, the United States would ensure peace with a preventive war. Conversely, many saw the intervention as an intervention which did not respect national sovereignty. For many then, the United States' intervention in the Islamic world was intended to expand democracy, while others saw it as a covert colonization (Abrahamian).

The concept of "imminent threat" made acceptable the use of force and would justify any intervention of Wonder Woman, or George W. Bush, in foreign countries (Lang). This is not the first time a super-hero intervenes in the affairs of foreign war in order to prevent deaths, one of the clearest examples being the Superman's intervention in Qurac, a country clearly built in the likeness of Iraq and Kuwait (Wolfman), but it is the first time a superhero with political office makes such intervention. Diana supposedly represents other interests besides herself when acting outside the U.S. borders, in her role as ambassador.

In *Wonder Woman* Vol. 2 #196 (Nov. 2003) Veronica Cale, one of the main villain in Rucka's run, appears for the first time. Darrel Keyes also appears, and he will be used by Cale as the public face behind the campaign that will discredit Diana using the religious and philosophical ideas contained in Diana's book "Reflections" as weapons.

Cale and Keyes instruct a group of people to find "controversial" ideas in Diana's book, which can be used against her. Keyes, who is "executive manager for Protect Our Children" would use the "non-traditional" ideas of family displayed in the book as an argument to attack Diana. The episode ends with a win for Keyes: elementary and high schools officially prohibit the "cult of Wonder Woman" and any student club or organization of teenagers bearing the name of the amazon princess is dismantled. This situation is reminiscent of the "backlash against the U.S. Muslim community" that took much of the world after the 9/11 (Abrahamian 538). Amid the paranoia caused by the terrorist attacks, everyone who belonged to one of the countries considered "enemies," any person belonging to Islam, anyone who dresses in clothes associated with countries of the Middle East could be considered "suspicious" and put under caution, especially at airports. The rise of islamophobia which increased after 9/11, built a barbarian "other" (Lazar 45–6) whose religious and philosophical ideas are so radically opposed to Westerners that it seemingly produces an inevitable "clash of civilizations" leading to a decline for fear of reprisals of religious activities in schools in the Western world (Huntington 3). That "other" is constructed in opposition to a universal "one," who is occidental, white, Christian, heterosexual, and male. Anyone who does not respond to these categories in its entirety is framed as "other."

It is in Themyscira where the geographical and multicultural boundaries blur in an uncomfortable coalition. The Amazons native of the island, commanded by General Phillipus after the resignation of Diana and her mother Hippolyta, must share their land in an alliance full of distrust with the Egyptian Amazons of Bana-Mighdall,[3] led by Artemis. Both tribes cohabit, trying to take the island to a new era without war, but with a permanent distrust toward the "other" one. Phil Jiménez, the author that highlighted the alliance among the tribes, describes the Amazons of Bana-Migdhall as "less politically powerful but more technologically advanced" (*Out Magazine*, Mar. 2001, 64).

The amazons from Middle East were conceptualized when George Pérez was the primary *Wonder Woman* creator as uncivilized, brutal, responding to the dialectic between "bourgeois and barbarians" since whenever "we see warriors in Africa or the Middle East we tend to see barbarians" (Coker). The fear of others and the dissolution of borders becomes more complex in this game of mirrors where the Amazons are seen as potential enemies, while within the island that fear is reiterated in another dichotomy between civilized and barbaric. Maybe for this reason Rucka addresses in 2003 the conflict among the amazon tribes. In *Wonder Woman* #198 it is specified that the amazons do not approve of the entrance of the western men, since they use the island's resources in an unequal relationship: "They ate our food, they use our goods and services, they bring nothing in trade, and the gods alone know what they're doing to our security" (Rucka, "Down ... Part Three"). Fears of colonization are clearly shown: a nation, under the excuse of a diplomatic intervention to increase commercial exchange or spread democracy, goes into another country extracting from it all the desirable resources without leaving anything in return.

For some authors the terrorist attacks can be framed in a competition caused by globalization (Baudrillard) in which a particular country wants to demonstrate its superiority to another one, thus hiding their envy (Agathangelou). This may be what Al Qaeda wanted when attacking the symbols of American power and civilization. Terrorists want to demonstrate that they reached the same levels in its system of technological and armament production provoking a "symbolic impact" that leaves this fact engraved in the audience's retinas (Baudrillard). In the globalized world, powers come closer together and borders are erased, forcing a sometimes uncomfortable proximity, similar to the issues the two tribes of amazons living on Themyscira face in Rucka's tale.

Nations want to show their power and establish sovereignty to avoid falling into a process of perceived feminization that present them as dependents of greater (male) powers (Agathangelou). This fear of a possible slide into a process of feminization and this envy of the power of the neighboring nation is what appears to afflict Dr. Veronica Cale in Rucka's run on *Wonder Woman*. What Cale cannot stand is people proclaiming Diana as a prototype of a strong or modern woman. Cale sees Wonder Woman as born with undeniable advantages: superhuman strength, wisdom granted by the gods, invincible and magical weapons, superhuman beauty, etc. Cale considers the praise of Wonder Woman to be akin to worshipping a false idol that distracts the people from the real women who should be examples of womanhood. Women like herself, who with tenacity and great sacrifice made it out of a life doomed to poverty (her mother was a stripper and her father does not recognize her as his child), accumulating a fortune using her intelligence: a human intelligence, not granted by the gods (Rucka, "Leaks"). To attack Diana she uses as an excuse Wonder Woman's "extreme" (fundamentalist?) ways of life, her religion which strongly contrasts with Christian values. What Cale wants to do is "invade" Wonder Woman, reduce her using prejudices and people's preconceptions about sexuality, religion, and ideology to make sure public opinion will be on her side. Cale considers herself the ideal role model of the American Dream come true, someone who built an empire working hard and making good use of the opportunities. For this confrontation Cale will have an unquestionable ally: the media.

Audiovisual media present events as unquestionable truth, even after an editing process, while anything that doesn't take place on a screen, ironically becomes virtual due to the absence of images, That which is not preserved by images in the media ceases to be real, it becomes a non-event (Merrin). This is easy to see from the images repeated over and over again, as in a temporal loop, of the exact moment in which the hijacked planes impact on its target on 9/11, or the towers collapsing in a time that seems to be always present, even though it happened years ago. However, the images of the attack on the Pentagon have not been shown, leading to all sorts of speculation about possible deception and lies. As Diana significantly says in *Wonder Woman* #199 (Feb. 2004), "the first casualty in war, after all, is truth" (Rucka, "Down ... Part Four").

As a strategy to defeat Wonder Woman, Veronica Cale uses her economic power to make some networks join her in her attack on the Amazon Princess. In issue #198, the embassy staff is embarrassed as a TV news show manipulates certain words uttered by Diana to Flash, where she asked him to allow a forest fire to burn since fire is necessary for the renewal of nature. However, what is shown on television is a Wonder Woman unconcerned about what might happen to the residents close to the burning forest, and even when the video is clearly edited, people will eventually believe "what they want to believe" (Rucka, "Down ... Part Three").

In *Wonder Woman* #210 (Jan. 2005) Diana defeats Medusa in a televised battle, thwarting a plan hatched by Circe wherein Medusa would look directly at the cameras transmitting the match live and every citizen watching the event would be magically turned into stone by the gaze of the Gorgon. However, to win the battle, Wonder Woman blinds herself with the acid poison from a pair of snakes decapitated from Medousa's head, preventing Medusa's gaze from harming her. The vignettes of men and women in the streets, in homes, in bars and cafes watching the event with an anguished stare of terror undoubtedly mirrors the global reactions provoked by seeing in a TV screen the attack on the Twin Towers, an act that was "instantaneously relayed throughout the globe, thanks to the technology and communications network" (Lincoln 17). As Baudrillard argues, terrorists use as a weapon "the real time of images" to spread fear, to paralyze the masses at the horror show that is taking place in front of millions of citizens. With the Medusa battle, this idea is literal: the real-time images become a weapon of mass destruction where all the people watching their TV screens may die petrified in fear.

A final point should be noted. While all the above-mentioned happen, a "virtual" war (because it is not meant to be seen by human eyes) takes place. The gods battle for Zeus' throne, who should move on due to the new times.[4] In this battle between Ares, Athena and Zeus, the Amazons become "collateral damage" and Themyscira, which had the blessing of gods and floated over the world, falls into the sea (Rucka, "Down ... Conclusion), causing extensive damage and leaving the amazons helpless in the eyes of a very powerful enemy: the United States. Themyscira is now near the Carolinas and with the excuse of "humanitarian" help for the wounded amazons and the material losses, ships of war surround the island, which has always been coveted by the patriarch's world.

The U.S. invasion of Iraq or Afghanistan under the idea of "preventive war" or a "spread of democracy" produced and still produces controversy even today (Lichtenberg; Chomsky), and that position is mirrored in the fictional President Jonathan Vincent Horne's position towards Themyscira in these issues of *Wonder Woman*. "In the aftermath of 9/11, President George Bush declared that the United States would act pre-emptively to fight the two major threats it faced: terrorism and rogue states" (Colonomos 85). A preventive war does not require "conditions of direct necessity" (Colonomos 87), the possibility of threat is sufficient to initiate it: "Offensive action is justified on the basis of a threat, remote in the case of prevention" (Colonomos 87). But as the definition about what country or region can be considered a "possible" threat is very subjective, the preventive wars can be guilty of a colonialist color: a conquest war disguised as preventive war (Colonomos 87).

During the meeting at the White House in *Wonder Woman* #208 (Nov. 2004) the U.S. government and the ambassador of Themyscira, with Artemis and Phillipus, come together to try to solve their border issues through diplomacy. The U.S. government shows its true colors when they make their proposal: defend and respect the Amazons' territory in exchange for the purple healing ray that Themyscira keeps (Rucka, "Stoned Part Three").

At this point an interesting dialogue begins between the different parties, in which the Amazons try to defend, through diplomacy, their frontiers, while the government of U.S. begins to frame Themyscira as a sovereign nation of warriors which can be seen as a "potential security threat" due to their levels of technological sophistication and advances in the art of war. A preventive war looms.

Rucka solves this potentially controversial topic with a classic comic book method. An attack by Medusa takes place and the dialogue is interrupted, never to be resumed. After a series of adventures which leave no time for the debate to be addressed anew, Greg Rucka leaves the series which is rebooted with a new issue number one at the hands of Allan Heinberg in 2006. Though the diplomatic debate is never concluded, the U.S. government uses Wonder Woman's actions following their attempts at diplomacy, most notably when video of her killing Maxwell Lord surfaces, to deepen the image of the amazons as dangerous, a latent threat that must be preventively neutralized. What the government and military clearly want is to invade and colonize the island, claiming its resources and inventions under a conquest's war. It is easy to draw a parallel between this, the Bush presidency, and the protests of vocal segments of society who claimed that the U.S. invasion of Afghanistan was a war for the oil and the gas which the country produces (Rall).

But the invasion did not take place: the gods decide to grant a favor to the Amazons and Paradise Island is again made invisible to the patriarchal world's eyes. This event in turn closes not only Rucka's storyline, but also the embassy itself. Diana is no longer an ambassador, since Themyscira is out of the globalized world and diplomatic relationships have no meaning. Thus, Rucka leaves the character free from any ties for the next writer, who can address Diana from any point of view. This is the last time in which readers see the characters that populated the embassy all these years.

In Greg Rucka's time as writer there was no explicit reference to attack on the Twin Towers, although there are events which are reminiscent of the catastrophe (the fall of Themyscira to the ocean in *Wonder Woman* #200 (Mar. 2004). Both the Medusa attack (which took place in the White House), and the new Silver Swan's strike in *Wonder Woman* #200 (Mar. 2004) can be considered terrorist attacks. In fact, Diana continually asks for Silver Swan to not be named as a terrorist by the government because under the villain's mechanical suit is Vanessa Kapatelis, a friend of hers, who was brainwashed and surrounded it with metal, circuits and technology to be a living threat (Rucka, "Stoned Part Three").

Border problems abound throughout the years, both within and outside the island. The frontiers at risk of being crossed and attacked are not just geographic: they are religious, cultural and ethnic. Wonder Woman must defend her book and her religion from intolerance towards other religions and ideas. She must defend her position, her identity, and that of all the amazons who are continually in danger of being discursively constructed as "barbaric" and therefore in need of being conquered and civilized. This can clearly be seen in the events following the murder of Maxwell Lord, when Diana must face the consequences of killing a being that does not look monstrous, a being who is not an "other." In a heated argument with McCarthy, he presents to Diana the problems with the law which Lord's death will bring and how people's distrust towards the amazon will increase in the coming days. She recalls that she killed before and that that murder was broadcast live (Medusa), but McCarthy reminds her that the Gorgon was a monster, something different, while Lord was human, American, white and male. What McCarthy is trying to say is that the murder of the "other" is permitted, is forgivable. Not so the murder of one of "us." Making parallels with the bloody battles after the 9/11, it is possible to say that the killing of the terrorists and the innocent people who lived near them, is a necessary evil. But it is not measured in the same way as the murder of Westerners.

The clearest example is, of course, Ferdinand, the epitome of the "other": a minotaur chef who works and lives, advises, respects and is respected by others when he is not even fully human. Ferdinand is perfect "other": the minority taken to another level. This coexistence reaches its point with the romance between Ferdinand and Dr. Leslie Thompkins.

That budding romance was not addressed after Rucka's departure from *Wonder Woman*. Perhaps if Greg Rucka returns at some point to write for Wonder Woman, he can address to tension of diplomacy/war that is at the core of the main character, perhaps giving her much needed internal coherence. And maybe Rucka (or anyone else) should bring back Dr. Thompkins and Ferdinand, a transgressive romance that can join two cultural contexts in peace.

NOTES

1. Recently, the character went through at least one "official" reboot in the fourteen issues written by J. Michael Straczynski and Phil Hester (#600–614), and another with the new Wonder Woman written by Brian Azzarello from the reboot of the entire DC universe in "The New 52."

2. "Because you and all of your sisters preach peace but know war!" Jonah McCarthy says to Diana in *Wonder Woman* Vol. 2 #220 (Rucka, "Affirmative").

3. If the amazons of Paradise Island are "Europeans" for their connection to ancient Greece, the amazons of Bana-Mighdall are more related to the Middle East as it is in those regions where they migrated when the originals amazons were separated into two tribes.

4. In fact, in Rucka's run, the gods dress, in their majority, in contemporary clothes, with exceptions suchas Zeus who dresses in a classic toga.

WORKS CITED

Abrahamian, Ervand. "The U.S. Media, Huntington and September 11." *Third World Quarterly* vol. 24, no. 3 (2003), pp. 529–544.

Agathangelou, Anna. "Power, Borders, Security, Wealth: Lessons of Violence and Desire from September 11." *International Studies Quarterly* 48 (2004).

Baudrillard, Jean. *The Spirit of Terrorism*. Trans. Chris Turner. New York: Verso, 2003.

Baxter, Kylie, and Shahram Akbarzadeh. *U.S. Foreign Policy in the Middle East: The Roots of Anti-Americanism*. New York: Routledge, 2008.

Chomsky, Noam. *The Culture of Terrorism*. London: Pluto, 1989.

_____. *Pirates and Emperors, Old and New: International Terrorism in the Real World*. New Ed. Cambridge, MA: South End, 2002.

Coker, Christopher. "War Without Warriors." In *Global Responses to Terrorism: 9/11, Afghanistan and Beyond*, edited by Mary Buckley and Rick Fawn, 284–295. New York: Routledge, 2003.

Colonomos, Ariel "Preventive War à l'Américaine: In the Fog of Norms." In *War, Torture, and Terrorism: Rethinking the Rules of International Security*, edited by Anthony Lang Jr. and Amanda Russell Beattie, 85–102. New York: Routledge, 2008.

Danieli, Yael, Danny Brom and Joe Sills. "The Trauma of Terrorism: Contextual Considerations." In *The Trauma of Terror: Sharing Knowledge and Shared Care*, edited by Yael Danieli, Danny Brom and Joe Sills, 1–17. New York: Haworth Maltreatment and Trauma, 2004.

Dreher, Tanja. *Targeted. Experience of Racism in NSW After September 11, 2001*. Broadway, NSW: UTS, 2006.

Ferrante, Joan. *Sociology: A Global Perspective*. Enhanced 7th ed. Belmont, CA: Wadsworth, 2011.

Fetzer, Joel, and Christopher Soper. "The Roots of Public Attitudes Toward State Accommodation of European Muslims' Religious Practices Before and After September 11." *Journal for the Scientific Study of Religion* vol. 42, no. 2 (Jun. 2003), pp. 247–258.

Huntington, Samuel. "The Clash of Civilizations?" *Foreign Affairs* 72:3 (Summer 1993), pp. 22–49.

Lang, Anthony. "Rules and International Security: Dilemmas of a New World Order." In *War, Torture, and Terrorism: Rethinking the Rules of International Security*, edited by Anthony Lang Jr. and Amanda Russell Beattie, 1–22. New York: Routledge, 2008.

Lazar, Annita, and Michelle Lazar. "Enforcing Justice, Justifying Justice: America's Justification of Violence in the New World Order." In *Discourse, War and Terrorism*, edited by Adam Hodges and Chad Nilep, 45–65. Lancaster: University of Lancaster, 2007.

Lichtenberg, Judith. "Pre-emption and Exceptionalism in U.S. Foreign Policy. Precedent and Example in the International Arena." In *Wars on Terrorism and Iraq: Human Rights, Unilateralism, and U.S. Foreign Policy*, edited by Thomas Weiss, Margaret Crahan, and John Goering, 61–73. New York: Routledge, 2004.

Lincoln, Bruce. *Holy Terrors: Thinking About Religion After September 11th*. 2d ed. London: University of Chicago Press, 2006.

Merrin, William. *Baudrillard and the Media*. Cambridge, UK: Polity, 2005.

Rall, Ted. *Gas War: The Truth Behind the American Occupation of Afghanistan*. Lincoln, NE: Writers Club, 2002.

Rucka, Greg (w), and Drew Johnson (a). "Down to Earth Conclusion." *Wonder Woman* Vol. 2 #200 (Mar. 2004). New York: DC Comics, 2004.

_____. "Down to Earth (Part I of V)." *Wonder Woman* Vol. 2 #196 (Nov. 2003). New York: DC Comics, 2003.

_____. "Down to Earth Part Three." *Wonder Woman* Vol. 2 #198 (Jan. 2004). New York: DC Comics, 2004.

_____. "Down to Earth Part Four." *Wonder Woman* Vol. 2 #199 (Feb. 2004). New York: DC Comics, 2004.

_____. "The Mission." *Wonder Woman* Vol. 2 #195 (Oct. 2003). New York: DC Comics, 2003.

_____."Stoned Conclusion." *Wonder Woman* Vol. 2 #210 (Jan. 2005). New York: DC Comics, 2005.

_____."Stoned Part Three." *Wonder Woman* Vol. 2 #208 (Nov. 2004). New York: DC Comics, 2004.

Out of the Refrigerator

Gail Simone's Wonder Woman, 2008–2010

ALISON MANDAVILLE

Wonder Woman's gender may have been the brainchild of a woman, Elizabeth Marston, wife of William, the psychologist credited with creating the new heroine in 1941,[1] yet it was not until 2008 that the *Wonder Woman* comic series would gain its first regular, ongoing female writer, Gail Simone.[2] Perhaps the most popular late twentieth century symbol of female power,[3] nevertheless, the superheroine[4] can be critiqued as less than empowering of women: in all her incarnations, Diana is a curvy, stereotypically attractive figure defined through the equally stereotypical "feminine" emotions of love and compassion and originally portrayed primarily through her relationship to a man (Steve Trevor). Awareness of the sexist portrayal of female superheroes bodies recently reached critical mass with the initiation of "The Hawkeye Initiative" launched December 2, 2012, on Tumblr. Fans post parody renditions of the male superhero, Hawkeye, in the same poses in which female superheroes have been drawn, past and present — illuminating the degree of sexism present simply in superhero comics' character poses (thehawkeyeinitiative.com).[5] Simone's version of Wonder Woman does not entirely dispel these critiques of the sexism inherent in depiction of her main character — in the five story arcs she authored, collected as *The Circle, Ends of the Earth, Rise of the Olympian, Warkiller* and *Contagion,* Diana remains a sexy, busty woman with an attraction to men and a hankering for love and compassion. But the narrative world in which this superhero moves has changed significantly. Simone's complex narratives explicitly extend Marston's vision of an ethical female superhero in the cultural context of late twentieth century "third wave" U.S. feminism. Simone not only builds on and takes for granted second wave feminism's achievements of increased gender equity in the home and workplace but her diverse characters also assume women's rightful places in global arenas. Instead of linking women's narrative worth solely to their relationships with men, Simone centers women's relationships with each other. And, rather than minimizing differences between men and women, Simone's narratives draw on and even revel in gender differences, emphasizing the power of the female body and female sexuality.

Women in Refrigerators (WiR) and the Third Wave

Gail Simone is perhaps best known, in the comics world at least, for her 1999 coinage of the term "Women in Refrigerators," which she created to mark the common, and in her opinion, seriously problematic, use of violence against women as a plot device in superhero comics. Run a search on "Women" and "Refrigerators," in academic databases — the first page of search results features a remarkable number of social science studies linking women to the appliance. The many titles include "Beauty Queen, Bulletin Board, and Browser: Re-scripting the refrigerator" (Watkins), "Three Greek Women: The Insignificance of an Appliance" (O'Rourke) and my personal favorite in the context of this piece, "'Preserving Women': Refrigerator Design as Social Process in the 1930s" (Nickels). These studies reflect contemporary Western culture's enduring association of women with the domestic sphere — and inadvertently parody the long history of women killed, raped and maimed in the service of male superhero narratives, a history long frost-bitten and hidden at the back of the superhero freezer. By 1999, for Simone, it was time to "rescript the refrigerator."

The refrigerator is used, perhaps without irony but apparently not coincidentally, in the comic *Green Lantern* #54 (Aug. 1994) to "preserve" the body of the hero's murdered girlfriend (Marz); a plot device that engenders the story of vengeance that follows. It is also an image and phrase that will become symbolic of such violent tropes in 1999 when Simone, after an exchange of letters among friends about treatment of female comics characters, creates and posts online a list of scenes of gratuitous violence against female superheroes. She introduced the list, writing, "These are superheroines who have been either depowered, raped, or cut up and stuck in the refrigerator. I know I missed a bunch. Some have been revived, even improved — although the question remains as to why they were thrown in the wood chipper in the first place." The website provoked both support and backlash. She posted some of the backlash — and her response: "I have a secret. I love superheroes ... [but] it had been nagging me for a while that in mainstream comics, being a girl superhero meant inevitably being killed, maimed or depowered, it seemed"

("Women").[6] The seemingly frozen narrative fate of the "girl superhero" that had long been "nagging" Simone was now out of the refrigerator — and Simone herself would soon play a pivotal role in thawing and re-shaping the narrative space of these female characters.

Not long after she became widely associated with the critique now known as "Women in Refrigerators" or "WiR," Simone combined a life-long love of comics and her skills as a writer to begin work in the comics industry, soon becoming known for her storylines centering on women characters in DC's *Birds of Prey* series and most recently as writer of *Batgirl*.[7] In 2007, she agreed to become the ongoing writer for *Wonder Woman*[8] and began creating story arcs that, almost offhandedly, depict and counter the gender stereotypes and inequities that first and second wave activists struggled to make visible.

Simone's particular treatment of these themes anchors this incarnation of *Wonder Woman* firmly in the third wave of gender activism in the U.S., a movement characterized by its critique of second wave feminism and emphasis on cultural production and the female body as a source of social change. The "first wave" of gender activism in Western countries, spanning the late eighteenth to early twentieth centuries achieved basic property and voting rights for (mainly white) women. The "second wave" from the late 1950s through the 1970s made significant gains towards gender equity in the workplace, reproductive choice, and recognition of, if not always protections against, gendered violence. Simone ties her interest in *Wonder Woman* directly to that second wave context. In a 2007 *New York Times* interview, she says of the character: "She was a princess who didn't need someone to rescue her. I grew up in an era — and a family — where women's rights were very important, and the guys didn't tend to stick around too long. She was an amazing role model" (Gustines).

Third wavers are defined as the women (and some men) who came of age in the 1970s and 1980s, as did Simone, in a context of second wave feminist struggles, achievements — and faults. Indeed, critique of second wave feminism has been a centerpiece of the third wave. In 1995, Rebecca Walker edited the anthology of essays *To Be Real: Telling the Truth and Changing the Face of Feminism* in an attempt to speak to the sense that, as she says in a later foreword to *The Fire This Time: Young Activists and the New Feminism* (2004), "capital F Feminism needs an overhaul" based on "critique ... by the majority of the world's women, including but not limited to indigenous women, Third World women, American women of color, and working-class women" (xiv). Similarly acknowledging the ways second wave feminism at times ignored how race, class and other constructions of difference interact to produce different experiences of gender oppression, in *Not My Mother's Sister: Generational Conflict and Third Wave Feminism* (2004) Astrid Henry writes, "If the third wave has been schooled in the lessons of the second wave, as some third wavers argue it has been, then it must conceive of feminism as more than just a movement to empower white economically privileged women" (45).Yet, beyond this critique, there is little agreement on the definition of "third wave feminism." In *Third Wave Agenda* (1997) Heywood and Drake "define feminism's third wave as a movement that contains elements of second wave critique of beauty culture, sexual abuse, and power structures while it also makes use of the pleasure, danger, and defining power of those structures" (3). In *Manifesta: Young Women, Feminism and the Future* (2000) Jennifer Baumgartner and Amy Richards define the Third Wave by its historical and pop-cultural context as "the core mass of the current women's movement in their late teens through early thirties, roughly speaking — the ones who grew up with Judy Blume books, *Free to be ... You and Me* and *Sesame Street*" (402). By 2004, Henry notes "there are as many competing narratives of the third wave as there are of the second" (45).

These varied definitions of third wave gender activism do share three things: a strong connection to second wave feminism, whether building upon or critiquing it, a desire for a more inclusive movement, and a deep investment in cultural production — particularly popular culture (trade books, TV series, music, beauty culture) — as a site not only for gendered critique, but also for gendered creativity, power and change. In the *Wonder Woman* comic books Simone authored, while characters still live in a world of sexism and stereotype, diverse women confront these injustices as a matter of course, taking the accomplishments of the second wave largely for granted. They work as soldiers, medics and movie producers. They parent. They travel the world. While the central characters are still white and regular inclusion of racially and ethnically diverse characters often seems color-blind to the differential ways women may experience gender inequities, Simone's women characters, both good and bad "guys," are nevertheless complex. They value their own lives and their relationships with other women. While Diana, at times, chooses to set aside her personal desires, as she does of her romantic interest in co-agent Tom Tressor in the story arc *Rise of the Olympian*, this never means confining love and compassion to the private, domestic sphere; Diana's family is diverse and global (even universal), a kind of Sisterhood 3.0, and, as Tom's induction into the Amazon tribe illustrates, a community no longer limited by gender. Where second wave feminism began to articulate connections between the personal and the political,[9] through Simone's spotlight on the inner workings of the Amazon sisterhood, which is, effectively, a sister-citizenship, she seamlessly reconnects the gendered division of public political (male) and domestic family (female) spaces, expanding an inclusive ethic of love and care for others to a global-political level. Perhaps most characteristic of the third wave, in Simone's

Wonder Woman women and girls can be creative masters and celebrants of an explicitly female body image and beauty culture with which second wave feminism struggled, and, at times, rejected wholesale.

The Female Body and the Gaze of Comics

First wave feminism did not, in general, take up a critique of the construction of female body. Rather, in the foundational first wave equal rights manifesto, the 1948 Seneca Falls "Declaration of Sentiments," references to men's "chatisement" of their wives and a "different code of morals" merely hint at concerns about gendered violence and sexual double standards. For the most part, these will not be addressed systematically until the second wave agitates for legal protections against domestic violence, rape, sexual harassment, and for reproductive health choices. But even as the second wave confronted key issues directly impacting women's bodies, they also resisted essentialist arguments against gender equity that were based on biology, often minimizing biological sex differences.

Third wave gender activism emerged not only from a critique of perceived second wave exclusiveness, but also in response to a conservative backlash against second wave feminism marked most visibly in the legislative and judicial erosion of reproductive rights in the two decades following Roe V. Wade U.S. Supreme Court decision in 1973 that legalized abortion. As Trina Robbins says of third wave feminism in *Girls to Grrrlz: A History of Women's Comics from Teens to Zines*,

> the daughters of [third wave feminists] grew up understanding the concept of sexism, and taking for granted many of the gains made by that earlier movement. Along came the backlash, and young women found their security rudely shattered by threats to their reproductive rights, and by a new wave of sexism and homophobia. They were still not free to walk down the street without being harassed. They were mad as hell and they weren't going to take it [125].

The female body clearly still mattered — and the third wave not only sought to defend it, but to celebrate and create through it. The third wave often framed itself through cultural productions in which the female body figured prominently: music (all-female bands Bikini Kill and Bratmobile from Olympia, Washington), zines (*Riot Grrrl* was one of many self-published and distributed "zines" by young women), fashion and performance (bookended in time by Madonna and Lady Gaga). This cultural work went hand-in-hand with a deliberate inhabitation and depiction of a material female body that was powerful, mobile, sexy, and decidedly having fun with the very images of femininity that second wave feminism had so often critiqued as problematic. This pointed to a turn in gender activism of the 1990s, not away from political action, but towards cultural production and aesthetics as its sustainable form, recharged by its own creative juices.

The increasingly visual nature of popular culture in the late twentieth and early twenty-first centuries (television, web media, music videos) perhaps made inevitable the third wave's increasing centering of the body as a site (sight?!) of power and resistance. In Simone's *Wonder Woman*, gender role stereotypes based on constructions of women's and men's bodies abound, among both gods and humans. Paralleling a landscape of lingering real world gender inequity, the background conflict throughout these story arcs is Zeus' distrust of the Amazons and Diana based on their gender. He says to Apollo "Hippolyta's daughter has had YEARS to change this world. But, really, what has she accomplished?" Apollo replies "It is time to recognize what you and I have both known for centuries. Changing the world is not a job for WOMEN.../...it is a job for MEN" (*Rise* 7). In another example of the hostile environment women still face as they enter traditionally male spaces to go about their business of saving the world, when Diana seeks cooperation from several other (male) heroes in a drinking hall, she is mistaken for a prostitute and called a variety of gendered epithets including "wench" and "slattern" (*Ends* 10, 21). The archaic language remarks on the long history of gender bias. Simone also makes clear the ubiquitous threat of sexual violence women still face from both "good" and "bad" men. The words of an enemy mercenary soldier "I did wanna see that wonder chick, though. I'd know how to make good use of HER" (*Circle* 76) are nearly identical to previous comments by her soon-to-be ally Beowulf when he says, "I deem you ill-used, girl. I could find but MANY happier uses for you" (*Ends* 23). Secure in her power, Diana merely says to Beowulf in reply as she breaks his nose, "Funny, I was about to say YOU might try being something other than a warrior, YOURSELF. But you're too ugly to be a whore." When called a "trollop," she comments humorously and matter-of-factly, "Odd how limited men's vocabularies become when faced by a woman who is their better" (*Ends* 58).

Yet, true to a third wave sensibility that rejects a wholesale separatist impulse that was a small, but sensationalized part of second wave feminism, Simone's Diana recognizes the sexism that runs throughout the world — from leaders to enemies to allies — is a challenge that must be called out, but that it needn't get in the way of strategic alliances and getting things done. In Simone's narratives, sexism is neither ignored nor whitewashed, but neither is it given significant narrative power. Narrating from a strongly female perspective, Simone has succeeded in shifting and, to use her own word from WiR, "depowering" a male-dominant narrative perspective — the "male gaze" — in traditional superhero comics.

"Looking" is central to reading comics, an explicitly image-based narrative form. Key to Simone's comics version of *Wonder Woman* is a third wave effort to reclaim and maintain power within an increasingly globalized industry of beauty and the related, often limiting, visual narratives of girls and women. The third wave focus on cultural production as a site of female and feminist power stems from a critical awareness and reorienting of what second waver Laura Mulvey, in her 1975 essay "Visual Pleasure and Narrative Cinema" termed "the male gaze." Analyzing male dominance in film narrative Mulvey writes of "Woman as image" and "Man as bearer of the look," arguing that "Woman then stands in patriarchal culture as signifier for the male other, bound by a symbolic order in which man can live out his phantasies and obsessions through linguistic command by imposing them on the silent image of woman still tied to her place as bearer of meaning, not maker of meaning" (n.p.). Importantly, reorienting the male gaze is not just about changing the view, but about changing the *story* that view tells about our lives.

By 1990, arguably the beginnings of the third wave, feminist critics such as Mary Devereaux are questioning Mulvey's suggestion that the medium of film is itself patriarchal and oppressive, or that women themselves gaze only from a male perspective. In an interview published in 2011, Mulvey claims that she intended her argument to be "polemic" and a "manifesto" saying "I think, in retrospect[,] from a more nuanced perspective, about the inescapability of the male gaze (Sassatelli 128)." She states that "Visual Pleasure" emerged from a particular historical moment, before the technologies of video and digital imaging that allow broader creative access to cinematic media and much greater interaction and control by a "viewer" or "reader" of visual narratives. In her introduction to a special issue of *Signs* in 2004 Mulvey notes that "New technologies can transform the way that the cinema of the past is seen and thus understood" (1288). Mulvey's later reevaluation of her stance points, as she says, to a significant shift in the control of the "gaze" and its apparatuses:

> Implicitly, as the female spectator is now able to manipulate and control the image, she can reverse the power relationship so central to the cinema of 24 frames a second, in which the female spectator was amalgamated into the male look, and the male protagonist controlled the dynamism and the drive of the image. Now that relationship can be reversed [Sassatelli 141].

Nevertheless, Mulvey's early work was critical in turning the gaze back on the eye behind the camera to better understand the effects of visual narratives constructed through this determining gaze. And although Mulvey limited her argument, saying "This complex interaction of looks is specific to film," the idea of the "male gaze" offered a useful tool to engage images across a world of increasingly visual communications and narrative media (n.p.).

In a comics format, the reader has always had far more control over narrative pace and the consumption of images than she has had with cinematic media. Moreover, the comics form also offers an in-your-face awareness of what it means to "frame" an image. As in many contemporary comics, in Simone's *Wonder Woman* frame shape varies over the course of a single narrative — sometimes breaking into long horizontal or vertical frames, sometimes shattering a single scene into multiple frames, so that, in either case, readers themselves "close" — as Scott McCloud has termed it — the narrative gaps. Sometimes the narrative expands into a splash page of one panel that bleeds to the page edges, fully immersing the reader in an overwhelming scene. And, as McCloud has noted, the types of moves *between* frames also shifts: Sometimes the narrative frames advance from moment to moment, or event to event, and at other times, the narrative slows in time to explore, aspect by aspect, in multiple frames, a single moment. Framing strategies shift often enough in most comics to keep the reader from entirely naturalizing perspective as she usually does when watching a film.

The particular awareness of framing in comics is emphasized in Simone's *Wonder Woman* to remind the reader how all story comes with a "perspective." When Diana and Tom Tresser have a heart-to-heart talk about where their relationship is headed, Diana's lasso of truth becomes the frame, standing in contrast to, and so illuminating, "the usual" narrative frame as not necessarily offering "the truth" (*Warkiller* 60–63). And when the same lasso-framing technique is used as the creature "Genocide" torture's Diana's best friend Etta Candy with the stolen lasso, it is clear that even perspectives of "truth" are selected and constructed frames, tools that can be used for good — and evil (*Olympian* 112–114, 118).

The play of perspective in Simone's *Wonder Woman* exposes the way a sexist gaze has been constructed and normed for all readers, as Mulvey noted in "Visual Pleasure." It took many of my students and me several scenes of the story arc *The Rise of the Olympian* to realize that the monster character "Genocide" is, in fact, female. Because of our internalized gender stereotypes, the introductory image of Genocide's hard, muscular body together with the creature's stated goal of human death and destruction (under the broad auspices of Ares, the god of war) lead us *not* to expect a female in the role (21). When, finally, her breasts could no longer be ignored (for me, around page 42), I went back through the book and realized that, despite my long-time efforts towards a feminist awareness of gender bias, gendered narrative expectations limited my ability to "see" a more complex image of femininity. Upending gender stereotypes, Diana's body is portrayed by the artists in Simone's narratives as powerful not *in spite* of her femininity, but *because* of it. During one battle she faces the reader aggressively, the phallic Washington monument ironically at her back, arms and legs taking up space, abdominal muscles and breasts ridged together as one unbroken range of power (*Earth* 73). And images of strong male bodies are also explicitly framed as beautiful, even feminine, as when on the previous page of the same scene, Beowulf's long hair flows and curls just like Diana's as they confront their adversary together (72).

The explicit awareness of framing and perspective in comics might even be called "feminist"— or, at least, potentially feminist. Re-thinking Mulvey's early work on the "male gaze" Devereaux writes,

> Feminism in this sense offers a unique critical perspective. It provides resistance, and an alternative to, the male gaze. Admittedly, just as the male gaze involves a distinct political position, so too the feminist perspective [as Annette Kuhn writes] 'cannot be regarded as politically neutral.' Yet, as a way of seeing, it importantly differs from its male counterpart in acknowledging itself as a way of seeing [Deveraux 347, Kuhn 70, qtd in Devereaux].

In just one example among the many scenes in Simone's *Wonder Woman* that "acknowledge [themselves] as a way of seeing" and deliberately call attention to a naturalized dominant male narrative gaze, several women stand together appreciating the agent Tom's body, exposed at the back by an open hospital gown (*Olympian* 141). Notably, all the *reader* sees of his bare body are his lower legs — male-thin and rather scrawny compared to those of the powerful women characters. This scene not only reverses the gender of the "gazer" and the "looked at," but also shifts the ethics of gazing from being one of domination and objectification to being one of appreciation and respect; the body gazed upon is afforded a kind of modesty and the reader is left to imagine her own image of Tom's backside. Moreover, the stereotypical "powerful male" body is humorously undercut by what the reader *does* see of the man — his scrawny legs.

In 1990, at the advent of third wave feminism, Devereaux acknowledged that, up to that point, much feminist critique of had been negative: "Briefly summarized, the feminist critique of representation rests on the equation; the medium = male = patriarchal = oppressive" (338). Where second wave feminism may have gotten a bit stuck in an analysis of gaze and of visual media as irrecoverably patriarchal, the third wave takes back the gaze together with the media, arguing that one can critique media and visual narrative while retaining the possibility of an ethical visual appreciation of others' bodies. Simone's scene reverses the power of the gaze not in order to eliminate gazing — which seems, after all, a required element of narrative, especially comics narrative — but to make visible the ways in which the gaze can be played with, shifted, done differently to different effect. In breaking the objectifying and oppressive gaze by calling our attention to it, the possibility of a more equitable and pliable appreciation of bodies also emerges.

In another scene ripe for stereotypical imaging, in which Diana and Tom are holding each other and kissing, Simone again plays with gendered narrative expectations: The taller and more powerful Diana embraces a shorter Tom, hand on his lower back, leaning over him. Yielding to her pressure, his back arches as he awkwardly bends backward to receive her kiss. Their dialog afterwards makes clear the author and artists know exactly what they are doing in this visual reversal of a timeworn narrative trope of male sexual dominance:

> TOM: Uh ... This is...
>
> DIANA: Uncomfortable?
>
> TOM: I could get used to it, don't get me wrong./Really used to it. Like surprisingly used to it/I'd have to say I might even PREFER—
>
> DIANA: I was just thinking the same, actually. (*Rise*)

With this exchange, not only is the reader made aware of gendered expectations in romantic visual narrative, but also of the real physical and potential psychological discomfort such a "position" entails. Again, Simone's scene does not merely reverse expected gender roles. The accompanying dialog models communication as part of intimacy and explores questions of dominance and submission in relationship as not tied to gender, but as matters to be discussed and negotiated. Like the appreciation of bodies, such "roles" needn't be rejected as necessarily oppressive.

Presaging an increasing focus in the twenty-first century on gender continuums and trans-activism, in Simone's third wave world, the body and what one can do with it, from fighting to constructing one's appearance and sexuality, offers a powerful locus of creative agency and performance. In a scene from *Warkiller*, Diana meets with her superhero friend Dinah, aka The Black Canary, to plan next steps in their efforts to—as usual—battle bad folk. To infiltrate a club hiding their adversary, they must disguise themselves as sexy cage-fighters. That Dinah holds a thoroughly third wave awareness of the female body as a plastic and negotiable site of creativity, performance and power is clear when she says to her friend, "We can't exactly go as OURSELVES. We have an issue here—the sexier the outfit, the fewer questions asked. This I learned early on. But that means exposing our community's second most famous bosom [after Powergirl]" (12–13). Implicit in her comment is the way in which the male gaze can be "depowered" and turned to women's advantage. This manipulation of the gaze can be read as a reinforcement of stereotypes of women using their "feminine wiles" to manipulate men. One difference, however, in Simone's version of this familiar narrative pattern is the characters' explicit understanding of this version of femininity *as a con-*

struction—and just one choice among many that intersect and continually shift. Reminding us all of our participation in such a complex of constructions, from gender to nation, Dinah rebuffs Diana's professed ignorance about the "famousness" of her bosom with the words "you MUST know all that.. why else wear the American flag on your rumpus..." (*Warkiller*).

Simone's scenes like this seem to argue that if the image serves to manipulate, it is because the viewers are stuck in a limited perspective—yet, in another very third wave move, while the text works hard to help the reader be aware of and critique those limits, it does so with a sense of fun that not only undercuts reader defensiveness, but encourages and sustains participation in the critique; it is pleasurable. As they get their "sexy" outfits on, Dinah continues to model a running awareness of limiting gender images. She, for example, nails the stereotype of two women playing dress-up, *making fun* of the stereotype and nevertheless *having fun* at the same time: "I can't believe I'm having a MAKEOVER party with WONDER WOMAN. I feel like we should make fudge and talk about BOYS" (*Warkiller* 13). And fun as playing dress-up sexy woman is, Simone refuses to naturalize the stereotype: she later has Dinah eat her noodles with a hearty and very un-stereotypically-ladylike "SSHLLLLURRP" (*Warkiller* 31). For the Black Canary, not only is the body a powerful site of creativity, performance, and critique but also it is a site of *fun*. Diana later acknowledges to herself "I think I could use a little Black Canary every once in a while, If I'm honest. She does know her way around the idea of fun" (*Warkiller* 32).

In her reemphasis of the female body as a source of both power and pleasure, Simone critiques a second wave narrative of gender progress that deemphasizes a gendered physicality. In a sub-plot, about, ironically, the problems of representing Diana's character in a movie without resorting simplistic backlash stereotypes of powerful women, another female character, an executive in the movie industry, critiques the "real" Diana/Wonder Woman's presentation of her body, complaining, "What right do YOU have to hold yourself up as an 'inspiration' to little girls? You think violence solves EVERYTHING. And pardon me if I don't think wearing the FLAG on your barely covered rear END is any kind of good message for my daughters" (*Earth* 112). Diana answers the charge forthrightly, saying, "These colors have MEANING for me, Ms. Allison. And would you rather I be ASHAMED of my body?" By rejecting shame and affirming her version of the female body, Diana affirms bodies in a broader sense. By matter-of-factly giving significant air-time to these conversations and negotiations between female characters in her story arcs, Simone gives third wave proof to the success of second wave's efforts to center women's relationships with each other. She creates significant, embodied, female-female connections that certainly move beyond "mak[ing] fudge and talk[ing] about boys" (*Earth*).

Sisterhood 3.0

Virginia Woolf, in her collected essays on women and fiction "A Room of One's Own" (1929) points out that, up to that point in Western literary traditions, women appeared in canonical Western literature almost exclusively in relation to men — as their lovers, their wives, their daughters, their victims. Reflecting on the strangeness she feels upon finding two women friends and colleagues centered in a contemporary novel by a woman, Woolf writes, "'Chloe liked Olivia,' I read. And then it struck me how immense a change was there. Chloe liked Olivia perhaps for the first time in literature... All these relationships between women... So much has been left out, unattempted" (82). Nearly eighty years after Woolf's words, the *Wonder Woman* stories written by Simone take up and center women's relationships each other — not as the first to do so, but as a matter of course. Where second wave gender activism struggled to bring women and their lives and concerns into focus, and often viewed goals of family and career as being incompatible, Simone's stories, written firmly in a third wave tradition, assume women can hold the center of a story — and not just in the domestic sphere OR out in the public world, but in a world built of relationships that are part and parcel of politics, preventing wars, doing the messy work of holding communities of individuals together. Through women's relationships with each other, in Simone's stories the "personal" and the "political" are largely seamless: Amazons, after all, are sisters who are also fellow citizens — a total integration of public and domestic.

In this more integrated landscape of public and private, women's (and all individuals') concerns — about the repercussions of having children, of choosing romantic partners — are not dismissed as "private matters," but are depicted as having communal and political implications. Simone presents as fait accompli the second wave call to make the personal political. She directly engages second wave feminism's struggle over family roles perceived to limit women to the domestic sphere and tie them to the interests of men rather than to their own or those of other women, by enlarging ideas of family. In a flashback to the birth of Diana that begins in the story arc *The Circle*, Simone chronicles how Diana's mother Hippolyta, calls on the generative powers of the gods to form a child from the soil of Themyscira island (the Amazons' homeland) and her own blood. In response, other Amazons voice the critiques of some second wave feminists that family, especially a traditional heterosexual family and motherhood, are institutions so compromised by sexist roles limiting women that there can be no way for a woman to enter into these roles without losing power and threatening the interests of "sisterhood." Representing an Amazonian version of this view, Alkyone, sworn to safeguard her queen, Hippolyta, worries "We loved her beyond vision and memory. But she meant to betray us all. She meant to make a child a DAUGHTER. When the rest of us were BARREN for ETERNITY. It would be an INFECTION. A PLAGUE. Joy would turn to ENVY and ENVY to HATRED" (*Circle* 57). Likewise, the rest of the Amazon community fears their queen's choice to have a child, concerned it will weaken their sisterhood. They say "She'll ABANDON us. She'll care only for the BABE" and "The parcel of the gods [the baby Diana] will crack our island in half" (*Circle* 59).

Simone's portrayal of a kind of "maternal madness" experienced of some Amazons who repress their seemingly "natural" desire to have children stands as an oddly reactionary essentialism of femininity until seen in light of third wave critique of separatist elements of second wave feminism (elements that, in fact, were drawn out of proportion and misrepresented in the conservative backlash that sought to discredit all feminism as "extremism"). Simone later picks up this thread again, more explicitly trying to take back a definition of feminism from a backlash that would stereotype it, when Diana says, while witnessing the making of a "bad" movie version of her life, "Why is it that people feel that a belief in women equals a hatred of men?" (*Earth* 132). Hippolyta's act to become a mother, the eventual acceptance and support she and the baby receive from her Amazon sisters, and Diana's maturity into a strong, capable woman all offer critique of a view that defines motherhood as incompatible with female independence and strength. Simultaneously, and seemingly paradoxically, these narrative elements affirm an alternate option of female separatism and women's right to have children by themselves or with other women, raising them without fathers if they so wish.

That Diana herself appears to consider the more traditional option of having children with her male co-agent and main attraction Tom Tresser (*Ends of the Earth* 144), is less about traditional roles than it is about the reconnection of public and private for both men and women; enlarging the idea of family to a global level brings men *back* into the domestic sphere — a critical step towards gender equity and shared labor in all areas of family and community. Throughout Simone's *Wonder Woman* narratives both parenting and a variety family structures are portrayed in a positive light. Both a respect for female headed families as well as the desire to construct alternate families is naturalized in a scene in which Diana communes with a polar bear family in the Arctic wilderness (*Warkiller* 5–7). Embracing a large female bear, Diana says to the nearby cub "Respect your mother, strong one. Watch and learn" and then also remarks, as the cub chews on her hand "Ah the rebellion begins. Part of the plan, cub. Find your own tooth and claw. A family is not meant to be a prison." Reinforcing the idea of constructing, rather than inheriting, family, she extrapolates from the bear cub to herself, thinking "I COULD again be sister, daughter, disciple, princess. But then I would not be Diana. So for the first time I must make my OWN home. My OWN family" (7). Immediately after this scene, she returns to her apartment to be greeted and hugged by the white gorillas that have effectively become her family. As concerned as any family member, their leader squeezes her tightly and says "We thought we had lost you" (8). Immediately after this explicit proclamation on alternative family, the story focuses on Diana's close relationship with her female friend Dinah Lance "The Black Canary." This episode affirms the significance of female friendship and the idea that one can have more than one family; Diana's fellow super-heroes are another kind of family.

Even the human characters Simone creates offer positive alternate family models, such as the family of the woman film executive discussed above who is parenting two daughters alone. That the two girls have different skin colors — they may have different fathers or be adopted — is unremarkable in Simone's narrative (142–3). Born of an entirely female and racially diverse "household," to Diana this human family's all-female, racially diverse composition is unremarkable; she is more concerned with the woman's substance abuse problem and isolation (*Earth*, 141–44). The assumed value and importance of choosing and creating one's own family is again emphasized when the executive asks Diana "But ... what do I do on the nights where I DON'T have and Amazon visitor to keep me honest?" The superhero replies "Then I guess you find the Amazon that will never leave you" (143). Because earlier in this story arc, a man, Tom, has himself become an Amazon, this is less advice to find a partner of a particular gender, but rather to find (and *found*) a family that, whether created of sisters and lovers or fellow citizens, has your best interests at heart.[10] While there is here a white-identified writer's certain color-blind glibness, this is also a generational view, and marks the sensibility, if not material fact, of many children of the third wave. Teaching 18–22 year olds from a variety of backgrounds, including many multi-racial students, I see that racism as well as sexism, while acknowledged by this generation as still very limiting at times, are perceived as variable and challenging constructions, and not as the dualistic barriers they were for their grandparents.

Lassoing It All Together

Truth is not only information. Truth is revelation. In Simone's pragmatic third wave world of gods and magically strong superheroes, sexism remains an obstacle, but one that can be faced and overcome. With a keen and explicit awareness of the fine line between the gaze of appreciation and that of objectification, these stories go public with a female body that is a powerful sight to behold — a sight controlled and enjoyed by women. From how women shape and adorn their bodies, to whether (or not) they have children from and with those bodies, to whether (or not) they make their families with friends or with lovers or in a larger sense with their fellow citizens — Simone's is not a series of narratives particularly concerned with how men do or do not see women. Women characters in Simone's *Wonder Woman* stand on their own and in relationship to other women: sisters, friends, mothers and daughters, co-workers, citizens. Diana is far more upset when her good friend Etta Candy is captured and tortured than when she has to choose her mission over her relationship with Tom (*Olympian*).

Because of Simone's WiR critique, the scene in which Etta Candy is tortured by the Monster "Genocide" is a kind of test: Can a women can be violently tortured in a superhero comic without being a mere victim or plot device? In broad outline, Etta's plight is similar to Simone's list of gratuitously tortured women superheroes. Etta is abducted especially to torment the superhero in question (Wonder Woman). When Diana finally finds Etta's broken and comatose body, hanging with a note from Genocide that reads "She screamed a lot. She was *FUN*," the violence against her friend is the immediate excuse for the superhero's mission of revenge (112–114, 118, 128–9). However, Etta is a friend, not a lover or love-interest. Her abduction stands more in the tradition of buddy stories, where one character has to come to the aid of his fallen comrade. Moreover, in the scenes of torture that Simone writes, the reader sees only a defiant Etta, unbroken by either the pain or the creature's attempts to foster jealousy of Diana through her husband Steve Trevor's past attraction to her friend. While Simone's abducted female character is not invincible — Diana finds her broken and comatose — she is no easy victim, talking back to Genocide until the last frame in which we see her conscious: "I'll kill you. So help me, if Diana doesn't do it first ... I WILL kill you you worthless MONSTER" (118). And in a marked difference from WiR as plot device for admirable heroic action, Simone does not glorify Diana's subsequent reaction of anger and ruthlessness. Rather, she portrays revenge as an emotion that, while, perhaps natural, must and can be curbed to work towards larger goals of peace and compassionate justice. Diana is depicted as at her strongest when she overcomes blind rage and chooses in battle to let a helpless Genocide live. Simone makes it clear that Diana's efforts to contain Genocide must be made on behalf of the threat the monster poses all of humanity (and gods). Through the abduction of Etta Candy, Simone reshapes a male-centered narrative trope of personal, masculine glory at the expense of women to create instead a feminist story that extends a vision and definition of family beyond the personal, to the global arena. Women's roles extend to the global; men are drawn into the family.

Simone reorients the character and narrative of Wonder Woman from a simple tale of beneficial femininity set up in relation to a world controlled by men, to one of complexity in which the personal and the political are united and women and their relationships with each other are significant and centered. Characteristic of the third wave of gender activism, Simone uses a popcultural production — the superhero comic — to locate power in explicitly female bodies that are neither reactionary nor essentialist, but, rather, progressive and dynamic.

NOTES

1. According to Marguerite Lamb, when Marston first voiced his idea "for a new kind of superhero, one who would triumph not with fists or firepower, but with love," his wife advised "Fine ... [b]ut make her a woman."

2. Mindy Newell, Trina Robbins, and Jodi Picoult had previously contributed as writers to the series for shorter periods.

3. The Amazon princess' influence on several generations of women seeking gender equity and social justice, from Gloria Steinem to young girl fans is chronicled in the film documentary "Wonder Women: The Untold Story of American Superheroines" by Kristy Guevara-Flanagan (Vaquera Films, 2012), in which Simone is interviewed about her work on the character.

4. The terminology for women characters in comics is currently somewhat in flux. While Simone has used both "superhero" and "superheroine" to refer to female protagonists in comics, others want to use only the term "superhero" to refer to these women characters, feeling that "heroine" effectively "depowers" them. After this I will follow the convention of referring to all "super" characters as "superheros."

5. Simone herself has called "The Haweye Initiative" "the best thing in the history of historical anything ever in the universe or elsewhere" (Hudson).

6. As of 12/20/12 the WiR website, hosted by Godaddy.com, was marked for "renewal or deletion" and had been moved to http://www.lby3.com/wir/index.html.The term is all over the internet, with many followers of the reference on Tumblr.

7. Despite nearly a decade writing female-centered superhero comics, it seems the phrase and image Simone coined "Women in Refrigerators" has lost neither its currency nor iconic bite. When, as of Dec. 9, 2012, Simone announced via twitter that DC Comics fired her from that series, a news post on IGN Entertainment's website read, "Interestingly, when a follower tweeted at her, 'Did you not put enough women in refrigerators or something?' referring to her coining of the phrase about the treatment of women in comics ([Green Lantern] Kyle Rayner's girlfriend was murdered and stuffed in his fridge). Simone simply replied, 'Funny you should say that.'" But — just two weeks later, according to her twitter feed, she was rehired to write *Batgirl.* One comics news website speculated that perhaps the women of WiR fame is "now untouchable" (Morris).

8. Main artists who worked with Simone have included a diverse group of men and women: Terry Dodson, Rachel Dodson, Bernard Chang, Nicola Scott, Fernando Dagnino, and Aaron Lopresti, among others.

9. This term first appeared in 1970 as title to a piece by Carol Hanisch in a feminist publication *Notes from the Second Year.*

10. Hippolyta, Queen of the Amazons, says to Tom, "You are an Amazon now, Thomas. No matter what happens from now on, you must never forget that. You must be true to your sisters. For any of us would give our life for you without hesitation" (*Earth* 106).

WORKS CITED

Baumgardner, Jennifer, and Amy Richards. *Manifesta: Young Women, Feminism, and the Future.* New York: Farrar, Straus and Giroux, 2001.

"Declaration of Sentiments and Resolutions." Woman's Rights Convention, held at Seneca Falls, Jul. 19–20, 1848. The Elizabeth Cady Stanton and Susan B. Anthony Papers Project. Rutgers University. Web. Jan. 23, 2013

Devereaux, Mary. "Oppressive Texts, Resisting Readers and the Gendered Spectator: The New Aesthetics." *Journal of Aesthetics & Art Criticism* 48.4 (1990): 337–47.

Esposito, Joey. "Gail Simone Fired from Batgirl." *IGN Entertainment*. Dec. 9, 2012. Web. Dec. 10, 2012.

Gustines, George Gene. "Wonder Woman Gets a New Voice, And It's Female." *New York Times*. Nov. 27, 2007: 1. Academic Search Complete. Web. Dec. 10, 2012.

Hanisch, Carol. "The Personal Is Political." Personal Website. Jun. 25, 2011. http://www.carolhanisch.org/CHwritings/PIP.html (Originally published in *Notes from the Second Year*, edited by Shulie Firestone and Anne Koedt, New York: Self-published, 1970.)

"Hawkeye Initiative." Various artists on Tumblr site launched Dec. 12, 2012. Web. Jan. 23, 2013.

Henry, Astrid. *Not My Mother's Sister: Generational Conflict and Third Wave-Feminism.* Bloomington: Indiana University Press, 2004.

Heywood, Leslie, and Jennifer Drake. *Third Wave Agenda: Being Feminist, Doing Feminism.* Minneapolis: Minnesota University Press, 1997.

Hudson, Laura. "How to Fix Crazy Superheroine Poses in Comics? Swap Then With Hawkeye." *Wired*. Dec. 12, 2012. Web. Jan. 23, 2013.

Kuhn, Annette. *Women's Pictures: Feminism and the Cinema.* London: Routledge and Kegan Paul, 1982.

Lamb, Marguerite. "*Bostonia: The Alumni Quarterly of Boston University* (Fall 2001):1–3. Archived from the original on Dec. 8, 2007. Alumni Web, Boston University. Web. Dec. 23, 2012.

McCloud, Scott. *Understanding Comics: The Invisible Art.* New York: Harper, 1994.

Morris, Steve. "Gail Simone Rehired as Writer for Batgirl." *The Beat: The Newsblog of Comics Culture.* Dec. 21, 2012. Web. Dec. 31, 2012.

Mulvey, Laura. "Looking at the Past from the Present: Rethinking Feminist Film Theory of the 1970s." *Signs: Journal of Women, Culture and Society.* 30.1 (2004):1286–1292. Gale Publishing. Web. Dec. 23, 2012.

_____. "Visual Pleasure and Narrative Cinema." Wiki.Brown.Edu. Originally published in *Screen* 16. 3 (1975): 6–18. Web. Dec. 23, 2012. https://wiki.brown.edu/ confluence/ display/ MarkTribe/ Visual+Pleasure+and+Narrative+Cinema.

Nickles, Shelley. "'Preserving Women': Refrigerator Design as Social Process in the 1930s." *Technology and Culture* 43.4 (Oct. 2002): 693–728.

O'Rourke, Diane. "Three Greek Women: The Insignificance of an Appliance." *Journal of Modern Greek Studies* 30.1 (May 2012): 74–101.

Robbins, Trina. From *Girls to Grrrlz: A History of Women Comics from Teens to Zines.* San Francisco: Chronicle, 1999.

Sassatelli, Roberta. "Interview with Laura Mulvey: Gender, Gaze and Technology in Film Culture." *Theory, Culture & Society* 28.5 (2011): 123–43. Web. Dec. 10, 2012.

Simone, Gail (w), et al. *The Circle.* New York: DC Comics, 2008. Print.

_____. *Contagion.* New York: DC Comics, 2010. Print.

_____. *Ends of the Earth.* New York: DC Comics, 2009. Print.

_____. *Rise of the Olympian.* New York: DC Comics, 2009. Print.

_____. *Warkiller.* New York: DC Comics, 2010. Print.

_____. (GailSimone). "Here's a thing. Gail Simone is the new Batgirl writer. :) — GailSimone" Dec. 21, 2012, 1:06 P.M. Tweet.

Simone, Gail, and Beau Yarborough, et al. "Women in Refrigerators." Website developed in Mar. 1999. Web. Dec. 31, 2012. http://www.lby3.com/wir/index.html.

Walker, Rebecca. "Foreword: We Are Using This Power to Resist." In *The Fire This Time: Young Activists and the New Feminism*, edited by Vivien Labaton and Dawn Lundy Martin, xi–xx. New York: Anchor, 2004. Print.

_____, ed. *To Be Real: Telling the Truth and Changing the Face of Feminism*. New York: Anchor, 1995.

Watkins, Helen. "Beauty Queen, Bulletin Board and Browser: Rescripting the Refrigerator." *Gender, Place and Culture: A Journal of Feminist Geography* 13.2 (Apr. 2006): 143–152.

Woolf, Virginia. *A Room of One's Own*. Orlando: Harvest, 1989.

Greek, Roman or American?

Wonder Woman's Roots in DC's New 52

JOHN DAROWSKI and VIRGINIA RUSH

Ancient Greece and Rome have had a profound impact on the culture of the United States, from art and architecture to forms of government. One of the greatest contributions has been through their myths, which continue to influence American culture to this day. One needs look no further than the best-selling *Percy Jackson* series by Rick Riordan to see that mythology is still prominent in contemporary popular culture. Superheroes, oft considered a modern mythology, owe a great debt to these classical forbearers. Among the pantheon of American superheroes, few have closer ties to the Greco-Roman tradition than Wonder Woman. However, while acknowledging the relations between modern culture and their traditions, it is clear that contemporary differences in religion and lifestyle, to say nothing of advances in technology, have created a society vastly different than anything those older civilizations could have imagined. With this progress comes the need for new stories to reinforce modern values and traditions.

Ancient myths have become a narrative shorthand, archetypes that can be appropriated and reconfigured in a manner entirely displaced from their original context. In modern culture this happens to such a degree that distinct Greek and Roman traditions have often become conflated when used in new narratives (Korvacs 15). Superheroes are not immune to this pattern, either; each age brings about a repurposing to revitalize the stories for a new generation of readers. The September 2011 relaunch of the DC Comics universe, labeled the New 52[1] by the publisher, offers a version of *Wonder Woman* that hews closely to the character's classical roots. This story of gods and goddesses, of heroes and prophecy, as told by writer Brian Azzarello and artists Cliff Chiang and Tony Aikens, presents an opportunity to examine the appropriation of Greek, Roman, and American mythologies for a twenty-first century audience.

In repurposing mythology, the creators of *Wonder Woman* have naturally drawn on the pattern of such stories, identified and popularized by Joseph Campbell in *The Hero with a Thousand Faces*: the Hero's Journey. This journey consists of three main parts: Departure, where the call to adventure leads the hero away from home; Initiation, where the hero undergoes a series of trials to obtain treasure or knowledge; and Return, where the hero uses said treasure or knowledge to vanquish evil and restore order, often inheriting his father's role as leader afterwards. It should be noted that Campbell's work was meant to be descriptive, analyzing pre-existing texts, rather than prescriptive, an outline for future tales. As such, the heroes in Campbell's analysis are predominantly male. There is no female equivalent to the Hero's Journey, no Heroine's Journey, because women were not generally the protagonists of mythology in the ancient world. In fact, women were often viewed as possessions and were frequently the prize the hero won during Initiation (LoCicero 119). And while heroes were often demigods, demigoddesses either became queens or were raised to the level of minor goddess. Azzarello is able to circumvent this because (a) there is greater gender equality in the twenty-first century and (b) Wonder Woman is Princess Diana of the Amazons, a matriarchal society where she can aspire to rule.

The New 52 Wonder Woman's journey begins, as many myths do, with a prophecy. As foretold by Apollo's oracles: "There is a storm gathering just beyond the horizon and the one responsible shall rule in fire [...]It wears a crown of horns and a cape of blood, flowing from its shoulders onto a naked woman at its feet [...] Your family ... is broken, beaten and betrayed. By blood" (Azzarello, *Wonder Woman*, Vol. 1 17–19). Because of this prophecy, Zeus has abandoned his throne and disappeared. The oracles continue: "Well, your father has abandoned fate to someone who can blow away the smoke if they choose to" (Azzarello, *Wonder Woman*, Vol. 1 19–20). This results in a power struggle among the gods to claim the throne of Olympus, a conflict which centers on Zola, a mortal girl who was the object of Zeus's latest dalliance and is now pregnant with the newest demigod.

Hermes sends Zola to Wonder Woman for protection. This Call to Adventure takes on much more significance in this new continuity when Diana learns that she herself is a child of Zeus, making the unborn child and her mother, as well as many of the gods, family. Wonder Woman's first task is to stop Hera, who has a history of punishing those who consort with her husband, as evidenced by the goddess turning Diana's mother, Queen Hippolyta, who is now revealed to have had a relationship with Zeus, to stone and the rest of the Amazons into snakes. Wonder Woman manipulates Poseidon and

Hades into helping her destroy Hera's scrying pool, effectively blinding the goddess; but in the process Hades kidnaps Zola.

This leads Wonder Woman into undertaking one of the elite Initiation acts of the ancient heroes: a journey to the underworld (LoCicero 121). Diana frees Zola from Hades, only to run afoul of the siblings Apollo and Artemis. Their confrontation extends to Mount Olympus, where Apollo claims the throne of Zeus. Meanwhile, Zola gives birth, only to have the demigod child stolen by Hermes. After this first year of stories, Wonder Woman still has many trials to go before she can complete her quest.

One of the challenges the creators faced in tying this modern take on Wonder Woman to mythology is the portrayal of the gods. These divinities have been reconfigured ad infinitum over the millennia resulting in an expansive disjuncture with their relationship with humans anciently and how they are portrayed now (Dethloff 103). To the ancient Greeks, the Olympians were to be worshipped. A polytheistic society, they believed the gods had control over every aspect of their lives. Contemporary America, despite its cultural diversity and religious tolerance, does not believe the Olympians to be divine or even real, owing to the predominate Judeo-Christian sensibility inherited from its Puritan founding. When portrayed in popular culture, such beings are often shown dressed in togas and speaking a faux-archaic dialect to illustrate their disconnectedness from contemporary society and the utter absence of any relationship with the modern world.

The creators of this Wonder Woman relaunch chose to strike a balance between these two extremes by showing the Olympians not as gods to be worshipped but as powerful forces that influence every aspect of the world; an apt metaphor in a time when environmental, political, and market forces are ill-understood and still have a profound impact on individual lives. This balance is achieved by having the gods act in accordance with their character in ancient myth but update their appearance and speech with twenty-first century style. As Azzarello explained: "I think the gods are going to be much more fearsome. You're not going to see a white toga anywhere near this book" (Gartler).

We have already seen one example of a goddess acting in conformity with her ancient role with Hera punishing those women who have relationships with Zeus. Additionally, there are examples such as Apollo acting as the god of prophecy and Hermes as a trickster. But a deeper understanding can be gleamed by examining a classical text such as the chronicle of the Trojan War, *The Iliad*. In this Homeric epic, the Greek gods have incredible influence, sometimes participating directly in the conflict as an extension of their own familial squabbling. With such divine involvement one might have anticipated a quick resolution to the war. However, the war continued for ten years because the gods themselves were bound by two strictures: justice and fate (Lefkowitz 2, 54).

It was known early on in *The Iliad* that the Greeks were fated to win. It was only a question of how long and how much honor the gods could receive in the course of the war. The reason the war took a decade is that, even though fate cannot be avoided, it can be forestalled. The decision to enact or delay consequences fell to Zeus as the arbiter of justice. The gods would present arguments to decide the outcomes of battles based on which of the combatants had broken the laws. And if the gods circumvented Zeus's judgment, they would face the anger and punishment of the king of the gods.

Zeus's absence is keenly felt in *Wonder Woman*, as without his justice the Olympians turn to fighting amongst themselves for power; well, more fighting than usual. And while Zeus never abandoned his post in ancient myth, his actions are consistent with those stories. The oracles prophesied that the family of gods would be betrayed and beaten by one of their own and there is a pattern of sons defeating fathers: Uranus and Kronos; Kronos and Zeus (LoCicero 71). Even though Zeus can dispense justice, he has no control of fate. This is why Zeus has left his post and why Apollo, who never sought for power anciently, is now determined to claim it. As Apollo explains when taking the throne of Olympus: "I have a destiny — and a prophecy — to forestall. There is a storm on the horizon. One that I plan to face down" (Azzarello, *Wonder Woman*, Vol. 2 105)

While the gods in *Wonder Woman* may act in a manner consistent with their past, their appearance is not. Classical paintings and sculptures show the Olympians to be human in form. But story after story reveals that this is an illusion and that the divide in power and intelligence between mortal and immortal is insuperable (Lefkowitz 17). There is no such illusion in this modern presentation. Artists Chiang and Aikens have developed an entirely new visual vocabulary to illustrate the gods. As Azzarello explains: "What we're going for is externalizing their personalities, or what they stand for" (Rogers).

And so Hermes is no longer a youth with winged sandals, but a blue-skinned man with actual bird feet. Poseidon is a giant sea monster. Hephaestus is a grotesque horror a mother might truly reject. Most interestingly, Hades is a child with a crown of melting candles, an image reportedly inspired by a French painting of Death (Campbell). Hand in hand with this comes a new set of names to externalize each individual's area of expertise: Hermes-Messenger; Hades-Hell; Apollo-Sun; etc.[2] There are only occasional references to their traditional names to provide the reader context. But renaming the gods is nothing new. It's been going on since antiquity with the Romans.

The Olympians aren't the only contribution the Greeks made to the

Wonder Woman mythos; they also originated the Amazons. This race of warrior women is most well-known through the ninth labor of Hercules, where the hero was tasked with stealing the magic girdle of Queen Hippolyta (LoCicero 103). They also make appearances in *The Iliad* and *The Aeneid*, each time on the losing side of the battle (*ibid.* 124). The reason the Amazons lose so often in myths is that they were meant to serve as a cautionary tale where the warrior women have to be defeated for social order to reign (Blondell 224). Particularly disruptive to the social order was the Amazons' form of conception, where they would capture men, sleep with them and then kill the men and any male children that resulted from the union. By modern standards this is horrifying to the Judeo-Christian morality, but to the Greeks horror resulted from the reversal of the male/female roles (Harris). This has been theorized to be the result of the conflict between the Minoans, a traditionally matriarchal society, and the Dorians, or Bronze Age Greeks. Portraying a female-only society as savage and barbaric made the Greek conquests into civilizing missions.

When William Moulton Marston created Wonder Woman in 1941, he appropriated the Amazons in name only. Instead of the barbarians of myth, he portrayed the women as an advanced civilization living in peace and harmony on Paradise Island, where they only used combat for sport. Marston wanted the Amazons to embody the generative power of women, and therefore they had the patronage of Aphrodite. Wonder Woman was sent out into the world to combat the destructive power of men, as embodied by Ares (Simms 117). This was done without a trace of irony for the fact that Aphrodite and Ares were traditionally portrayed as lovers and not rivals.

Azzarello chose to return the Amazons to their classical roots, raiding parties and all, though any male children are no longer slaughtered but traded to Hephaestus for weapons. This has been questioned as Wonder Woman has become a feminist icon and such a reconfiguring of Paradise Island can be interpreted as, at best, limiting the characterization of what had been a diverse society and at worst as a reversal of progress (Thompson). This is a case where recasting Wonder Woman so close to her mythological roots has, for some readers, regressive and negative results.

These tales of the gods and the Amazons were appropriated by the Romans; appropriation being one of the few traditions shared by most cultures, though no one did it better than Romans. In their conquests, the Roman Empire would allow civilizations to keep their religions as long as they paid a tribute to Rome. This resulted in the import of many deities, though none more significant than the Olympians. But as the Romans had different values and traditions, the stories were adjusted to emphasize their priorities, resulting in a different hierarchy of the gods.

What Romans valued most was family and the state. This is witnessed by Aeneas's journey to the underworld in *The Aeneid*. Aeneas is reunited with his father, who reminds his son of his destiny to found a great city and then shows him all the future leaders of the country. Aeneas understands that these future glories come from a strong state, which is the result of strong families. These values are reflected by the Romans placing Vesta (Hestia), the goddess of the home, and Mars (Ares), the god of war and soldiers, above other deities.

Family is essential to this reimagining of Wonder Woman due to her shift in status to a child of Zeus. When Marston created Princess Diana, she had been molded out of clay by Hippolyta and given life by Aphrodite. This falls in line with the miraculous birth archetype, most notably Pygmalion. But it is not a unique circumstance in myth: Athena sprung from the forehead of Zeus, Aphrodite from the genitals Zeus cut off from his father Kronos, and Dionysus was taken from the womb and sewn into Zeus's leg to gestate until birth (LoCicero 90). But while the miraculous birth was not uncommon, it was not usually the way of the hero. Most demigods were born naturally.

This isn't the first time there has been a reimagining of Wonder Woman's origin. During the Silver Age, writer Robert Kanigher made Diana the offspring of two mortals who was then given powers as gifts from the gods (Daniels 108). The repurposing in the New 52 again strikes a balance between ancient and modern traditions.

The shift in origin also serves as a reflection of contemporary society as it comes at a time when America is debating the definition of family. The nature of what family is has become troubled. The rise in divorce rates has caused a reconsideration of the family unit. Co-habitation allows for emotional bonds where there is no legal binding. Whether homosexuals have the right to marry and adopt has been an ongoing discussion for the entire opening of the twenty-first century. Making Diana part of a much larger family forces her decide which aspects of the filial structure to embrace and defend. As Azzarello explains: "She's got a family now, you know? She's got a dysfunctional family now and it's not all women. And how she deals with that family is what we're going to be dealing with for the next year" (Rogers). And no family defines dysfunctional like the Olympians. Fighting, kidnapping, affairs; as Hermes says: "Wounded? That's the point of family dinners on Olympus. You should join us sometime" (Azzarello, *Wonder Woman*, Vol. 1 101)

Family is a complicated issue with no clear cut answers for society or Wonder Woman, who spends the first year of the New 52 fighting her newly recognized blood relations in order to defend other new-found relatives. But Princess Diana shows that family, whatever an individual's interpretation of that might be, is worth fighting for. And that is a sentiment to which the Romans could relate.

The Roman Republic and later Empire was a militant society whose army was not only for conquest but also to provide peace and order throughout the known world. Military service was expected of its male citizens and was even a way to gain citizenship. As such Mars was a crucial figure in the pantheon, though the Romanized deities were not portrayed as often involving themselves in mortal battles as their Greek counterparts. They were much more spiritual figures or tools of propaganda (LoCicero 117).

While many of the Olympians have survived appropriation over the millennia with their dignity relatively intact, such is not the case for Mars. In the modern context he is invariably repurposed as a villain. He was Wonder Woman's first archenemy when she burst onto the comic book scene in 1941 and has remained so through many iterations. This is in part due to Marston's view of war as masculine and destructive, but also a reflection of the United States' traditional attitude, at least in rhetoric, of conflict as a necessary evil for defense, but something best to be avoided.

But Mars in the new *Wonder Woman* bears little resemblance in character or design to either the heroic god of the Romans or the robust villain of the twentieth century. Instead, Azzarello has recast Ares as a tired, old man. Artist Cliff Chiang, who based the design for War on Azzarello's appearance, explains:

> This is not the traditional Greek god who glorifies violence and is kind of a psychopath. Based on the look, you can see War [Ares] is someone who is a little more calculating, someone who has been worn down by the mantle. War has traditionally been Wonder Woman's villain, and he's not, here. He serves a purpose the way all gods do, and it's not this simple binary black-against-white [Josie Campbell].

This Mars is exhausted by the near constant stream of terrorist attacks and racial warfare throughout the world and doesn't want the additional burden of participating in this latest Olympian squabble. As such, he has been reconfigured as the epitome of contemporary society's attitude towards the global war on terror, which gained near unanimous support immediately after September 11, 2001, but whose popularity has since waned significantly in the face of the human and economic costs as the conflict enters its second decade.

Such social and political commentary is rife throughout the story as characters are configured to combine classical and modern tropes in such a way as to allow *Wonder Woman* to serve as a reflection on the prevalent trends and concerns of the day. When Apollo claims the throne of Zeus, Olympus is transformed from a mountain into a skyscraper (Azzarello, *Wonder Woman*, Vol. 2 122). This is representative not only of the shift of the centrality of business over religion in culture, but also endemic of the position of the economy in the public consciousness. Business has been constantly discussed throughout the recession, bailouts, and Occupy movement.

The transformation of Olympus also raises the specter of progress over tradition. "See, you've mistaken the awe of the old for the shock of the new," declares Apollo (*ibid.*). While this has been most predominately expressed in society in terms of the political dichotomy between conservative and liberal, it can also reference the near constant innovation in technology as well as the generation gap. This is especially true when contrasting Apollo's Olympus with Hades' underworld, which appears in the form of London without any of the distinctive modern features (Azzarello, *Wonder Woman*, Vol. 2 28). Hades shapes his domain out of the souls of the dead, and the use of London is not only meant to be an invitation for Wonder Woman, who is based out of London in these stories, but illustrates Hades' old world mentality (Azzarello, *Wonder Woman*, #0 31). Additionally, Hades is a first generation god whereas Apollo, a son of Zeus, is second generation.

At the end of the first year of the New 52, Wonder Woman and Superman shared a kiss in the pages *of Justice League* #12, cementing their status as a couple.[3] A controversial moment, it illustrates the risks DC Comics is willing to take to reconceptualize their characters for the twenty-first century. It also serves as one of the ultimate couplings of ancient and modern mythology: the Amazon princess of myth and the Man of Tomorrow. In appropriating Greco-Roman myths as metaphors for current anxieties, Azzarello, Chiang and Aikens have repurposed an American myth, Wonder Woman, as an access point. By staying true to classical roots while reconfiguring characters to reflect contemporary values and concerns, *Wonder Woman*'s appropriation of Greek, Roman and American mythologies helps keep these culturally defining myths relevant and accessible for a modern audience.

Notes

1. The New 52 was the marketing term for an event in which DC cancelled all of their ongoing titles and relaunched 52 new titles with #1 issues. This marked not only a change in the publishing schedule, but a reboot of the narrative universe. The new issues were meant to introduce the key elements of the characters, who were being reintroduced without the weight of decades of continuity.

2. For the sake of clarity, we will continue using the Greek or Roman names.

3. In the New 52 continuity, Superman and Lois Lane were never married.

Works Cited

Azzarello, Brian (w), and Cliff Chiang (a). "The Lair of the Minotaur!" *Wonder Woman* #0 (Nov. 2012). New York: DC Comics.

Azzarello, Brian (w), Cliff Chiang (a) and Tony Aikens (a). *Wonder Woman* Volume 1: *Blood.* New York: DC Comics, 2012.

_____. *Wonder Woman* Volume 2: *Guts.* New York: DC Comics, 2013.

Blondell, Ruby. "Hercules Psychotherapist." In *Super/Hero: From Hercules to Superman,* edited by Wendy Haslem, Angela Nadalianis and Chris Mackie. Washington, DC: New Academia, 2007.

Campbell, Joseph. *The Hero with a Thousand Faces.* New York: Barnes and Noble, 1949.

Campbell, Josie. "Chiang Reflects on New Gods, Gods and 'Wonder Woman.'" *Comic Book Resources*, Nov. 20, 2012. Accessed Nov. 20, 2012.

Daniels, Les. *Wonder Woman: The Complete History.* San Francisco: Chronicle, 2000.

Dethloff, Craig. "Coming Up to Code: Ancient Divinities Revisited." In *Classics and Comics,* edited by George Kovacs and C. W. Marhall. New York: Oxford University Press, 2011.

Gartler, James. "Azzarello Scares Up a New Take on Wonder Woman." *Comic Book Resources*, Sep. 21, 2011. Accessed Dec. 24, 2012.

Harris, Sonia. "Committed: Why Ancient Mythology Breaks in Contemporary Comics." *Comic Book Resources*, Apr. 18, 2012. Accessed Apr. 19, 2012.

Kovacs, George. "Comics and Classics: Establishing a Critical Frame." In *Classics and Comics,* edited by George Kovacs and C. W. Marhall. New York: Oxford University Press, 2011.

Lefkowitz, Mary. *Greek Gods, Human Lives: What We Can Learn from Myths.* New Haven: Yale University Press, 2003.

LoCicero, Don. *Superheroes and Gods: A Comparative Study from Babylonia to Batman.* Jefferson, NC: McFarland, 2008.

Rogers, Vaneta. "Spoiler Sport: Wonder Woman Creators on Her New Origin." *Newsarama*, Nov. 18, 2011. Accessed Aug. 17, 2012.

Simms, R. Clinton. "The Burden of War: From Homer to Oeming." In *Classics and Comics,* edited by George Kovacs and C. W. Marhall. New York: Oxford University Press, 2011.

Thompson, Kelly. "She Has No Head!— Is the Destruction of the Amazons the Destruction of Feminism in DC Comics?" Mar. 26, 2012. Accessed Feb. 19, 2013.

About the Contributors

W. C. **Bamberger** is the author, editor or translator of more than a dozen books. He has recently written about Stan Lee and translated Gershom Scholem, and a selection of his essays on music, *Of Fret Rattle and Underwater Skylabs*, appeared in 2013. He is working on a book-length study of Samuel R. Delany's *The American Shore*. He lives in Michigan.

John **Darowski** is in the Ph.D. program in humanities at the University of Louisville. He has presented research on comic books, anime and the Gothic at the national conference of the Popular Culture Association. He has an essay in *The Ages of Superman: Essays on the Man of Steel in Changing Times*.

Joseph J. **Darowski** is on the English faculty at Brigham Young University Idaho and is a member of the editorial review board of *The Journal of Popular Culture*. He is the editor of *The Ages of Superman* (2012) and forthcoming volumes on superheroes, including the X-Men, the Avengers, and Iron Man. He has also published on television shows such as *The Office, Chuck, Downton Abbey*, and *Batman: The Animated Series*.

Michelle R. **Finn** is the deputy city historian of Rochester, New York. She teaches courses in gender and women's studies at the University of Rochester. She also teaches U.S. women's history at Monroe Community College (SUNY). Her work on Wonder Woman is part of a larger project that examines the persistence of feminist ideas in American popular culture between 1920 and 1948.

Nicole **Freim** served as the area chair for the Comics and Comic Art area of the National Popular Culture Association for nine years and is on the editorial board for the *International Journal of Comic Arts*. She teaches and publishes on comics, film, television, and literature.

D. R. **Hammontree** is an assistant professor and an associate director of First-Year Writing in the Department of Writing and Rhetoric at Oakland University, Rochester, Michigan. He contributed to the *Encyclopedia of Comic Books and Graphic Novels* (2010) and the forthcoming *Comics Through Time*, edited by M. Keith Booker. He is a member of the executive board of the Michigan Council of Teachers of English.

Jeffrey K. **Johnson** is a World War II historian for the Joint POW/MIA Accounting Command in Honolulu, Hawaii. He is the author of *American Advertising in Poland: A Study of Cultural Interactions Since 1990* (2009) and *Super-History: Comic*

Book Superheroes and American Society, 1938 to the Present (2012) . He also has published several journal articles and is working on a book about Hawaii in World War II.

Donna B. **Knaff** is a military historian at the Joint POW/MIA Accounting Command in Honolulu, Hawaii, and former chief historian for the Women in Military Service for America Memorial at Arlington National Cemetery. Her book *Beyond Rosie the Riveter: Women of World War II in American Popular Graphic Art* won the PCA/ACA's Emily Toth Award.

Paul R. **Kohl** is an associate professor of media studies at Loras College in Dubuque, Iowa, where he teaches courses in television, film, and popular music. He has an essay in *The Ages of Superman*.

Jason **LaTouche** is an associate professor of sociology at Tarleton State University. His work on superhero comic books has appeared in *The Ages of Superman* and the *Critical Survey of Graphic Novels*. He has presented research on superhero comic books at the Popular Culture Association annual conference and has created and taught a course titled "The Sociology of Superheroes."

Peter W. **Lee** is a Ph.D. candidate in history at Drew University. He has contributed to *The Ages of Superman*, *Comic Books and the Cold War, 1946–1962*; *Web-Spinning Heroics*; *Comic Books and American Cultural History*, and the *Critical Survey of Graphic Novels: Heroes & Superheroes* reference set. His work has also appeared in *Thymos, The Bright Lights Film Journal*, and *Studies in Medievalism*.

Lori **Maguire** is a professor of British and American studies at the University of Paris 8 (Vincennes–St. Denis). She has published a number of essays and books on the political history and foreign policy of Great Britain and the United States. She has also published essays on the presentation of the Cold War in popular culture in *Cold War History*; *The Ages of Superman* and in *Star Wars and History*.

Alison **Mandaville** teaches writing and literature at Luther College. Her articles on comics literature and teaching comics have appeared in *The Comics Journal, International Journal of Comic Art* and *Philology;* and in the edited collections *Teaching the Graphic Novel*; *Comics and the U.S. South* and *Comics and American Cultural History*. She is writing a work on race, gender and politics in word and image.

Ruth **McClelland-Nugent** holds a doctorate from Dalhousie University in Halifax, Nova Scotia. She is an associate professor of history at Georgia Regents University in Augusta, Georgia. She has previously written about *Wonder Woman* in the contexts of Cold War domesticity and 1970s World War II nostalgia.

Joan **Ormrod** is a senior lecturer in the Department of Media at Manchester Metropolitan University. She has published in books on superheroes, adaptation and Edgar Allan Poe, masculinity and online fandom, and subcultural audiences. She also edits Routledge's *Journal of Graphic Novels and Comics* and is on the organizing team of the International Conference of Graphic Novels and Comics.

Fernando Gabriel **Pagnoni Berns** is a graduate teaching assistant at the Universidad de Buenos Aires in Argentina. He has published articles in *Imagofagia, Cine-documental, Stichomythia, Ol3media, Anagnórisis-Theatrical Research Magazine* and

UpStage Journal, and essays in the books *Undead in the West, Horrofilmico* and *The Culture and Philosophy of Ridley Scott.*

Virginia **Rush** has an M.A. in the humanities from Brigham Young University. Her master's thesis was titled "Reflections of War: Imitations of Statius' Thebaid in Ariosto's Orlando Furioso." She has taught Western civilization and the humanities at Brigham Young University for ten years.

Matthew J. **Smith** is a professor of communication and director of cinema studies at Wittenberg University in Springfield, Ohio. He has published six books, the latest three in collaboration with Randy Duncan: *The Power of Comics: History, Form and Culture,* a textbook for comics studies; *Critical Approaches to Comics: Theories and Methods,* and *Icons of the American Comic Book.*

Craig **This** is a lecturer at Sinclair Community College in Dayton, Ohio. He teaches the popular culture course Comic Books and American Culture. He has published essays in *Nazisploitation: The Nazi Image in Low-Brow Cinema and Culture* and in *Icons of the American Comic Book.* He is a member of Comics Association of Professionals and Educators.

Francinne **Valcour** teaches and is a coordinator of academic services at the Community College of Vermont. She earned a Ph.D. in history from Arizona State University. Her dissertation, "Manipulating the Messenger: Wonder Woman as an American Female Icon," examines the process by which Wonder Woman became an icon and what that process tells us about gender and commodity production.

Index